DIVERSIFYING RETAIL AND DISTRIBUTION IN THAILAND

DIVERSIFYING RETAIL AND DISTRIBUTION IN THAILAND

ENDO GEN

Silkworm Books

ISBN: 978-616-215-057-9

This edition first published in 2013
Silkworm Books
6 Sukkasem Road, T. Suthep
Chiang Mai 50200 Thailand
info@silkwormbooks.com
http://www.silkwormbooks.com

Typeset in Cronos Pro 10 pt. by Silk Type

Printed in Thailand by O. S. Printing House, Bangkok

5 4 3 2 1

CONTENTS

LIST OF ILLUSTRATIONS

Figures

Tables

PREFACE

This volume is a revised and updated English translation of a book I wrote in Japanese entitled *Sinkokoku no ryutsu kakumei: Thai no mosaic jo shohi sijo to tayoka suru ryutsu* [Distribution Revolution in an Emerging Market: The Consumer Market of Mosaic Structure and Diversifying Distribution in Thailand] (Tokyo: Nippon Hyoron Sha, 2010). When I first began my research, I initially focused on the competitive relationship between transnational and leading local Thai retailers. Looking back, I can see that this hardly embraced the whole system of Thailand's retail and distribution industries. This was, in part, due to the overwhelming focus of earlier studies and newspaper articles on the rise of new retailing formats and what was assumed to be the fall of traditional retailing formats, but also due to the fact that data and earlier studies on traditional retail and distribution industries were very limited. As my research progressed, I came to broaden my outlook. This led me to try to understand the changes in retail businesses within Thailand's entire retail and distribution system, including consumer goods manufacturers and intermediate distribution. However, I was still heavily influenced by the commonly held view that new retailing formats were strong, whereas traditional retail and distribution businesses were weak and, thus, destined to decline.

I first began to doubt this common view when I had the opportunity to interview many consumer goods manufacturers (and sales companies). Every manufacturer told me that it attached weight not only to its dealings with new retailing formats such as hypermarkets, but also to dealings with traditional retail and distribution businesses, leading provincial wholesalers in particular. Thus, I extended the scope of my research to the wholesale industry. While information and statistics on retail and distribution industries in Thailand were generally insufficient for my research, data on the wholesale industry was even scarcer. This lack of documentary sources made interview-based research all the more necessary. I first compiled fragmentary data on various industries and leading wholesalers and then, from this preliminary database, selected appropriate persons to interview.

However, I often had no connections with the companies in my database. In the case of Bangkok-based leading companies, I could expect to get to know the companies to some extent through introductions by some of my Thai professors or persons I knew connected with the industry. In the cases where I couldn't find any formal referrals, I went directly to the companies' offices and gave them a document in Thai that provided a self-introduction and a description of my research project. In some cases, I was permitted an interview, if not on that day, then a few days later. Nevertheless, it was very difficult to replicate this process with provincial wholesalers dispersed throughout the country. I, therefore, searched for the addresses of the companies I hoped to visit and the name of their representative director from company files maintained at the Commerce Ministry's Business Development Department, and then sent them inquiry letters. I had no other choice but to rely on such an unassured method. To my surprise, the attempt was more successful than I expected. Many of the companies must have been surprised to receive a letter from overseas requesting an interview. Some kindly replied by fax or e-mail, while others took the trouble to make an international telephone call to my home in Japan. When I actually met them, I was pleasantly surprised at the warm welcome given to me, as a lone foreign researcher. During the most important interviews and store observations, I was often struck by the foresight and robustness of these provincial wholesalers.

As my field research progressed, the actual situation of intermediate distribution—which had been almost entirely overlooked by previous studies on Thailand's retail and distribution industries—came sharply into focus. I was, thus, gradually freed from the view that the "distribution revolution had bypassed wholesalers," and ended up completing my research in a very different way from what I had first imagined. As a result, I argue, in this book, that the recent changes in the distribution system in Thailand remain so partial that we cannot regard the current situation as a "revolution" in the strict sense of the word. In other words, Thailand's retail and distribution industries are, for the time being, heading toward diversification rather than uniformity, the latter phenomenon being generally associated with the advance of multinational corporations.

Throughout the research and writing of this book, I have been assisted by many people and institutions. First of all, I would like to express my great appreciation to Professor Suehiro Akira of the University of Tokyo for his practical comments on an earlier draft and for all his academic advice over many years. Without his guidance, I would never have stood on my own feet as a scholar. I would also like to thank Professor Arai Yoshio of the same university and Professor Kikkawa Takeo of Hitotsubashi University for their constructive comments on my research. I only truly began my Thai studies when I entered the master courses of my graduate program at the University of Tokyo. I owe my basic training in area studies to the strict but warm teachings of the late Professor Takahashi Akira. My special gratitude also goes to Professors Tomosugi Takashi, Akagi Osamu, Kitahara Atsushi, Tasaka Toshio, Murashima Eiji, Yamamoto Hiroshi, Takahashi Masaki, and Tamada Yoshifumi, who have always encouraged me in my studies. I am equally indebted to the following scholars of Thai studies: Yokoyama Mitsunori, Higashi Shigeki, Miyata Toshiyuki, Oizumi Keiichiro, Nagai Fumio, Kakizaki Ichiro, Mieno Fumiharu, Ihara Motoi, and Natenapha Wailerdsak. I am similarly indebted to my colleagues at Daito Bunka University, especially to Associate Professor Garren Mulloy for his kind advice on English-language usage. The comments and encouragement of my old friend Tozawa Fuyuki have been invaluable as well.

Naturally enough, I was also greatly helped by many people during my field research in Thailand. Dr. Sompop Manarungsan, president of the Panyapiwat Institute of Management, and Mr. Ukrist Pathmanand, associate director of the Institute of Asian Studies, Chulalongkorn University, consistently encouraged me in my research, and Dr. Pasuk Phongpaichit and Dr. Nualnoi Treerat of Chulalongkorn University kindly accepted me as a visiting scholar in their Faculty of Economics from April 2006 until March 2007.

I am grateful to all of the interviewees, but particularly to Mr. Kanda Masao, Mr. Manu Lilanuwat, and Mr. Chaloemchat Nakharangkun. While I cannot acknowledge all the interviewees because of limited space, I would like to thank them here again.

I am also grateful to Mr. Sombun Rujikhajon, a reporter for the Brand Age Company, and to the staff of the company's information center for generously helping me with my data collection. The Ministry of Commerce's Business Development Department and Internal Trade Department as well as the Ministry of Interior's Urban Planning Department provided me with valuable materials and data on many occasions. I was also able to use the excellent facilities of a number of institutions for my research, particularly the Bank of Thailand, the National Statistical Office, and the Central Library of Chulalongkorn University.

The Japan Society for the Promotion of Science, the Institute of Developing Economies of the Japan External Trade Organization, and Daito Bunka University, to which I belong, granted funds for my fieldwork during various periods between 2000 and 2012, without which it would not have been possible, and the publication of this book was supported by a Grant-in-Aid for Publication of Scientific Research Results provided by the Japan Society for the Promotion of Science (JSPS).

My special thanks go to Ms. Florence Lahournat and Dr. Lisa S. Keary, who sincerely edited my manuscript, as well as Ms. Trasvin Jittidecharak and Ms. Susan Offner at Silkworm Books for their professionalism and friendship.

Finally, my deepest gratitude goes to my wife, Yoshie, and my three children, Banri, Tamaki, and Mitona, who are always the source of my energy. Without their cooperation, I would not have been able to finish this book.

ENDO Gen
Daito Bunka University

INTRODUCTION: THE "DISTRIBUTION REVOLUTION" IN EMERGING MARKETS

OVERVIEW OF RETAIL AND DISTRIBUTION INDUSTRIES IN EMERGING MARKETS

Since the 1990s, the big retailers based in Western countries have actively advanced into emerging markets around the world whose economic growth rates are relatively high. Behind the scenes, host countries have undergone such change that transnational corporations (TNC) have regarded these rapidly growing economies as an attractive consumer market. At the same time, investors from advanced countries have found that big retailers are unable to expand their businesses in their respective domestic markets due to matured markets, the "oligopoly" of the retail industry, and increased government regulation. This combination of push and pull factors has stimulated a rapid transnationalization or internationalization of the retail business, with emerging markets as its new stage. With this major change, we can no longer argue that retailing is, unlike manufacturing, essentially a domestic industry.

It can be said that transnationalized Western retailers have competitive advantages over local retailers in emerging markets in such areas as capital, retail technology, including information technology (IT) and logistics, as well as foreign direct investment experience. A widely shared opinion is that if Western retailers advance into emerging markets, they will occupy a dominant position. Another view sees transnational retailers as the catalyst that could bring a distribution revolution into emerging markets. It is true that France-based Carrefour, the second largest retailer in the world, has taken a dominant position among Taiwan's mass-merchandising store chains by introducing a new format—the hypermarket—along with a new method of store management. However, as is also widely known, Carrefour was not successful in establishing businesses in Japan and has already withdrawn from the country. In Korea, too, domestic companies have maintained such an advantageous position up until now that Carrefour had no other choice but to leave that country as well.

In short, and contrary to original prospects, transnational retailers have failed to advance into certain emerging markets. That the results of the same TNC differs depending on the host country it enters clearly suggests that success comes from not only the company's management strategies but also from the host country's particular circumstances; in other words, the local context surrounding the retail industry in the host country. In this respect, it is interesting to look at the retail industry in a given emerging market from the viewpoint of area studies and business histories, which highlight the specific context of this market. The target of this study is Thailand, one of the most popular host countries for transnational retailers.

THE RETAIL INDUSTRY IN THAILAND

In recent years, modern retailing has grown in Thailand. Up until the mid-1980s, there was little modern retailing in the country, with the exception of department store and small-scale supermarket formats. Since the late 1980s, however, new retail formats such as cash-and-carry, hypermarkets, convenience stores, and so on, have emerged one after another. These new retail formats together with previous modern retail formats, like department stores, are generically referred to as the "modern trade" and have attracted considerable attention. With the monetary and economic crisis in 1997–98, transnational retailers took the lead in these new formats, and foreign-led retailing chains further accelerated their new store openings and rapidly increased their sales volume in Thailand.

These new retail formats succeeded in offering low-price sales and improved purchasing convenience by making full use of their huge buying power and advanced IT. The hypermarket,[1] a hybrid format between a large-scale discount store and supermarket, in particular, coincided with the needs of Thai consumers wishing to save on household expenditures under the post-crisis depression. The hypermarket became Thailand's leading format in the retail industry within a short period of time. It is generally believed that with the change in these industry circumstances, domestic retailers were heavily damaged, forcing many of them into closure or into reducing the size of their businesses. The same thing happened with the middle-standing department stores as well as with traditional retailers, like small-scale grocery stores. The impact of the new retail formats also extended to traditional wholesalers and consumer goods manufacturers. As a result, Thailand's traditional distribution system, which had been built with big consumer goods manufacturers as the leader, seemed to be confronting a structural change.

On the one hand, such a change could possibly spur modernization and increased efficiency in the distribution system, while on the other hand it might drive many traditional retailers and wholesalers, at least for a short term, into closure and result in serious employment problems. The media frequently reports on the difficulties facing traditional retailers and the opposition by small-scale retailers to store openings of new foreign-led retail formats. There are also reports of cases of consumer goods manufacturers forced to accept unfavorable transaction terms from large-scale retailers, who have become their main customers. Retail sales and distribution has become one of the most important political issues in Thailand at the moment, for which the government has tried to adopt various policies.

A general survey of the present situation of the distribution industry in Thailand would lead us to formulate the hypothesis that Thailand is a typical host country where transnational retailers have succeeded in business and where the distribution revolution is rapidly ongoing with transnational retailers playing a leading role. However, is this hypothesis, which is now becoming a common view, really supported by sufficient data and methodology?

THE RETAIL INTERNATIONALIZATION PROCESS

Changes relatively similar to those occurring in Thailand can be observed broadly in other emerging markets, including East and Southeast Asian countries and regions. Studies on transnational retailers' advance into emerging markets have recently flourished, and Thailand, one of the most popular host countries for transnational retailers, often appears as a case study.[2] Many of these studies aim to clarify the retail internationalization process from a commercial science perspective, and tend to focus on the activities of transnational retailers. They then try and analyze to what extent transnational retailers transferred their business systems, standardized in their home countries, into the host countries, and to what extent they attempted to adapt to the new circumstances of the host countries. Yahagi (2007), in particular, succeeded in categorizing the localization process of Japan-based and Western-based general mass-merchandisers (e.g., general merchandise stores and hypermarkets) on the basis of an extensive reading of theoretical studies and his own ample research on this topic.

The experiences of Wal-Mart Stores Inc. and Carrefour have shown that the success and failure of the same company seems to vary according to the host country. Why is this? As Yahagi (2007) has suggested, we cannot attribute the causes of failure only to differences in the business strategy of transnational retailers. This is because the retail industry calls for greater attention to the local context of the host countries than does the manufacturing industry due to the extent of the involvement by retailers in the local context. While studies on the retail internationalization process examine, to a certain extent, the local context of the host countries, they do not necessarily pay sufficient attention to specific particulars, such as the structure of consumer markets in the host countries; their traditional and changing distribution systems; the commercial practices and actions of local companies and businesses; governmental laws and regulations; and so on.[3] This may be because such studies highlight transnational retailers as the leading actors.

This is understandable when we take into consideration that only a few studies actually focus on the domestic distribution industry in emerging markets. Moreover, basic data, including commercial statistics, are not readily accessible in emerging market countries.[4] That is why, in this respect, area studies focusing on the specific circumstances of these markets can contribute to the field and can complement the methodology and research results of retail internationalization process studies.

STUDIES BY THAI RESEARCHERS

Recently a number of Thai researchers have been studying the distribution industry from a different viewpoint from retail internationalization process studies. These studies can be roughly divided into two kinds: (1) current reports on business developments of new retail formats in Thailand,[5] especially of transnational retailers, and (2) positive (as opposed to normative) analyses concerning the impact of new retail formats upon traditional retailers.[6] Both types of studies pay much attention to the competitive relationships between modern and traditional retailers, foreign-led and local retailers, or large-scale and small-scale retailers. In other words, they tend to focus on the "horizontal relationships" in the distribution system. These studies have undoubtedly provided valuable information on the changes and problems that the retail industry in Thailand is confronting. However, partly because all-inclusive data on the Thai retail industry is unavailable, these studies have not always examined such things as new retail formats market share as a percentage of the entire retail industry, or the impact of new formats on the traditional retail industry. In addition, these studies tend to overlook the trends in a country's retail industry in relation to its entire distribution system. Needless to say, since the retail industry lies at the end of the entire distribution system (that consists of production, wholesale, and retail stages), it is necessary to pay equal attention to "vertical relationships," such as retailers' business connections with manufacturers and wholesalers, in order to gain an in-depth understanding of the changes and problems in the retail industry.[7]

Some important studies in this respect were recently published. One such study is by Niphon et al. (2002), which fully analyzed, for the first time, the impact of transnational retailers on the entire Thai distribution industry. The authors did this by looking at both traditional retailers and traditional wholesalers. Their study is especially valuable for its detailed research on consumer purchasing behaviors, something seldom studied in a full-scale way. Aruni (2003) similarly studied and excellently explained the impact of new retail formats on the Thai traditional distribution system, while also looking at business connections between large-scale retailers and consumer goods manufacturers. There is also the case of an anonymous ex-employee of a leading local consumer goods manufacturing company who disclosed the hidden side of business connections between leading consumer goods manufacturers and large-scale retailers, presenting outsiders with valuable information (*Mr. Re-Tell*, 2002). However, these studies do not pay enough attention to the building of marketing channels by taking specific cases of consumer goods manufacturers and wholesalers as the leading actors in vertical relationships.[8] In addition, they only have an incomplete perspective for understanding the current changes in the Thai distribution system within a historical context. As a result, they tend to excessively emphasize the present prosperity of the new retail formats.

Jirapha (2003), to the contrary, gives a concrete explanation for the development of marketing channels, using the cases of the local-based Saha

Pathanapibul Plc and Charoen Pokphand (CP) groups and the foreign-based Unilever-Thai. Although her study is important, as it throws light on the roles of consumer goods manufacturers in the Thai distribution system, it tends to rely too much on newspapers and magazines for data, and overlooks the roles of traditional wholesalers. Nevertheless, studies by Thai researchers provide a counterpoint to retail internationalization process studies.

CHARACTERISTICS OF THAILAND'S CONSUMER MARKET

Most of the earlier studies, whether they were studies of horizontal relationships by Thai researchers or retail internationalization process studies by Western and Japanese commercial scientists, tend to overestimate the urban middle class when considering the consumer market. Income differentials within emerging market countries in the midst of industrialization are generally wide.[9] It is certain that the urban middle class plays an important role in providing pulling power for consumption, but it doesn't necessarily occupy the largest consumer base. As will be shown in chapter 2, using positive analysis, the low-income class in Thailand is still large, especially in provincial agricultural areas. It, thus, becomes necessary to examine the entire consumer market, including the lower-income bracket, because the low-income class is likely to be important customers, particularly in the case of daily foods and necessities with their relatively lower income elasticity of demand.

Here, careful attention should be paid to the possibility that the purchasing behavior of consumers can differ widely across income levels. For example, even within the same category of goods, there will inevitably be differences among geographical areas and differences among income classes with regard to the extent to which greater importance is attached to price or brand. Distributors (i.e., wholesalers and retailers) and manufacturers must both provide various responses to the segmented consumer market. In some cases, within emerging consumer markets, local companies may have more advantageous access than TNCs and, similarly, among domestic companies, provincial companies may have better access than leading metropolis-based companies. In other words, when researching the distribution system in an emerging market characterized by wide income differentials, Thailand being a typical case, focus should not be solely on the urban middle class consumer market, but rather the perspective must be widen to include the entire consumer market and its income differentials.

THE DISTRIBUTION REVOLUTION IN THE CONTEXTS OF JAPAN AND THAILAND

In the 1960s, Professor Hayashi's argument regarding the distribution revolution aroused an important controversy in Japan. Hayashi (1962) argued that during the period of rapid economic growth in the 1960s, mass production and mass consumption were achieved in Japan, while the traditional distribution system began to malfunction. He explained that the traditional system, characterized by small-scale stores, an excessive number of retailers, and multi-level transactions by wholesalers, was evolving into a new one. In this new system, emerging large-scale retailers (e.g., supermarkets) made direct dealings with large-scale manufacturers, bypassing wholesalers. In other words, it was a drastic change from "thin and long" distribution channels to "thick and short" distribution channels. This, of course, meant that the roles of wholesalers were declining.

Since then, mass-merchandisers, such as supermarkets and general merchandise stores (GMS), have rapidly expanded. Nevertheless, wholesalers have not systematically declined in Japan. Three reasons account for this. First, large-scale retailers regarded wholesalers as useful because of their various functions, including physical distribution. Second, large-scale retailers invested a lot of money and manpower into expanding their chains, so that they could not afford to internalize the functions wholesalers had previously assumed. And third, many wholesalers succeeded in reforming their business; for example by expanding to the national level, strengthening their operations, etc.

Let's now compare the Japanese experience with the case of an emerging market like Thailand. The case of Thailand differs from that of Japan in several respects. During the period of rapid economic growth in the 1960s, the Japanese middle class increased in number, and consumption patterns became homogeneous. By contrast, the Thai middle class remains the minority, and the income differentials among classes and areas are still wide. Nevertheless, the studies mentioned earlier often put too much emphasis on the middle class as a pulling power for consumption. In the case of daily foods and necessities in which the income elasticity of demand is relatively low, the lower-income class should also be regarded as an important group of customers.

In addition, whereas the development of a chain operation system and the full-scale introduction of information technology did not occur at the same time in Japan, the modern retail industry in Thailand has introduced these two retailing innovations simultaneously. As a result, traditional retailers and wholesalers in Thailand have had less time to cope with these drastic changes, while the new retail formats equipped with efficient physical distribution systems can bypass wholesalers. This suggests that the development process of wholesalers in Thailand is undoubtedly different from that in Japan.

POINTS AT ISSUE

The objective of this study is to uncover the actual situation of the Thai distribution system by primarily investigating the daily processed foods and necessities that have been most seriously damaged by the rise of the new retail formats. This study concentrates on the period beginning around 1990, when new retail formats emerged one after another, and continues until the mid-2000s, when the retail issue became sharper in Thailand. The study also goes back in time whenever necessary, and focuses on a number of specific issues and perspectives, as follows.

The first chapter presents the characteristics and formation process of the traditional distribution system in Thailand. This information is indispensable for understanding Thailand's distribution system in its historical context.

The next two chapters examine the structural characteristics of the Thai consumer market, keeping in mind the relationship with the distribution industry. In order to offer a better view of the consumer market as a means to analyze the entire distribution system in Thailand, the study pays special attention not only to the urban middle class but also to other classes, especially the low-income class, which still comprises the majority of the population.

The actual situation of the new retail formats operating in Thailand on the basis of positive data is also examined (chaps. 3 and 4). As mentioned previously, many of the earlier studies emphasized the rise of new retail formats in Thailand with insufficient positive data.[10] They also share a tendency to deal with the new retail formats collectively as the "modern trade." This study investigates the actual situation of the new retail formats by looking at the competition between formats and between companies, while also considering the problems with which the various formats are confronted.

Basing the discussion on the daily processed foods and necessities channels, the study shows how vertical relationships in the Thai distribution system are changing with the rise of new retail formats (chap. 5). The study also highlights the marketing channel strategies of consumer goods manufacturers as well as the business connections between manufacturers and large-scale retailers (the new retail formats). It then focuses on the roles of traditional wholesalers as channel members, mostly overlooked in earlier studies. The objective here is to understand the situation of the Thai distribution industry as a whole, while making careful use of governmental statistics since the earlier studies (heavily influenced by the media) tend to emphasize the fall of traditional wholesalers and retailers without sufficient positive data.

The study also elucidates the reactions of the parties (retailers and wholesalers) within the industry and the government's policies towards various distribution issues (chap. 6). Ever since distribution issues in Thailand first emerged, the government's distribution policies have greatly wavered, as a result of the reactions and pressures of the domestic industry. These policies have also become very complicated. The study analyzes the implications and problems of Thailand's distribution policies, while paying full attention to the behavior of the interested parties.

The last chapter focuses on the actual nature of the "distribution revolution" in Thailand, one of the most popular host countries for transnational retailers. It also suggests prospects for future comparative studies with other emerging markets, while considering the significance of the case of Thailand.[11]

SOURCES

Few sources on the Thai distribution industry are available at present. While academic papers and current reports written in Thai in this field have recently increased, the sum total remains insufficient. Therefore, the author placed considerable efforts into collecting information from Thai-language newspapers and business magazines. This was done as extensively as possible in order to build an original database on the trends of the Thai distribution industry. A list of Thai-language newspapers and business magazines used in this study is provided in the reference section at the end of the book.

Sources concerning individual companies also played an important role. For example, the author made his best efforts to obtain documents such as company histories, company profiles, and so on. While company histories per se are rarely written in Thailand even by leading long-established firms,[12] there is a tradition, when a socially well-known person dies, to compile a book consisting of that person's life history and achievements, and the history of the field in which that person played an active role. These commemorative books for funerals, or *nangsue chaek ngan sop* in Thai (sometimes *nangsue chaek* for short), are meant for distribution at the funeral, but are often written in cooperation with professionals and can be a valuable document as a substitute for company history, if the deceased was an influential businessperson (Suehiro 1995).

Regarding the financial statements of each company, listed companies' annual reports and prospectuses, including detailed financial statements of the last few years, are available. In the case of non-listed companies, the list of shareholders and financial statements of each company are available for viewing (following prescribed procedures) at the Department of Business Development, Ministry of Commerce. To access these documents, however, the registration number or exact Thai-language name of the company is necessary. In the case of a chain store operated in the same name by other separate companies in the same business group, the documents of those companies are not classified as the same chain. Data gathering in this case, as sometimes seen in department store chains, is more problematic. In addition, financial statements of non-listed companies lack detail in comparison with those of listed companies, and most of the other available data are not particularly useful, with the exception of shareholders' lists. Nevertheless, in the absence of other sources, this company data is still very valuable.[13] The limited data of non-listed companies is supplemented by the above-mentioned database of industry trends.

As to financial statements, which are very important in studying companies, some data of all registered companies, listed or non-listed, is available. The problem is that governmental organizations and private institutions have limited corporate statistics on the distribution industry in Thailand as a whole. For example, the National Statistical Office (NSO) of the Thai government organized commercial and industrial censuses several times and published the number of establishments by type of industry, size, and so on (see chap. 5), but neither governmental organizations nor industrial associations have sufficient data regarding financial indicators such as sales volume by type of industry and by format, or the number of stores by company and by format.[14] Therefore, the author built an original database of financial statements and the business development of retail and wholesale companies in Thailand by gathering data on individual companies one by one. The corporate statistics required for arguments in the subsequent chapters rely on this database.

For the reasons stated above, the very first step in this research involved collecting as much data as possible regarding individual companies and industrial trends in order to build an original database. On the basis of this database, the author conducted interviews with many persons connected with the industry. During the interviews, the author asked questions mainly concerning qualitative data, such as each company's business connections and channel strategies, which is difficult to get without interviews. Interviews were also used as a means to check the veracity of other information collected in advance of each interview. Because of the lack of well-organized documents on Thai local companies, interviews become a particularly important tool in the research conducted for this study.

KEY TERMS

To avoid possible misunderstandings in subsequent chapters, it is necessary to explain some of the key terms used throughout this research.

The term "modern trade" appearing at the beginning of this chapter is widely used in Thailand, not only by the mass media but also by governmental committees, private think tanks, and other institutions, including academic circles. Modern trade consists mainly of new retail formats, specifically identified as cash-and-carry, hypermarkets, supermarkets, convenience stores, and some other forms of retail business that appeared in Thailand from the late 1980s to the mid-1990s. Department stores, the only modern retail format in the past, are sometimes included in modern trade. This term is used in contrast with the term "traditional trade" which refers to traditional wholesalers and retailers. In this study, however, there are some cases of traditional wholesalers, as discussed in detail in chapter 5, who have reformed the traditional style of business into a new format equipped with some factors of the modern trade.

The terms "cash-and-carry" and "hypermarket," are both part of the new retail formats, but still unfamiliar in some countries and need to be defined briefly. Cash-and-carry refers to membership warehouse clubs that sell daily processed foods and necessities in bulk at low prices mainly to small-scale retailers and restaurants with membership privileges. Cash-and-carry may also sell other categories of goods, such as clothing, DIY (do-it-yourself) goods, home electronics appliances, toys, etc. Stores are built in a low-rise warehouse style in which the interior cost is minimized, and are also equipped with a large parking lot. In this type of store, customers have to pay in cash and carry out the purchased goods by themselves, hence the name "cash-and-carry." Cash-and-carry are nominally wholesale businesses but are also involved in retail services. This study regards this format as a kind of retailing. A "hypermarket," on the other hand, is a large-scale retail format that combines a supermarket and a discount store. While a hypermarket has such common points with the cash-and-carry format as a low-rise, warehouse-style store and large parking lot, a wide range of goods, self-service, and low prices, hypermarkets are also characterized by a rich selection of foods, including perishables. In Thailand, hypermarkets partially compete with cash-and-carry, because the former has a corner in its store dedicated to daily processed foods and necessities in big lots and also partly functions as a kind of cash-and-carry wholesaler for small- and medium-scale wholesalers and retailers. Actually, these two formats are often dealt with collectively in Thailand. Therefore, in this study, cash-and-carry and hypermarkets are generically referred to as general mass merchandisers (Yahagi 2007, 11). The differences between the two formats are further discussed in chapter 4.

Other terms regarding intermediate distribution also require the readers' attention. First, "sales company" is a form of a wholesale business, but in this study the author distinguishes it from general wholesalers and identifies it as a distributor who exclusively sells products of specific manufacturers at the wholesale level. Although one usually thinks that a sales company is established with the capital of a manufacturer who is the parent company, the percentage level of the investment does not matter in this study. It is because of two major companies, Saha Pathanapibul Plc and Diethelm Co., Ltd., that the author considers sales companies as greatly different in function and scale from general wholesalers, while in terms of investment, they do not come under the ordinary definition of a sales company. By using the term "sales companies," the author is referring to two types of sales companies, those that belong to a manufacturing business group and those that are independent from a manufacturing group.

As for general traditional wholesalers, there are some terms peculiar to the Thai context. While wholesalers are typically called *phu prakopkan kha song* or *phu kha song* in the Thai language, traditional wholesalers, in particular, are also often called *yi pua* in Teochiu. Therefore, the word *yi pua* is sometimes used in this study when mentioning traditional wholesalers. In addition, there are certain distinctions between independent wholesalers (*yi pua*) and agents (*tua thaen jamnai* in Thai) that enter into a contract with a manufacturer to exclusively sell its products. However, since both in reality overlap in many cases, as discussed in detail in chapter 5, the study does not distinguish between them, if it is not necessary to do so.

It should be noted that *yi pua* hold an intermediate position within the entire distribution channel. *Yi pua* purchase goods from a manufacturer or importer (*thao pua*) and resell the goods to a secondary wholesaler or a retailer, or *sa pua*. This means that *yi pua* aren't always wholesalers. In reality, as will be explained later in the study, *yi pua* often run wholesaling and retailing simultaneously. However, Thai traders don't necessarily divide their activities between wholesaling and retailing; therefore, the author uses the term *yi pua* to also refer to traditional wholesalers. On the other hand, since *sa pua*, that is secondary wholesalers, only play a limited role in the intermediate distribution of daily processed foods and necessities, this term is not used in this study, but rather the term *cho huai* (in Teochiu) is used for small-scale grocery stores that occupy the largest portion of Thai traditional retailers.

1

FORMATION OF THAILAND'S TRADITIONAL DISTRIBUTION SYSTEM

CHINESE MERCHANTS

SAMPHENG: THE CENTRAL COMMERCE DISTRICT

In one corner of Chinatown in the southeastern part of old Bangkok, there is a district called Sampheng. It was formed in 1782 when the Rattanakosin kingdom was first established and its capital was moved from Thonburi on the right bank of the Chao Phraya River to Phra Nakhon (Bangkok) on the left bank. Chinese merchants were subsequently forced to move to Sampheng, located outside the castle wall.

From the beginning of the Rattanakosin era, the Sampheng district played an important role in trade with China, which at the time was Thailand's main trading partner. Sampheng-based Chinese merchants collected special products from various localities and exported them. They also imported goods to sell in Thailand's domestic market. Commonly exported goods included rice, cayenne (red pepper), white-rumped swift nests, sugar, and so on. Imported goods from China consisted mainly of ceramic ware, silk fabrics, gold and silverware, glassware, Chinese medicine, roofing tiles, and Chinese traditional processed foods (Janjutha 2006, 93–96). When a junk (Chinese traditional sailboat) carrying imported goods arrived at the Chao Phraya River, these goods were traded on board and unloaded at the Ratchawong Wharf in the Sampheng district (Khomsan 2006, 360–62). It can be said that at that time the Sampheng district was the economic front linking Thailand with foreign countries, China in particular.

After Thailand concluded the Bowring Treaty with the United Kingdom in 1855, and similar treaties with other Western countries in successive years, its trade with Western countries as well as with China expanded. The conveniently located Sampheng district increasingly prospered as the central business district where Chinese importers and wholesalers were concentrated. The construction of many new roads around the district under the reign of Rama V (1868–1910) also contributed to accelerating the prosperity of Sampheng (Piyanat 2006, 5–11). Ratchawong Road, Jakkrawat Road, Anuwong Road, and Songwat Road were some of the main streets constructed during this period. Since Sampheng Lane—the core of the district, with shops on both sides—was too crowded to be widened, Yaowarat Road was constructed to the north, parallel to Sampheng Lane. As a result, the Sampheng district became even more convenient as a location for business, improving its status as the central business district.

In this way, Chinese merchants in the Sampheng district established a predominant position both in external trade with foreign countries and in internal trade in the Thai domestic market. It is important to note that the practice of selling on credit had spread among local merchants, as some earlier successful merchants became involved in money lending (TDRI 1999, 10–12). Distribution from the Sampheng district was extending all over the country, as the wholesaler-led distribution channel centering on credit was gradually formed and the extension of the railways from Bangkok to the provinces brought more Chinese immigrants to provincial cities.[1]

EUROPEAN TRADING COMPANIES

Prior to the conclusion of the Bowring Treaty, that is before the free trade system was established in Thailand, Chinese merchants were so deeply engaged in trade on behalf of the Thai royal family that all trade was virtually under their control. Beginning in the latter half of the nineteenth century and continuing until the first half of the twentieth century, however, European trading companies advanced into Thailand one after another. In the 1870s, in particular, when the primary means of transportation for trade was changing from junk to steamboat, Europeans became strong competitors with Chinese traders because they had the advantage of capital and transportation technology (Van Roy 2006, 26–28). The percentage of junks in Thailand's trade with foreign countries decreased drastically for twenty years between the 1870s and 1880s—even the steamship route between Bangkok and Swatao (Shantou) in China, which was the main route at the time, was controlled by European companies. Although a number of Chinese traders established their own shipping companies as a countermeasure, they were always confronted with great difficulties in their competition with the Europeans (Suphang 2006, 85–89).

European shops were established one after another in Bangkok during this period and enjoyed popularity. For example, Messrs. Harry A. Badman & Co., which opened in the walled city of Bangkok around 1880, dealt in accessories for the royalty, nobility, and upper classes and uniforms for civil officials and the military, as well as furniture, wristwatches, jewelry, and so on. These goods were directly imported from Europe via the Purchasing Office in London. Outside of the walled city, too, many European trading companies were established, including the S.A.B. Store, which opened in 1907 and imported high-quality watches and jewelry made in Belgium (Anek 1999, 130–53).

However, the decline of the Chinese shipping business didn't mean that the role of Chinese merchants in Thailand's trade and commerce was decreasing (Skinner 1957, 102). This is an important point to which we should pay attention. European trading companies mainly sold high-priced goods and luxuries, targeting the Bangkok upper class, while Chinese stores dealt in some high-priced goods but mainly focused on daily foods and necessities. Therefore, Europeans and Chinese didn't always compete with each other. For example, Kee Chiang & Son, H. Swee Ho, and Young Lee Seng, all of which were well-known Chinese stores in Bangkok at the time, mainly sold alcoholic beverages, medicine, goods, and tools imported from China (Santi 2001, 44–50). It is important to add here that European businessmen needed Chinese small-scale ships and many Chinese laborers (coolies) to unload their cargo, and also depended on Chinese merchants' distribution channels in the Thai domestic market, in which the Sampheng-based wholesalers played leading roles (Khomsan 2006, 363).

DOMESTIC DISTRIBUTION CHANNELS

European trading companies and Chinese merchants actually interacted in a complementary relationship in some aspects of their trade. With regard to domestic distribution, in particular, Chinese merchants played indispensable roles as trade partners for European trading companies because they were more familiar with the Thai consumer market than European businessmen, and they had built up closer relationships with provincial Chinese retailers in Thailand. Moreover, Chinese merchants had learnt how to treat Thai officials over several centuries and had always cooperated with the royal family in trade. They, therefore, enjoyed special privileges, like the reduction and exemption of tax as well as certain financial aid, all of which European trading companies were unable to benefit from. By contrast, Europeans, who spoke neither Thai nor Chinese, could only have access to limited and indirect business information (Skinner 1957, 99–102).[2]

Chinese merchants thus played a leading part in Thailand's domestic retail as well as wholesale businesses, except for a few types of high-priced goods. As European businesses further expanded, Chinese businesses grew as well. The Sampheng-based Chinese merchants, in particular, gradually increased their controlling power. For instance, even Switzerland-based Diethelm, which established its Thai affiliated company in 1906 and concentrated on import businesses until around World War II, had no other choice but to depend on Chinese merchants in its domestic trade within Thailand (Somjai 2004, 236–39).[3]

It was the withdrawal or reduction of many European trading companies following the outbreak of World War I and the postwar depression that definitively established the predominant position of Chinese merchants in domestic distribution channels (Samrit 1992, 223–24). Chinese merchants regarded this as an ideal business chance. They purchased the businesses of European trading companies and entered into the vacant market after the Europeans' withdrawal. However, under the nationalistic policy of the pre-war Phibun government (1938–44), economic activities of foreigners, especially the Chinese, were strictly regulated. Despite these unfavorable circumstances, Chinese merchants actually weathered their hardships, for the most part, not only by changing their Chinese surnames and trade names to Thai to ease the oppression, but also by forming close relationships with the military and politically influential persons. A similar thing occurred during the post-war Phibun government (1948–57), under which economic intervention by the military and bureaucracy further intensified.

In this way, Chinese merchants, especially Sampheng-based wholesalers, came to occupy an overwhelmingly predominant position in domestic distribution channels. However, by around 1950 at the latest, some of the Chinese and European importers began to worry that they would lose opportunities for extending their businesses if they continued to depend on the Sampheng-based wholesalers' distribution channels, and became dissatisfied with these channels. Indeed, Sampheng's wholesalers dared not go to the provinces to sell their goods but waited for provincial wholesalers to come and purchase goods in Sampheng (Somjai 1990, 43–44).[4] Another cause of dissatisfaction with Sampheng's wholesalers was that they did not have full respect for the product differentiation policy of the consumer goods manufacturers and importers, and neither did they have sufficient knowledge regarding new goods successively introduced on the market. Furthermore, Sampheng's wholesalers did not provide feedback on sales data to the manufacturers and importers (Kao Industrial 1986, 53). These limitations of the old distribution channels became even larger obstacles when the companies entering the manufacturing industry in the 1960s under the import substitution industrialization (ISI) policy made efforts to expand the market for their products.

THE OPENING UP OF DOMESTIC MARKETS

Faced with this situation, certain consumer goods manufacturers and importers started to voluntarily open up markets to free themselves from their dependence on Sampheng's distribution channels. One of the earliest examples is Osotspa Co., Ltd., which started its business by selling pharmaceutical products and soon extended its activities into pharmaceutical compounding and pharmaceutical products manufacturing. Osotspa started to sell its goods on provincial markets during wartime in 1944, and then began to use advertising trucks equipped with a film projector to promote their products. According to one former employee of the company, who was engaged for a long time in the opening up of provincial markets, Osotspa employees, in groups of three, loaded pharmaceutical products and a projector onto an advertising truck and worked together to handle the sales, collection and remittance of funds, screening of a film to attract villagers, the driving of the vehicle, etc. (Thanit 2001, 11–17). By around 1970, Osotspa had twenty-five teams of advertising trucks (seventy-eight persons in total) and each team showed films in twenty villages and sold goods to residents from approximately sixty villages each month (ibid., 29). The use of films to open up provincial markets and attract customers was soon adopted as a marketing strategy by many local and foreign companies as well.

Thai Shin Phanit Co., Ltd., which was the sole import agent for Kao products in the 1950s before the advance of Kao into the Thai market, used Sampheng's wholesalers as its selling agent, but also actively sought new markets for itself.

The company first concentrated on the Bangkok market, and soon thereafter began to enter provincial markets. The company eventually succeeded in expanding its business to such an extent as to have dealings with five hundred stores in Bangkok and seven hundred provincial stores. It also made efforts to record information about the stores with which Thai Shin Panit had dealings, including the names and addresses of those stores and the banks they used, as well as photos of the store owners' families and signatures for verification purposes (Kao Industrial 1986, 22–35).

Saha Pathanapibul Plc (hereafter abbreviated as Saha Pat) also started to seek new provincial markets for its products from the early 1950s onwards. The forerunner of Saha Pat was a small store named Hiap Seng Chiang (協成昌有限公司). It was established in 1942 on Songwat Road (located between Sampheng Lane and the Chao Phraya River) by the founder of the Saha Group, Thiam Chokwatthana (李興添, 1916–91).[5] Although it was a small-scale wholesaler and retailer at the beginning, the store rapidly grew into an importer (*long thao*) by setting up a branch in Hong Kong. It imported goods such as clothes, medicine, canned foods, socks, shoes, undershirts, pens, glasses, tooth powders, and ironware, 90 percent of which came from Hong Kong and the remaining 10 percent from the US, Netherlands, and Japan (Saha Pathanapibul Plc, n.d., b: 5–8).

The commercial practices at the time were such that importers only sold goods to Sampheng's wholesalers and were not directly involved in domestic markets. In spite of these practices, Thiam not only did business with Sampheng's wholesalers but also had direct dealings with Bangkok's large-scale retailers. In addition, he began to seek new markets for himself by sending salespersons to the provinces beginning in the mid-1950s.[6] The commemorative book published to mark the fifty-year history of the company cites two reasons for why Thiam looked to extend his business (Saha Pathanapibul Plc, n.d. b: 10). First, the company recognized the necessity to open up other distribution channels for its products since its sales were insufficient using only the Sampheng-based wholesalers' channels. Second, the company found that relying on only the Bangkok market was not enough to grow its business. Although Sampheng's wholesalers were dissatisfied that Saha Pat was not using the Sampheng wholesalers as middlemen to enter the provinces, at a time when telecommunication was not as developed as it is now, they had no way to fully grasp the ramifications of Saha Pat's locating new markets in the provinces by itself, and thus did not regard it as a particularly big problem.[7] To find new markets in the provinces, Saha Pat would send salespersons to each region (four persons in total at first), where they had dealings with six to seven provincial traders per region.[8] The salespersons received goods from the head office in Bangkok at a hotel where they stayed for a short period and did business with the hotel on a temporary basis. Later on, they formed cash van teams that traveled around the provinces, while simultaneously using advertising trucks with film projectors to promote their business.

As consumer goods manufacturers and importers started to recognize the limitations of the Sampheng-based wholesalers' channels, they poured their efforts into seeking new markets. At the time, however, this was done without any deliberate plans and it had yet to reach a level in which these companies could build their own marketing channels. In fact, the Sampheng-based wholesalers still held such a strong control of distribution channels that manufacturers and importers had little choice but to rely on these already established channels.

THE BUILDING OF MARKETING CHANNELS

Early in the 1960s, some importers began to establish joint ventures with foreign companies, which had previously been their trading partners, in order to enter the manufacturing industry under the Thai government's import substitution industrialization policy. For example, in 1964, Thai Shin Phanit Co., Ltd. (the sole import agent for Kao) became a joint-venture partner with the Japan-based Kao Group that had established Kao Industrial (Thailand) Co. Ltd. (hereafter abbreviated as Thai Kao). Saha Pat Co., Ltd. similarly entered into a joint venture with the Japan-based Lion Group to establish Lion Corporation (Thailand) in 1967. Both of these newly formed companies, Thai Kao and Lion Corporation, began in full swing to manufacture and sell laundry detergent. This same phenomenon can be observed in the field of durable consumer goods, such as automobiles, home electronics appliances, textiles and garments, and so on (Suehiro 1984, 10–13; Suehiro 1989, 225–39).

As import substitution industrialization progressed, a wider variety of goods came to be distributed in the Thai market in larger volume.[9] Despite significant changes, as far as production was concerned, the old distribution channels in which the Sampheng-based wholesalers played a leading role were retained, even though they were beginning to malfunction. Faced with this situation, it is not surprising that companies with rapidly increasing productivity came to find it indispensable to build their own marketing channels for their products.

During the first period following its establishment, Thai Kao relied on the distribution channel of its joint-venture partner, Thai Shin Phanit, and similarly relied on cash transactions through the company's cash van sales and credit transactions, which at that point was handled through Sampheng-based agents (wholesalers). However, four of the seven Sampheng agents were garment wholesalers and had never dealt in laundry detergents, the main product of Thai Kao. The other three Sampheng agents were also agents for "Fab," the laundry detergent made by Colgate-Palmolive (Thailand) Co., Ltd. (hereafter Thai Colgate) as well as the laundry detergent "Omo" manufactured by Unilever Thai Co., Ltd. (Thai Unilever). Thai Kao obviously could not expect the Sampheng agents to sell its products more eagerly than its competitors' products. In addition, Thai Shin Phanit had only three teams of cash van sales, while Thai Colgate and Thai Unilever had twenty-eight and sixteen teams, respectively (Kao Industrial 1986, 41). This is why Thai Kao increased its cash van teams to eight in 1967 and then to fifteen in 1970, and also began to build direct sales channels bypassing the sales agents.

While Thai Kao's Sampheng agents naturally resisted this attempt, Thai Kao managed to reach an agreement to abolish the contract it had with them by paying the Sampheng agents a fixed amount of money for their long-standing cooperation. Thai Kao also started sorting out the new business connections that Thai Shin Phanit had developed, and went on to separate its sales and marketing departments from its manufacturing department to keep up with business expansion. In 1975, Thai Kao founded the sales company, Kit Siam Commercial Co., Ltd., whose name was changed to Kao Commercial (Thailand) in 1991 (hereafter abbreviated as Thai Kao Sales). Despite promoting the creation of direct sales channels by establishing this company, Thai Kao Sales' direct dealings with retailers at the time amounted to about only 15 percent of total sales, with the remaining 85 percent coming from dealings with about sixteen hundred wholesalers all over the country (Kao Industrial 1986, 53–56, 70–72).

Switzerland-based Diethelm (Thailand) Co., Ltd. (hereafter abbreviated Thai Diethelm) established warehouses both in Bangkok and in each of Thailand's major regions, so it could build direct marketing channels to sell its goods to retailers in the capital and the provinces, thereby bypassing Chinese middlemen (Somjai 2004, 239). The UK and Holland-based Thai Unilever made similar efforts to construct a direct-sales system by establishing warehouses in each region of the country.

However, establishing its own warehouses caused much additional cost, as Thai Unilever proceeded to further open up provincial consumer markets. In addition, there were initially some limits involved in covering the vast provincial markets by oneself. As a result, Thai Unilever selected "stockists" or warehousemen from among provincial wholesalers and entrusted them with the setting up and management of the warehouses for Unilever products (Sombun 2005b, 50–51). The role of these stockists was mainly to establish and manage these warehouses, while the company's principal business affairs, such as delivery, selling, and accounting, were under the responsibility of Thai Unilever. In reality, however, even Thai Unilever, despite having warehouses in each region, wasn't able to establish thorough, direct dealings with every single retailer, and, just as its competitors had no other choice but to depend on the distribution channels of leading wholesalers in each area, so, too, did Thai Unilever.[10]

Saha Pat, unlike Thai Diethelm and Thai Unilever, set up a selling-agent system in the 1960s, in which it selected agents (*saha rung rueang*) from among influential wholesalers in each locality. In other words, Saha Pat made the best use of external managerial resources without persisting in building its own direct-sales channels.[11] This is due to the fact that Saha Pat, a latecomer in the laundry detergent business, attached importance to provincial markets while avoiding the Bangkok market where the two European companies, Thai Colgate and Thai Unilever, already occupied strong positions (Somjai 1990, 70–73). It seems that Saha Pat needed to lower its selling prices in provincial markets as much as possible and did this by minimizing the costs involved in building marketing channels. Saha Pat's selected agents found that Saha Pat not only supplied its products on more favorable conditions than it did to general wholesalers, but it also set out to build closer business connections with its agents by giving them opportunities to participate in meetings and factory observation in Bangkok (Saha Pathanapibul Plc, n.d., b: 94–95).

Many consumer goods manufacturers poured efforts into building their own marketing channels. These new channels, in turn, enabled them to free themselves from much of their dependence on the Sampheng-based wholesalers' channels.[12] Nevertheless, they still had to rely most often on the selling power of provincial wholesalers spread across the country.[13] Yet, even if certain consumer goods manufacturers were using leading provincial wholesalers as their stockists or selling agents, this did not stop provincial wholesalers from entering into similar contracts with other consumer goods manufacturers.[14] These contracts did not strictly limit their activity with competitors. In other words, Thai Chinese or local manufacturers, not to mention foreign manufacturers, had no means to directly control provincial distribution channels.

THE BIRTH AND DEVELOPMENT OF DEPARTMENT STORES

FOUNDING OF CENTRAL DEPARTMENT STORE[15]

European trading companies, which had advanced into Thailand since the latter half of the nineteenth century, opened many Western-styled retail stores in Bangkok, most of which disappeared in the period between the two world wars. Yet, larger-scale Chinese retail stores, such as Tai Far Store and Maeo Dam Store, thrived along Yaowarat Road in the Sampheng district before and after World War II, but then gradually declined until not a trace was left of them in today's retail industry. In this sense, it can be said that Thai modern retailing, as we know it today, originated with the Central Department Store, which was born after the war.

Tiang Jirathiwat (鄭汝常, 1904–68), the founder of Central Department Store, was born on Hai Lam (Hainan) Island, China, in 1904 and immigrated to Thailand with his wife Wan and first son Samrit in 1927. A few years after their arrival, Tiang opened a small grocery store in Thonburi. Only after World War II did the Jirathiwat family really expand its business. When Tiang discovered that the importing of Western-language books started by Samrit and his friend was a promising business, he closed down his small grocery store in 1947 and established the Central Trading Store for Western-language books in partnership with Samrit. "Central" was named after Tiang's hope that the new store would become the center of commerce.

Central Trading Store was first located in the Si Phraya district of Bangkok, southeast of Sampheng. Four years later, Tiang and his son bought a piece of land in the Suriwong district and moved the store there. The Suriwong district was located along the southern portion of Jaroenkrung (Charoen Krung) Road that extended to the old town, which was very convenient for transportation. The new store not only had a large floor with a frontage three times as wide as before, but also introduced a new display style. In response to the demands of its customers who saw advertisements in magazines, Tiang and Samrit soon came to deal in foreign ready-made clothes and cosmetics in addition to the import and sale of Western-language books and magazines.[16] Father and son dealt mainly in high-quality articles and became the sole agents for some well-known brands.[17] In short, it appears that a clear line was drawn between the Central Trading Store and other stores that dealt in convenience goods like daily processed foods and necessities. In this way, Tiang and Samrit's Central Trading Store garnered popularity from the upper class in Bangkok because of such novel foreign goods that only they sold.

A major turning point for Tiang came in 1956 with the opening of the first branch of the Central Department Store in Wang Burapha, a new commercial district west of Sampheng. The idea for the branch store originated from the observations that Tiang and Samrit had made of modern retail formats during their many trips abroad. Soon after the opening, the department store introduced a no-discount sales policy for the first time in Thailand, and so succeeded in creating an image of a high-class store that other older stores with price negotiations systems couldn't rival. This Wang Burapha branch of Central Department Store became the model for the many Thai department stores established afterwards (Wirat, Pandop, and Somsak 2003, 16–17).

The success of the Wang Burapha branch made Tiang determined to expand his business, and he eventually established a second branch along Yaowarat Road in the Sampheng district (data on when it was established is not available). In this district, where a population of frugal Chinese consumers densely lived, the Yaowarat branch, however, gave the impression that its goods were too expensive, so it did not succeed and finally had to withdraw after only two years. Following that, in 1964, Central Department Store opened its third branch in Ratchaprasong, east of old Bangkok, where the newest commercial institutions were increasingly concentrated at the time. But the Ratchaprasong branch, which did not front the main street, was inconveniently located. Moreover, it did not look as good as the newly opened Japan-based Daimaru Department Store, which had the newest facilities, including central air-conditioning and escalators, which were being used in Thailand for the first time, and so, Tiang's third branch also ended in failure (Wirat, Pandop, and Somsak 2003, 16–17).

Although Central Department Store did not always expand its business satisfactorily during its first years, Tiang was able to gain financial support from Thai-Chinese bankers, who trusted him greatly, whenever Tiang's department store business needed a large investment sum (Wirat, Pandop, and Somsak 2003, 19–23). One example is the opening of Central's first branch in Wang Burapha.

Tiang borrowed 3 million baht from Bangkok Metropolitan Bank (京華銀行), managed by Uthen Tetchaphaibun (who bears the same family name, *sae* 鄭). When Tiang opened his fourth branch on Silom Road, a new central business district at the time, to recover from the failure of the second and third branches, he was able to raise 10 million baht in total from the Bangkok Metropolitan Bank and Bangkok Bank. With this financial support, Tiang opened the Silom branch in 1968, a luxurious store with nine floors equipped with the first air-conditioning installed in the district.[18]

It is worth mentioning here that the Silom branch separated daily processed foods and necessities from other goods, such as clothes, for the first time in the history of Central Department Store. Items were located on different floors in different departments to clearly distinguish between them. It seems that Central found it necessary to manage its various departments in its store separately, considering the wide differences among the types of goods it sold, particularly with respect to such things as purchasing routes, the nature of the goods, inventory turnover, and so on. In addition, the branch hosted exhibitions for foreign goods (e.g., Italy Week) in cooperation with the appropriate embassy concerned, and won popularity from its customers. This was also the first attempt of this sort in Thailand. In short, it can be said that, at this point, Central Department Store became a "modern department store" both in name and in reality.

DEPARTMENT STORE BOOM: 1970S TO EARLY 1980S

At the beginning of the 1970s, while gradually putting the Silom branch on track, Central Department Store was again determined to establish a large-scale store in Chidlom near Ratchaprasong, where it had once opened a store but had shortly withdrawn. In 1974, the Chidlom branch opened as the first full-scale "one-stop shop," thus becoming the most advanced department store in Thailand.[19] This branch was particularly attractive in terms of its concern with expedited services for its customers, and thus appealed to the people of Bangkok who had become more time conscious due to their increasingly busy lives. Two years earlier, in 1972, when a student-led nationalist movement arose that began with a boycott of foreign-made goods, Central Department Store had established the Central Garment Factory Co., Ltd. to produce clothes accounting for 30 to 40 percent of Central's sales through this manufacturing subsidiary that did not depend on imports. It was also the first attempt in Thailand where a department store diversified into manufacturing. The company soon entered into a license contract with famous Western brand-makers to achieve "import substitution manufacturing" for some of the clothes that had previously been imported.

Beginning in the mid-1970s, the success of Central Department Store prompted other department stores to enter the Thai department store industry. Table 1.1 shows the development of the modern retail business in Bangkok from the opening of Central Trading Store, the forerunner of Central Department Store, to the rapid emergence of new retail formats up until the end of the 1980s, which caused drastic changes in the Thai retail industry. Though the leaders of the newly born department stores were Thai Chinese, they were seldom regarded as a foreign ethnic group. The term "local" will, therefore, from here on in, include Thai Chinese, in contrast to the term "foreign," which will refer to Western and Japanese ethnic groups.[20]

TABLE 1.1 Modern retailing in Bangkok, 1947–1987

Year	Events
1947	Establishment of Central Trading Store (foundation of the Central Group; import and sale of foreign books, clothes, cosmetics, and groceries)
1956	Opening of Central Department Store, Wang Burapha branch (1st store)
1964	Establishment of Japan-based Thai Daimaru Department Store on Ratchaprasong Road, a newly-developing commercial district
1968	Establishment of Harng Central Department Store Co., Ltd.; opening of Central Department Store, Silom branch
1972	Establishment of Foodland Supermarket in Phloenchit
1974	Opening of Central Department Store, Chidlom branch (head office also moved to this store)
1975	Establishment of Pata Department Store in Pratunam
1976	Establishment of Tang Hua Seng Department Store in Banglumpoo
1977	Establishment of Merry Kings Department Store in Wang Burapha
1978	Establishment of Banglumpoo Department Store in Banglumpoo
1979	Establishment of Robinson Department Store in Siam Square (1st store) and in Anusawari (2nd store); establishment of Kaeo Fa Plaza (affiliated with New World Department Store); opening of Foodland Supermarket (2nd & 3rd stores)
1980	Establishment of Cathay Department Store on Yaowarat Road and Asia Department Store in Phrakhanong; establishment of Rainbow Department Store and Ratchaprasong Shopping Mall; opening of Merry Kings Department Store, Saphan Khwai branch and Thai Daimaru Department Store, Phrakhanong branch

Year	Events
1981	Establishment of The Mall Department Store in Ratchadamri (1st store), Dao Khanong Department Store, Metro Department Store, N'mark Department Store, Amonraphan Department Store, and Edison Department Store
1982	Establishment of Lotte Department Store in Ngamwongwan; opening of Pata Department Store, Pin Klao branch
1983	Full-scale expansion of department stores and shopping centers into the suburbs (e.g., Thonburi, Samrong); establishment of Central Plaza (Central Department Store, Lat Phrao branch), a large-scale commercial complex consisting of a department store, shopping center, conference hall, and hotel; opening of The Mall Department Store, Hua Mark branch (2nd store) on Ramkhamhaeng Road (The Mall Department Store also started to focus on its advance into the suburbs); establishment of Excel Department Store on Phetburi Road (later bought by Charoen Siriwatthanaphakdi and transformed into an IT mall, Panthip Plaza); establishment of Imperial Department Store in Samrong and Nonthaburi, respectively; establishment of Japan-based Tokyu Department Store on Rama I Road (in MBK Shopping Center)
1984	Establishment of Japan-based Sogo Department Store on Ratchaprasong Road; establishment of New World Department Store in Banglumpoo; opening of The Mall Shopping Center on Ramkhamhaeng Road; opening of the Robinson Department Store, Silom branch
1985	Establishment of Welco Department Store on Ramkhamhaeng Road; establishment of Japan-based Jusco in Ratchadaphisek (1st store); establishment of MBK Sirichai Supermarket in MBK Shopping Center; opening of Banglumpoo Department Store, Bang Pho branch; opening of Merry Kings Department Store, Wong Wian Yai branch; purchase of Bang Kapi Department Store by Imperial Department Store
1986	Establishment of Setthakit Dao Khanong in Dao Khanong; opening of The Mall commercial complex in Bang Kapi; opening of Welco Department Store, Phrakhanong branch
1987	Establishment of ATM Department Store in Phrakhanong; opening of Imperial Department Store, Phongphet branch; opening of Japan-based Jusco in Senanikhom (2nd store)

SOURCE: Samrit (1992, 209–50); Supphachai (2006, 52–87); Thai Retailers Association, ed. (n.d., 39–123); Thanawat (2000, 80–89); Thanawat (2001, 348–65); Yutthasak (2001a); Athiwat (2002, 118–36); Wirat, Panthop, and Somsak (2003, 48–49); author interviews.

NOTE: Emphasis is on large-scale stores, such as department stores; "establishment" refers to the establishment of the first store of the company, while "opening" refers to the opening of the second and all following stores.

It can be observed from table 1.1 that intermediate-scale department stores, like Pata, Tang Hua Seng, Merry Kings, Banglumpoo, Cathay, and Asian, opened mainly in or around the old town, one after another between the latter half of the 1970s and the beginning of the 1980s. It was also during this period that Robinson Department Store, a powerful rival to Central Department Store between the 1980s and the first half of the 1990s, opened its first store by poaching some Thai managing staff from Thai Daimaru. Robinson's second store, the Anusawari branch, met with great success at the time, due notably to its convenient location, which had a high concentration of bus stops.

In 1981, The Mall Department Store, one of the two major department store chains today (the other being Central Department Store), opened for business. Supphachai Amphut, the founder, had first succeeded in the entertainment industry, including movie theater management. He then decided to advance into the department store business based on his experience during an observation trip in America (Supphachai 2006, 45–61). The first store he opened in Ratchadamri, however, soon had to close down due to its inability to boost sales in the aftermath of the second oil crisis of 1979, and exhausted by the competition with the Thai Daimaru Department Store, a leader in the same district. In 1983, the company opened its second store on Ramkhamhaeng Road in the suburbs to avoid direct competition with rival department stores. From that point on, The Mall Department Store succeeded in the department store business and managed to rapidly expand its chain of stores.

ADVANCE INTO THE SUBURBS AND POPULARIZATION: 1983 TO LATE 1980S

The next big change in the Thai department store industry originated from the establishment of Central Plaza, a mega-project of Central Department Store.[21] In 1979, Central Department Store was determined to develop a large-scale commercial complex in the Lat Phrao district of a northern suburb of Bangkok. The building site, leased on a thirty-year contract from Thailand Railway Public Corporation, was located at the intersection of Phahonyothin Road (National Highway Route 1) and Viphavadi Rangsit Road, connecting the center of Bangkok and Don Mueang International Airport. Although the location was potentially convenient for transportation, the area was so deserted at the time that there were only a few public bus routes. Even worse, the Thai economy at the time was suffering the aftermath of the second oil crisis with inflation and high interest rates, causing many companies to suspend big investments. Despite such circumstances, Central Department Store went ahead with the project, bringing criticism from the mass media and from the parties concerned in the industry.

In spite of the unfavorable wind against him, Samrit believed the Lat Phrao district to be promising, as he compared it with other cases in developed countries. In Tokyo, for example, a commercial district had expanded from

Ginza to Shinjuku. Samrit was able to raise funds amounting to a total of one billion baht. He obtained this sum through loans from Western banks (Bank of America, Société Générale, National Bank of Canada) as well as three local banks (Bangkok Bank, Bangkok Metropolitan Bank, Krung Thai Bank), with which Central Department Store had long, close relations. The Central Plaza project was not merely a department store but a commercial complex that included a large-scale shopping center and a high-end hotel with an international conference hall. Given the scale of the project, Central Department Store established Central Plaza Co., Ltd. in 1980 to manage the project as a developer.[22] With the establishment of this company, the Jirathiwat family business, with Samrit as its leader, clearly showed the direction of the company's development toward a family-owned conglomerate that consisted of a retailing business with Central Department Store as the core, a manufacturing and wholesaling business, as well as a hotel and resort business, a fast food business, and a real estate development business.

The influence of the Central Plaza project extended beyond the Central Group and throughout the Thai department store industry. As shown in table 1.1, around the same time, The Mall Department Store opened its second branch along Ramkhamhaeng Road in the Hua Mak district, in an eastern suburb of Bangkok and then actively expanded its chain in the suburbs. Among other department stores, as well, the advance into the suburbs and the development of shopping centers with a department store as the core tenant became a trend. Around this time, the Japan-based Tokyu Department Store and Sogo Department Store both opened for business in Bangkok, while the Thai Retailers Association, which consisted mainly of leading local department stores including Central Department Store, requested the Thai government to regulate the entry of foreign department stores, but this ended in failure (Thanawat 2000, 88). Naturally enough, the competition in department store openings led to the oversupply of stores. In addition, price competition during the period of economic stagnation in the mid-1980s caused difficulties for small- and medium-sized department stores that lacked funds (Khunathip 2001, 39–40).

Since the Saha Group (e.g., I.C.C. Co., Ltd.) and the Central Group controlled the supply of many big-name brand clothes and accessories through joint ventures with foreign capital and sole import agent contracts, medium-sized department stores with less buying power were purchasing those goods on unfavorable conditions.[23] From the very beginning, even if medium-sized department stores in the suburbs had had a large assortment of luxury items, those goods would not have met the needs of customers in the area. In this way, price competition within the Thai department store industry (except some stores in central Bangkok), especially among medium-sized department stores located in the suburbs, as well as a wider assortment of goods that appealed to price-conscious customers, resulted in the popularization of department stores. It allowed department stores, which had previously been the only actual modern retailing business, to compete directly with the new retail formats emerging one after another since the end of the 1980s, and caused many medium-sized department stores to withdraw and finally close down.

THAILAND'S DUAL-STRUCTURE RETAIL INDUSTRY

As we have seen, department stores, starting with Central Department Store, opened one after another after World War II. Department stores can thus be considered as virtually the first modern retailing business in Thailand's retail industry, where small-scale grocery stores (*cho huai*) originally occupied an overwhelming majority. While small-scale grocery stores mostly sold daily necessities and processed foods to general consumers, department stores, selling primarily big-name brand clothes, accessories and cosmetics, targeted the upper middle class and upper class. Such a dual structure in Thailand's retail industry can be said to be a reappearance of the prewar industrial structure, in which Chinese-led general stores and European-led trading companies' stores for the more well-to-do were coexisting. In this sense, Thailand's retail industry as a whole held many traditional characteristics until the 1980s. For this reason, this book refers to the distribution system in Thailand up until the 1980s as a "traditional distribution system."

However, as the competition among department stores in opening new branches intensified with the advance into the suburbs and price competition, the popularization of department stores progressed and the dual structure of Thailand's retail industry began to dissolve. Under such conditions, new retail formats since the end of the 1980s have entered Thailand's market one after another, thereby forcing the traditional distribution structure to confront drastic changes.

2

ECONOMIC GROWTH AND THE DIVERSIFICATION OF DOMESTIC BUSINESS GROUPS

RAPID ECONOMIC GROWTH AND THE CONSUMER MARKET

INVESTMENT AND CONSUMPTION BOOMS: LATE 1980S TO MID-1990S

New retail formats began emerging in Thailand's distribution industry one after another at the end of the 1980s, drastically affecting the traditional distribution system. In the early mid-80s, Thailand's economy had fallen into a depression due to a slump in the international commodities market. An investment boom began around 1987 and notably brought a sharp inflow of foreign direct investment, which completely changed the situation and directly caused a high rate of economic growth. According to the Board of Investment of Thailand (BOI), in 1986 the number and sum of investments (representing applications approved) amounted to 298 cases and 34.8 billion baht (including 154 cases and 25 billion baht of foreign investment), one year later, in 1987, this had increased to 626 cases and 67.7 billion baht (representing 385 cases and 50.1 billion baht of foreign investment), and then by the next year, in 1988, it rose again, this time quite sharply, to 1,461 cases and 201.4 billion baht (of which 892 cases and 157.5 billion baht represented foreign investment) (BOI 1989, 13).

While there are various causes for such a record-breaking investment rush, the devaluation of the US dollar originating in the Plaza Accord (signed by the G5 in September 1985) is generally given as the primary international cause. As a result, a great number of Japanese firms and firms in the Asian NIEs (Newly Industrializing Economies) were confronted with rapidly increasing currency values, such that they had little choice but to expand overseas. Thailand was one of the most popular destinations for these investors, because it provided a number of favorable internal conditions compared to other Southeast Asian countries, such as a relatively stable political situation, good economic performance, a full investment promotion policy, as well as abundant low-wage workers. The investment rush allowed Thailand's economy to rapidly improve.

While the real GDP growth rate was around 5 percent until the mid-1980s, it jumped to 9.5 percent in 1987 and exceeded 10 percent annually between 1988 and 1990, as shown in table 2.1. From then on and until 1995, Thailand's real GDP maintained a high growth rate of 8 to 9 percent. The growth rate of private consumption shows almost the same tendency as well. Moreover, since Thailand's population growth rate in this period was relatively low, GDP per capita (at current market prices) rose steeply from 15,933 baht (US$731) in 1981 to 70,474 baht (US$2,830) in 1995.[1] Generally speaking, when GDP per capita exceeds US$3,000, it tends to cause a consumption boom in the country concerned. By the mid-1990s, Thailand had almost reached that level.

TABLE 2.1 Thailand's economic growth and consumption boom, 1981–1995

	GDP	Per capita GDP			Private consumption expenditures	
	at 1988 prices	at current market prices		at 1988 prices	at 1988 prices	
Year	growth rate (%)	baht	growth rate (%)	growth rate (%)	million baht	growth rate (%)
1981	5.9	15,933	12.4	3.7	620,549	2.2
1982	5.4	17,277	8.4	3.2	634,507	2.2
1983	5.6	18,538	7.3	3.5	682,669	7.6
1984	5.8	19,513	5.3	3.8	712,971	4.4
1985	4.6	20,484	5.0	2.7	723,199	1.4
1986	5.5	21,586	5.4	3.7	748,896	3.6
1987	9.5	24,332	12.7	7.6	813,783	8.7
1988	13.3	28,710	18.0	11.4	885,008	8.8
1989	12.2	33,633	17.1	10.4	984,184	11.2
1990	11.2	39,104	16.3	9.9	1,110,935	12.9
1991	8.6	44,307	13.3	7.1	1,171,164	5.4
1992	8.1	49,410	11.5	6.7	1,273,031	8.7
1993	8.3	54,563	10.4	6.9	1,380,385	8.4
1994	9.0	61,815	13.3	7.7	1,489,070	7.9
1995	9.2	70,474	14.0	8.0	1,597,952	7.3

SOURCE: NESDB (www.nesdb.go.th).

STRUCTURAL CHARACTERISTICS OF THE CONSUMER MARKET

From the early 1980s until the mid-1990s, especially in the latter half of this fifteen-year period, Thailand's consumer market expanded considerably. Naturally enough, however, this growth phenomenon was limited to a certain part of the country and a certain segment of the population. In order to get a better understanding of this, let's analyze the structure of Thailand's consumer market. Table 2.2 shows household income by geographic area in Thailand at four points in time (1981, 1986, 1990, and 1994). While GDP-based statistics are often used to estimate income differentials, the table and this chapter instead make use of NSO's *Household Socio-Economic Survey*, which more precisely reflects the actual income levels of the local population.[2]

TABLE 2.2 Thailand's household income by region, 1981–1994

	1981		1986		1990		1994	
Region/area	income	index	income	index	income	index	income	index
Whole kingdom	40,536	100	43,572	100	67,500	100	99,144	100
Bangkok and vicinity	71,664	177	83,388	191	140,688	208	197,016	199
Center	43,980	108	48,072	110	69,924	104	104,688	106
Municipal areas	64,608	159	79,440	182	106,896	158	153,312	155
Sanitary districts	45,240	112	58,728	135	74,112	110	126,396	127
Villages	40,932	101	41,316	95	63,276	94	91,860	93
Northeast	30,144	74	30,660	70	42,348	63	67,188	68
Municipal areas	66,876	165	81,540	187	89,748	133	156,828	158
Sanitary districts	39,168	97	44,652	102	61,968	92	98,100	99
Villages	27,468	68	25,980	60	38,292	57	56,712	57
North	34,632	85	37,272	86	56,628	84	75,120	76
Municipal areas	70,620	174	79,080	181	120,612	179	154,044	155
Sanitary districts	38,112	94	37,872	87	67,176	100	85,584	86
Villages	30,852	76	32,616	75	48,396	72	64,944	66
South	39,072	96	43,884	101	61,836	92	96,168	97
Municipal areas	75,060	185	79,452	182	99,636	148	149,724	151
Sanitary districts	39,300	97	50,628	116	67,968	101	113,016	114
Villages	33,396	82	36,132	83	54,876	81	84,528	85

SOURCE: NSO, *Report of the Household Socio-Economic Survey*, various annual editions.

NOTE: Provinces in the Bangkok vicinity include Nonthaburi, Pathum Thani, and Samut Prakan; the central region excludes Bangkok and its vicinity. Income figures represent the average income per household and are in Thai baht.

From this table, we can observe the following. When considering household income as a whole, the growth rate from the latter half of the 1980s is higher. When comparing household income by region, the gap between the Bangkok metropolitan area and the provinces is wide.[3] Similarly, the urban-rural income disparity within each region is also wide. Yet, differentials between provincial cities and the Bangkok metropolitan area are unexpectedly small. Even though the Thai distribution industry and professionals in this field tend to overlook it, this last point is especially important, as will be later shown.

Table 2.3 shows the percentage of households by monthly household income in 1994 according to geographic region. As this table demonstrates, income differentials within each region are significant. In the Bangkok metropolitan area, for example, more than 20 percent of the total households falls within the high-income bracket, earning more than 20,000 baht a month, while the low-income bracket, earning less than 8,000 baht a month, occupies about one-third. According to an NSO survey, the Gini coefficient of household income in the Bangkok metropolitan area grew steadily in the 1980s (from 0.283 in 1981, 0.315 in 1986, to 0.356 in 1990). In 1994, it dropped slightly (to 0.336), but was still relatively high compared with the period 1981–86 (NSO, *Household Socio-Economic Survey*, annually). The same tendency can also be observed in each region outside of the Bangkok metropolitan area.

TABLE 2.3 Percentage of Thailand's households by monthly income level, 1994

Household income (baht)	Whole kingdom (%)	Bangkok and vicinity (%)	Other regions		
			Municipal areas (%)	Sanitary districts (%)	Villages (%)
Less than 4,000	39.7	7.9	17.0	34.3	50.3
4,000–7,999	30.9	24.6	29.8	32.2	32.1
8,000–10,999	10.4	17.3	15.6	12.2	8.0
11,000–19,999	11.9	27.9	21.8	14.2	6.9
20,000 and over	7.1	22.3	15.8	7.1	2.7
Total	100.0	100.0	100.0	100.0	100.0

SOURCE: NSO, *Report of the 1994 Household Socio-Economic Survey*.

NOTE: Provinces in Bangkok vicinity include Nonthaburi, Pathum Thani, and Samut Prakan.

When comparing the provincial municipal areas with the sanitary districts in table 2.3, there is an important difference between the percentages at the lowest stratum (less than 4,000 baht a month) and the highest stratum (more than 20,000 baht a month). The differentials between sanitary districts and villages are important as well. According to Hiranaka (1995, 18), president, as of 1995, of the Japan-based Siam-Jusco, the upper-half of Bangkok's population, in terms of income, was the target for modern retailers by the mid-1990s. Table 2.3 suggests that this corresponds to the strata of monthly household income of more than 11,000 baht. The strata corresponding to it in provincial urban areas (municipal areas) occupies nearly 40 percent of all the households, while in semi-urban areas (sanitary districts) it stands at a little more than 20 percent, and in villages slightly under 10 percent. This data clearly brings out the growing consumer market in provincial cities, as well as the remaining wide differentials among provincial urban areas, semi-urban areas, and villages.

Given this data, a few points should be mentioned in relation to the development of new retail formats. First, even though Thailand's consumer market as a whole had been expanding from the 1980s until the mid-1990s, income disparities between geographical regions and between strata remained. In analyzing the development of new retail formats, it is vital, therefore, not to simply emphasize the consumption boom but to take into consideration the consumption structure as well. A second point to consider, as far as per capita income is concerned, is that consumer markets in provincial cities are in no way inferior to that in Bangkok. Although the provinces outside of Bangkok were generally not targets for modern retailers, especially department stores, provincial cities in Thailand are actually attractive destinations as well, despite the fact that the population of each provincial city is quite small in comparison to Bangkok's 6.35 million people (as of 2000).[4] Nakhon Ratchasima in the northeast, Chiang Mai in the north, and Hat Yai in the south, each of which is that region's central city, had, as of 2000, a respective population of 205,000, 174,000, and 188,000, representing only about one-thirtieth of the population of Bangkok (NSO, *The 2000 Population and Housing Census*). Certainly it is necessary to recognize the fact that in Thailand the definition of "urban area" is limited to municipal areas, which are usually very small. But even if we were to imagine a virtual Thai provincial city that included the neighborhoods beyond the municipal area, the population of each city in the provinces is by no means large.

The third point to be made, in response to Thailand's complex income distribution and consumer market structure, is that retail and distribution companies tend to adopt diversification strategies rather than concentrate on the expansion of their chains by specializing in a specific format. Finally, it should be noted that semi-urban areas and even villages can be important consumer markets, if not for high-priced durable consumer and luxury goods, then for daily foods and necessities.[5] This is an important aspect of the market that the Thai distribution industry and specialists in the field have so far overlooked, but which is dealt with in detail in the next chapter, since it is related to the development of the distribution industry from the mid-1990s onwards.

THE DEVELOPMENT AND DIVERSIFICATION OF DOMESTIC BUSINESS GROUPS

THE THREE MAJOR DEPARTMENT STORE GROUPS

Thailand experienced rapid economic growth and a consumption boom from 1987 until the mid-1990s. In concert with the consumption boom, various kinds of modern retail businesses quickly developed. Among them, the department store was the first format to show rapid growth. For example, the number of department stores newly opened in Bangkok from 1985 to April 1992 reached thirty-six, which exceeded the cumulated number of stores opened by 1984. In addition, the average surface area per store increased from approximately 10,000 square meters in 1985–89 to roughly 20,000 square meters in 1990–92 (Japanese Chamber of Commerce-Bangkok, 1993). Among Thailand's department store chains, three major ones—Central, Robinson, and The Mall—actively developed new stores.

Table 2.4 classifies the development of the three major department store chains' branch stores, from which two notable items can be observed. One is that the three chains actively opened a number of new branches beginning in the early 1990s. The sheer number of store openings by Central and Robinson department store, in particular, is remarkable. Also of important note is that both Central and Robinson expanded their branches into provincial cities.

TABLE 2.4 Development of the three major department stores in Thailand, up until the mid-1990s

Chain	No. of stores	Branch name (year of opening)
Central[a]	14	*Bangkok and vicinity:* Wang Burapha (1956), Silom (1968), Chidlom (1974), Lat Phrao (1983), Huamak (1988), Silom Complex (1991), Raminthra (1993), Bangna (1993), Pinklao (1994), Fashion Island (1995), Rangsit (1996), Phraram 3 (1997) *Provincial cities:* Chiang Mai (1992), Hat Yai (1994)
Robinson[b]	20	*Bangkok and vicinity:* Anusawari (1979), Silom (1984), Ratchada (1989), Don Mueang (1989), Sukhumwit (1990), Bangrak (1992), Bangkhae (1993), Seacon Square (1994), Future Park Rangsit (1995), Fashion Island (1995), Lat Ya (1996), Siracha (1997) *Provincial cities:* Udon Thani (1995), Phuket (1995), Nakhon Si Thammarat (1995), Hat Yai (1995), Chiang Mai (1996), Ubon Ratchathani (1996), Ratchaburi (1997), Chanthaburi (1998)
The Mall[c]	7	The Mall 2 (1983), The Mall 3 (1986), The Mall 4 (1986), Tha Phra (1987), Ngamwongwan (1991), Bangkhae (199), Bangkapi (1994)

SOURCE: Thanawat (2000, 80–89); Robinson Department Store Plc (2000); Thanawat (2001, 348–65).

[a] In 1989, Central Department Store, in addition to the branches cited above, opened ZEN, a new type of department store mainly targeting young executives and located in the World Trade Center (now Central World) in Bangkok. At the end of 2000, the Huamak and Fashion Island branches were closed down and remodeled to a power-center format with Big C as the core. Robinson Department Store, Siam Square branch (1st store) had already closed down. The Anusawari branch (2nd store) closed down in 2001.

[b] Robinson Department Store, Siam Square branch (1st store) had already closed down and the Anusawari branch (2nd store) closed down in 2001.

[c] The Mall Department Store, in addition to the stores cited above, established a commercial complex known as The Emporium, located on Sukhumvit Road, in a joint investment with the Sophonphanit family, a founding family of Bangkok Bank. In addition, the department store established a large-scale shopping mall in Nakhon Ratchasima in August 2000, two years later than the originally scheduled date, due to the currency crisis.

The opening of Central Department Store's Chiang Mai branch in 1992 was the first provincial branch of a Bangkok-based department store chain. After that, with the merger of the Central and Robinson groups, Robinson Department Store came to take the lead in rapidly opening provincial affiliate department stores (Endo 1998c, 165) by targeting a principal city in each region. Since consumer markets in provincial cities were in no way inferior to that in the Bangkok metropolitan area, as far as the purchasing power per inhabitant was concerned, it was natural that the competition among store openings in the Bangkok metropolitan area extended to provincial cities before long.

Thailand's domestic consumer market consists of what I call a "mosaic structure," characterized by significant disparities between urban and rural areas and between income strata, such that retail and distribution companies readily adopted diversification strategies. The leading retail business groups were dissatisfied with the sole expansion of the old department store format. With the cooperation of Western transnational retail companies and the introduction of their new business know-how, Thailand's retail business groups began to develop new retail formats one after another. One of the most active groups to have diversified its retail business was the Central Group.

TABLE 2.5 Diversification of Thailand's two major retail and distribution groups in the mid-1990s

Format	Central Group/CRC Group (Central Retail Corp.)	CP Group (marketing and distribution division)
Department Store	Central Department Store (1956) Robinson Department Store (1979) • affiliating provincial department stores under CR Co., Ltd. (1995) Zen (1989) • targeting young executives	No diversification in the domestic market
General Mass Merchandiser (Hypermarket, Cash-and-Carry)	Big C (1994) • joint venture with Australia-based Davids Holding • putting emphasis on the provinces as well as on Bangkok • joint venture with France-based Carrefour (1996) • joint venture with France-based Carrefour • starting to advance into the provinces	Makro (1989) • joint venture with Holland-based Makro • membership-system wholesale club • putting emphasis on the provinces as well as on Bangkok Lotus (1994) • starting to advance into the provinces • opening of their first store in Shanghai (1997)
Supermarket	Tops (1996) • joint venture with Holland-based Royal Ahold • remodeling supermarket division within department stores	Sunny's Supermarket (1994) • technical cooperation from Japan-based Seiyu

Format	Central Group/CRC Group (Central Retail Corp.)	CP Group (marketing and distribution division)
Convenience Store	Central Minimart (1987) FamilyMart (1995) • joint venture with Japan-based FamilyMart	7-Eleven (1989) • area license from US-based Southland Corp. • opening corporate stores and franchise stores, as well as sub-area stores in remote areas
Category Killer	Powerbuy (1996) • separated from the home electronics selling division within the group's department stores Super Sports (1997) • separated from the sporting goods sales division within the group's department stores Office Depot (1997)	Makro Office Center (1995) • selling of office supplies
Specialty Store	Marks & Spencer (1996) • franchise of UK-based Marks & Spencer B2S (1996) • separated from the book-selling division within the group's department store Watson (1996) • drugstore, joint venture with Hong Kong-based Watson	No specialty stores in the group
Distribution Center	Davids Distribution Co., Ltd. • 1st center (1994) • 2nd center (1997)	7- Eleven • a new center (1998) Lotus • 1st center (1996)
Foreign Investment	Plans for investment throughout Asia scheduled for at least the year 2000	Already started in China plans to extend throughout Southeast Asia

SOURCE: Companies' annual reports; Thai-language newspapers.

NOTE: Dates in parentheses represent the year the store first opened.

As table 2.5 shows, the Central Group began diversifying its business by establishing a convenience store (Central Minimart) in 1987, and then expanded by opening a large-scale discount, general mass merchandising store (Big C) in 1994, in the form of a joint venture with the Australia-based Davids Holding Co., Ltd. After the Central and Robinson groups merged, they jointly established a hypermarket (Carrefour) with France-based Carrefour and a supermarket (Tops) with Holland-based Royal Ahold, both in 1996. The group also expanded into new formats such as category killers (Power Buy, Super Sports, and Office Depot) and specialty stores (Marks & Spencer, B2S, and Watson) by means of joint ventures and franchise contracts with Western companies (Endo 1998c, 168).

CP GROUP

The Charoen Pokphand (CP) Group, Thailand's largest agribusiness group, similarly advanced into the retail and distribution industry during Thailand's investment and consumption booms. Since the end of the 1980s, the CP Group had been developing into conglomerate-subsuming, high-tech industries, property development, financial businesses, and so on, as well as expanding its presence in the agriculture-related industry, which was the group's traditional business (Suehiro and Nanbara 1991, 73–108). The full-scale entry into the distribution industry was also part of the group's strategy.

As shown in table 2.5, the CP Group established its first Makro store (cash-and-carry) jointly with the Holland-based Makro Group and its first 7-Eleven store (convenience store) by means of an area license from the US-based Southland Corporation (now 7-Eleven, Inc.). Both stores opened in 1989. The group then expanded most notably into Lotus (hypermarket), Sunny's (supermarket), and Makro Office Center (category killer). Among the CP Group's new ventures, Makro became the first threat to the leading retail companies at the time (see also Endo 1998c, 168).

Makro was able to achieve low price sales by using a "cash-and-carry" format, lowering the cost of its stores' interior design, and implementing an effective inventory management system, which rapidly increased the number of its customers. A "cash-and-carry" format is basically a membership wholesaler targeting small-scale retailers, restaurants, and other juridical persons. It was not supposed to directly compete with modern retail businesses, such as department stores, in its assortment of goods and customer service. In reality, however, Makro stores' customers included many general consumers. Partly because Thailand's consumer market remained immature, differentiation among formats was insufficient. As a result, Central Department Store, which had long ranked first in sales in Thailand's retail industry, was outrun by Makro as early as 1993–94 (Endo 1998c, 165).

It is important here to emphasize that, from the very beginning, Makro (Siam Makro Co., Ltd.) depended on its Dutch joint venture partner for all of its actual management, though it was certainly playing a part in the CP Group's retail and distribution division. For example, as of 1996, five of the company's nine executive board members were foreigners, including the managing director, while the chairperson of the board of directors was Thanin Jiarawanon, the leader of the CP Group (Siam Makro Plc 1996, 11). In other words, the competition in the distribution industry between the Central Group and the CP Group at the time already contained an aspect of competition between local capital (Central Group) and foreign capital (Holland-based Makro).

STRATEGIC ALLIANCE BETWEEN THE CENTRAL AND ROBINSON GROUPS

Confronted with the rise of the CP Group in the distribution industry, in May 1995, the Central Group embarked on a strategic alliance with the Robinson Group, the second largest department store group in Thailand. Figure 2.1 shows the ownership structure of the group after this alliance, from which it can be observed that the Robinson Group and the main part of the Central Group's retail business were amalgamated under the leadership of the Central Group both in name and in reality, with CRC (Central Retail Corporation) as the common holding company. With this amalgamation, Central Group accelerated the expansion and diversification of its retail business in the mid-1990s.

At the end of December 1996, the board of directors of the CRC holding company consisted of eighteen members, thirteen of whom were founding family members of the Central Group and five were from the Robinson Group. Sutthichat Jirathiwat from the Central Group's founding family took office as CEO and chairperson of the board of directors. In this way, both groups were amalgamated with the core company CRC. However, both groups continued to hold their own specific roles. For example, Central Department Store specialized in high-quality stores targeting upper-middle and upper classes, while Robinson Department Store specialized in popular stores and made efforts to expand provincial affiliate department stores. Central also took the lead in establishing general mass merchandisers (including hypermarkets) and supermarkets, while Robinson took the lead in integrating existing convenience stores into the Japan-based FamilyMart, a convenience store franchise chain. In this way, the Central Group prepared for competition that was emerging with the CP Group's rapid expansion of its presence in the domestic retail industry.

Before long, however, it became clear that the amalgamation of Central and Robinson had two serious problems. One was a financial problem that arose from affiliating provincial department stores under the leadership of Robinson.

FIGURE 2.1 Ownership structure of Central Group, as of the end of 1996

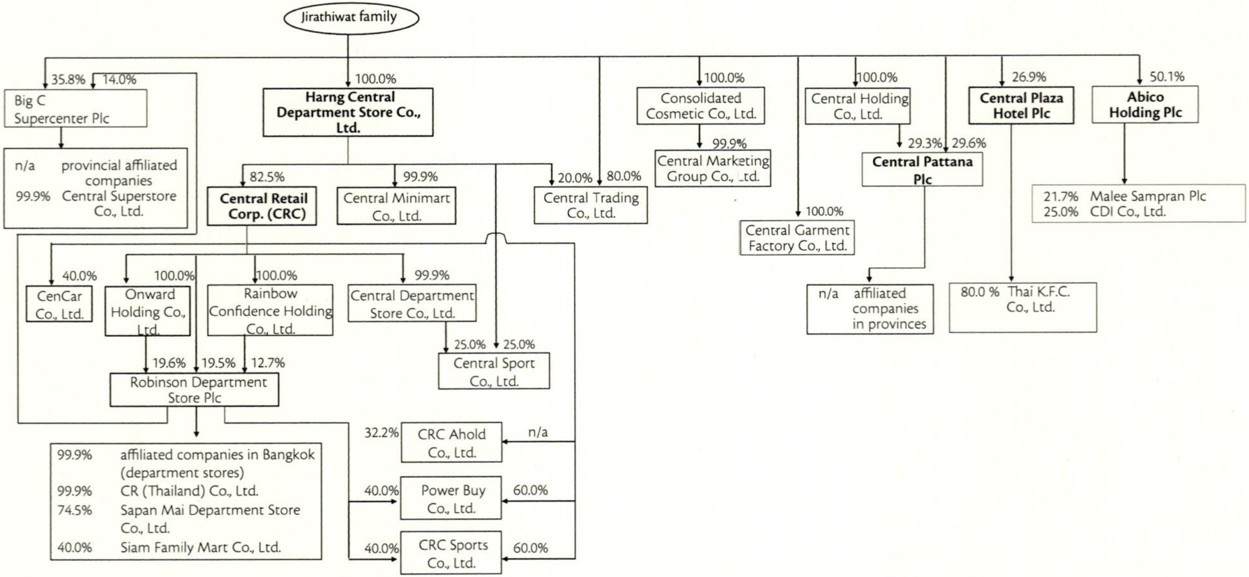

SOURCE: Based on list of company stockholders provided by Business Development Department, Ministry of Commerce and companies' annual reports.

NOTE: Numbers represent percentages of ownership; boldface represents the holding companies of the group; owner families of Robinson Department Store hold 16.8% of Central Retail Corporation's stocks, and CRC Corp. appears to hold a substantial part of CRC Ahold's stocks, but the details, as of 1996, were unclear due to insufficient data.; n/a indicates exact percentage. was unable to be identified.

Efforts to establish provincial affiliate department stores had been made since mid-1995 under the leadership of CR (Thailand) Co., Ltd. (established in June 1995), a subsidiary company of Robinson Department Store. To tell the truth, many provincial department stores were willing to seize the opportunity of the affiliation because at the time they were suffering from the burden of the enormous investment forced on them by the consumption boom and the subsequent financial difficulties brought about by over-competition. Actually, the provincial affiliate department stores weren't able to succeed in improving their business performances, and in 1996 all six of Robinson's affiliate stores and six of its seven stores in 1997 suffered net losses.[6] This financial problem devolved upon CR Co., Ltd., which had invested 50 to 90 percent in provincial department stores, and the problem further extended, naturally enough, to its parent company, Robinson Department Store, as well.

The second problem of the Central-Robinson amalgamation was deep-rooted and lay in the difference between each group's corporate culture. Even after the currency and economic crisis had abated in 2000, the ownership and management of the Central Group (now merged with the Robinson Group) was still under the strong control of Central's founding family, and the group was taking relatively conservative action (Endo 2002, 291–303). As suggested in figure 2.1, the group gradually proceeded with listing stocks on the Stock Exchange of Thailand from the group's non-core companies, while its core companies, such as Central Department Store Co., Ltd. (CDS) and Harng Central Department Store Co., Ltd. (HCDS), still remained unlisted and have so until now. By contrast, the Robinson Group had maintained a separation of ownership and management since its foundation,[7] so the group was not concerned about maintaining a family business. Robinson was also the first in Thailand's retail industry to list stocks. This difference in corporate culture was vividly reflected in the borrowing behavior of each group. Central was prudent in borrowing foreign capital involving exchange risk, while Robinson actively engaged in this practice.[8] As a result, Robinson Department Store Plc suffered an enormous currency exchange loss after the currency crisis. Despite the fact that the two groups were amalgamated with CRC as the core company, it is very possible that they failed to develop into an integrated business group, partly, because of differences in corporate culture and, partly, because they jointly adopted a decentralized system, in which management was divided between each founding family line.

The rapid expansion and diversification, including Central Group's amalgamation with the Robinson Group, caused the Central Group to suffer dispersion of managerial resources and a deterioration of its financial structure. Despite some differences in degree, the CP Group encountered similar problems as well, which will be examined in detail in the next chapter.

THE RISE AND FALL OF PROVINCIAL DEPARTMENT STORES

PROVINCIAL DEPARTMENT STORE OPENINGS BOOM

Before the three major Bangkok-based department stores began to advance into the provinces, department stores established with local capital in provincial cities had already begun to open one after another. These stores succeeded in meeting the demand of the provincial consumer markets, whose per capita income rivaled that of Bangkok. In 1988, the PDS (Provincial Department Stores) Club was founded in an attempt to organize against the encroachment of the Bangkok-based department stores. While all the provincial department stores throughout the country did not join this business circle, most of the leading provincial department stores were members.[9] Table 2.6 shows a list of PDS Club members as of 1994 as well as details and a brief history of their stores.

As table 2.6 demonstrates, the greatest number of department stores was founded in the 1980s, although many stores had already been established prior to the mid-1980s. This suggests that the opening of provincial department stores was not necessarily a transient phenomenon accompanying the investment and consumption booms that occurred at the end of the 1980s, but rather that provincial cities (as well as Bangkok) already had favorable market conditions for the emergence of department stores prior to the consumption boom. Many of them were, however, relatively low-storied and small-scale stores.

Around 1990, provincial department stores rushed to open large-scale stores. In the same way as occurred in Bangkok, many of these were local capital-built, large-scale commercial complexes with a department store as the core tenant. As shown in table 2.6, large-scale stores, with a floor space larger than 10,000 square meters, also emerged in provincial cities. However, provincial-based consumer markets were characterized by a very small absolute number of the urban populace, though per capita purchasing power was sufficiently large. Under such conditions, there was a possibility that competition in opening stores could easily turn into over-competition. Moreover, some provincial department stores saw their financial structure rapidly deteriorate due to over-investment in these large retail projects. A typical example of this phenomenon is that of Tantraphan Department Store, which was seriously damaged in 1992 by the advance of the Central Department Store into Chiang Mai.

TABLE 2.6 List of PDS Club members, as of 1994

No.	Members names (owner)	Opening year	Basic size of store	Location	History/ remarks
			North		
1.	Tantraphan Department Store* (Tantranon family)	1951 1981 1992	1st store: 4,000 sq m 80 employees 2nd store: 7,500 sq m 200 employees 150 car-capacity parking lot 3rd store: 18,000 sq m 800 employees 700 car-capacity parking lot	Chiang Mai	Founded in the 1910s; became a leading northern Thailand retail business group; besides being a department store, advanced into supermarkets, convenience stores, shopping centers, etc.; sold their second department store in 1994; department store division taken over in 1995 by Bangkok-based Central Department Store.
2.	Rim Ping Superstore (Tantranon family)	1988 1991	1st store: 1,500 sq m 2nd store: 6,000 sq m	Chiang Mai	Affiliated with the Tantraphan Group (no. 1).
3.	SEASON Store (Luangchairat family)	1987	3 floors, 10,000 sq m 220 employees 60 car-capacity parking lot	Chiang Mai	Founded in 1936; began manufacturing and selling shoes; as of 1994, commercial complex under construction.
4.	Worawat Phatthana (Itsarachiwawat family)	1989	6 floors	Chiang Mai	
5.	Wang Kham Department Store (Khruawiwat-thanakun family)	1985	3 floors, 1,800 sq m (expanded in 1992)	Chiang Rai	Started in hotel management and the sale of building materials; advanced into department stores by buying out and rebuilding an existing store; as of 1994, planned a 2nd store.
6.	Api Plaza (Apiniwet family)	1985	2 floors, 3,000 sq m 205 employees	Chiang Rai	Started as a stationary wholesale business.
7.	Nara Department Store (Bunthon family)	1989	3 floors, 1,750 sq m 138 employees	Nan	Started by selling newspapers, cosmetics, stationery, and so on.

No.	Members names (owner)	Opening year	Basic size of store	Location	History/ remarks
8.	Topland Arcade* (Robbanjerd family)	1980 1992	6 floors, 8,500 sq m 10,000 sq m	Phitsanulok Phetchabun	Founded in 1957; commercial complex Topland Plaza under construction, as of 1994.
9.	The Great Department Store (Swattanasin family)	1990	4 floors, 3,000 sq m 173 employees	Kamphaeng Phet	Branch of the same chain as no. 16 located in Chaiyaphum; as of 1994, only the first and second floors were in operation.
10.	Thep Phrasit Department Store (Khru Jaroen family)	1989	3,500 sq m	Kamphaeng Phet	Planning to expand the store floor space up to 10,000 sq m and develop a supermarket chain, as of 1994.
11.	Fairy Land Department Store* (Kunawong family et al.)	1987	5 floors, 13,000 sq m 600 employees 500 car-capacity parking lot	Nakhon Sawan	Founded in the 1950s; started by selling cloth and expanded into home electronics and a shopping center; branches in Phichit and Kamphaeng Phet (closed down in 1996).
12.	Withithep Department Store (Klaiphrutsawan family)	1981	4 floors, 7,000 sq m 590 employees	Nakhon Sawan	Expanded with a hotel attached to the store in 1987; planning to develop a commercial complex, as of 1994.
			Northeast		
13.	Charoensi Plaza* (Dikthananon family)	1983	23,000 sq m	Udon Thani	Leading business group in the northeast; is an automobile dealer and manages a wet market, supermarket, and commercial complex.
14.	Fairy Plaza* (Phatthanaphiradet family)	1978	4 floors	Khon Kaen	Founded as a sewing and grocery store in 1961; opened a large store with a movie theater in 1987.
15.	Sentosa Department Store* (Chinchaturaphat family)	1984	2 floors, 3,000 sq m (expanded in 1986)	Khon Kaen	Founded as a grocery store in 1967.
16.	The Great Department Store (Suwatthanasin family)	1988	3 floors, 12,000 sq m 200 car-capacity parking lot	Chaiyaphum	Founded in 1960; second store (Chaiyaphum) under construction, as of 1994.

No.	Members names (owner)	Opening year	Basic size of store	Location	History/ remarks
17.	Yingyong Department Store* (Jonswat family)	1983	3 floors, 3,800 sq m (expanded in 1990)	Ubon Ratchathani	Started as a dress-making store in 1935; established a grocery store in 1952; started to retail and wholesale jeans in 1975; also manages a minimart and supermarket.
18.	Sakun Thai Department Store (Sikritsanarat family)	1978	2 floors, 2,500 sq m 206 employees	Ubon Ratchathani	Founded as a grocery store in 1962; planning to open a supermarket chain, as of 1994.
19.	Surin Plaza (Runthonkiat family)	1989	3 floors, 7,200 sq m 350 employees	Surin	Started as a fish retailer in wet markets; later established a fabric and sewing store; planning to open a branch in Si Saket, as of 1994.
20.	Phet Kasem Plaza (Lokkasemsan family)	1989	4 floors, 7,500 sq m 200 car-capacity parking lot	Surin	Managed a small-scale food-processing factory c. 1950; established a hotel in 1983.
21.	Thawikit Plaza (Rotjonsinwilai family)	n/a	n/a	Buriram	
22.	Klang Plaza* (Manasin family)	n/a n/a	1st store: 8,000 sq m 2nd store: 9 floors 50,000 sq m 500 car-capacity parking lot	Nakhon Ratchasima	Started as a stationery shop; built a commercial complex with the second store as its core tenant.
23.	Norris City (Sphasilaphrapa family)	1991	6 floors, 20,000 sq m 794 employees	Nakhon Ratchasima	Established a jeans shop in 1975 and opened a grocery store in 1980 (destroyed by fire); has a few branches.
			Central		
24.	Asia Department Store (Tantanasan family)	1986	1 floor, 1,200 sq m 60 employees (sales division)	Suphanburi	Commercial complex under planning, as of 1994.
			East		
25.	Ocean Department Store* (n/a)	1983	3 floors	Chonburi	n/a
26.	Laem Thong Department Store (Nokhon family)	1984 1991	1st store: 6 floors, 15,000 sq m 2nd store: 6 floors, 25,000 sq m 820 employees (both stores)	Chonburi (Si Racha)	Built a commercial complex near Laemchabang Industrial Estate, includes a department store, shopping center, hotel, condominium, and office.

No.	Members names (owner)	Opening year	Basic size of store	Location	History/ remarks
27.	Mike Department Store (Mekaworakun family)	1984	1 floor, 1,600 sq m 216 employees	Chonburi (Phatthaya)	Began as a clothing store; planning to build a commercial complex with department store, shopping center, and supermarket, as of 1994.
28.	Tawan Ok Plaza (Jaroenrunruang and Kotchawat families)	1983 n/a	1st store: 4,800 sq m 2nd store: 40,000 sq m	Chachoengsao	Built a commercial complex.
29.	Chanthaburi Plaza (Runsiriyunyon family)	1988	6 floors 300 employees	Chanthaburi	Founded in 1964; established a supermarket in 1972.
			South		
30.	Ocean Shopping Mall (O. C. Group)	1983	5 floors	Chumphon	Affiliated with O. C. Group; also manages department stores and shopping centers in Phuket and Songkhla.
31.	Phuket Shopping Center (Yongsakun family)	1986 1988 1990 1994	1st store: 5 floors, 4,800 sq m 2nd store: 800 sq m 3rd store: 3,600 sq m 4th store: 3,000 sq m	Phuket Phangnga Phuket Phuket	Began in tin mining, then shifted to retailing; first store had 364 employees.
32.	Ocean Mall Shopping (Sianghen family)	1981 1988 n/a 1992	1st store: 7 floors, 20,000 sq m 2nd store: 7 floors, 3,000 sq m 3rd store: 2,332 sq m 4th store: 3,000 sq m	Phuket	Established a men's clothing store in 1976 and has grown into a leading retail business group in the South (O.C. Group), managing supermarkets and convenience stores as well.
33.	Saha Thai Department Store (Panhakhunathon family)	1987	7 floors, 12,500 sq m 617 employees	Surat Thani	Established as a supermarket in 1983, with its main branch in Nakhon Si Thammarat.
34.	Saha Thai Department Store (Panhakhunathon family)	1988	6 floors, 6,000 sq m	Nakhon Si Thammarat	Established a clothing and grocery store in 1963; also has branch in Surat Thani.

No.	Members names (owner)	Opening year	Basic size of store	Location	History/ remarks
35.	Lucky Department Store (Uawonphrayun family)	1984	4 floors, 4,400 sq m	Nakhon Si Thammarat	Established a clothing store in 1970; as of 1994, had a commercial complex under construction in a joint investment with Saha Thai Department Store (see nos. 33 and 34 above).
36.	Diamond Department Store (Anantrawanit family)	1991	4 floors, 2,400 sq m 138 employees (sales division)	Trang	n/a
37.	Ocean Department Store (Sianghen family)	1986	8 floors, 7,000 sq m 550 employees	Songkhla (Hat Yai)	Established a clothing store in 1974.
38.	Diana Department Store (public limited company)	1983 1988 1993	1st store: 5 floors, 4,500 sq m 2nd store: 4,500 sq m 3rd store: 20,000 sq m	Songkhla (Hat Yai) Pattani Songkhla (Hat Yai)	Leading business group in the south; businesses originated from inter-urban trade in the south and international trade with Singapore; expanded into rubber and coconut palm plantations; commercial complex under construction, as of 1994.
39.	Walk Department Store (n/a)	1986	3 floors, 1,900 sq m 290 employees	Songkhla (Hat Yai)	Established a cosmetics and women's underwear store in 1981; later a shopping mall and minimart (3 stores).
40.	Hat Yai Odeum Thurakit (n/a)	1981	4 floors, 2,000 sq m 200 employees	Songkhla (Hat Yai)	Joint investment with ten local businesspersons.
41.	Hat Yai City Shopping Center (Manjaroensiri family)	1991 1992	department store: 8,000 sq m supermarket: 1,400 sq m	Songkhla (Hat Yai)	As of 1994, remodeling into a commercial complex and expanding the department store to 18,000 sq m.
42.	Super Department Store (Sirichai family/Sisamai Group)	1983 1987 1989 1991	1st store: 3 floors, 4,000 sq m 2nd store: 2,000 sq m 3rd store: 2,000 sq m 4th store: 3,000 sq m	Yala Pattani Pattani Narathiwat	Besides department stores, has five convenience stores in Yala, Pattani, and Songkhla.

SOURCE: PDS (1994); Thai-language newspapers.

NOTE: n/a signifies that data is not available.

* Represents a founder of the PDS Club.

THE CASE OF TANTRAPHAN DEPARTMENT STORE[10]

Tan Nguan Chun (1889–1950), the founder of Tantraphan Department Store, moved to Chiang Mai around 1910. Tan worked at first for a UK-based trading company, Borneo. There, he was in charge of receiving orders and became acquainted with high-profile customers, such as the old northern (Lanna) Thai royal families and bureaucrats, and came to benefit from their protection (Prani 1995, 142–43). Later, Tan resigned from the Borneo Company and, in 1916, started a grocery store, Tan Hua Nguan, in Warorot Market, which was the largest wet market in Chiang Mai. He ran this store by making use of the experience and personal connections he had made during his time at the Borneo Company. His store sold mainly foreign products like canned food and cigarettes as well as daily foods such as salt and *nam pla* (fish sauce), which he must have procured through trade with the Borneo Company. Even after his resignation from the Borneo Company, Tan deepened his friendship with the old Lanna Thai royal families and high-ranking officials living in Chiang Mai, who became important customers of his store (Prani 1980, 47–74). This presented favorable conditions that eventually evolved into the opening of a department store. Under the economic-nationalistic policy of the pre-war Phibun government, Tan changed his family name to a Thai-sounding one, Tantranon, and his trade name to Tantraphan, meaning "goods of the Tan brand."

After the Second World War, in 1949, Tan opened Tantraphan Store on Thaphae Road, one of the main streets in Chiang Mai. It was a big store for the time, with a 200-square-meter store surface. After Tan died in 1950, Tan's second son, Thawat (born in 1922), succeeded his father as the storeowner. Thawat adopted a fixed-price sales policy earlier than other stores in the area. In 1967–68, he expanded the Thaphae store into a two-storey building, with a 600-square-meter floor space. In 1969, he had an escalator installed in the store for the first time in any provincial city. In this way, Thawat actively introduced a new sales strategy and store layout, based on foreign models such as those of Hong Kong and Japan, to gradually achieve a modern department store format. Tantraphan Store sold goods such as clothes, cosmetics, and other daily necessities, mostly purchased from the large consumer product conglomerate, the Saha Group. Tantraphan also sold big name clothing brands purchased mainly from the Bangkok-based Central Group (Central Trading Company, in particular), amounting to 30 to 40 percent of Tantraphan's total turnover. Thawat simultaneously ran a foreign cigarettes import store and was a Nestle sales agent. Table 2.7 provides a timeline of the Tantraphan Group's business history, as well as retail and distribution trends in Chiang Mai from the 1910s to 1990s.

TABLE 2.7 Business history of the Tantraphan Group

Period	Tantraphan Group	Trends in Chiang Mai's Retail and Distribution Industries
1910s/1920s	The founder, Tan Nguan Chun, moves to Chiang Mai and starts a grocery store; later he also runs a money-lending business; the trade name becomes Tan Hua Nguan (陳和源).	
1930s		The founder of Si Suwan Group starts a grocery store and, in 1936, starts manufacturing and selling shoes.
1940s	In 1942, the trade name is changed to the Tantraphan. In 1949, a new store opens on Thaphae Road, the main street in Chiang Mai at the time.	The founder of So Kankha Group starts a grocery store.
1950s	After the death of Tan Nguan Chun, in 1950, his business is split among his three sons.	
1960s	In 1967–68, with the expansion of the Thaphae branch (store floor space increases to 600 sq m), the Tantraphan Store is gradually transformed into a department store; in 1969, escalators are installed.	So Kankha Group starts wholesaling clothes.
1970s	In 1974, the Thaphae branch is expanded again to 4,000 sq m.; the company diversifies into the wet market, transportation business, and mining, and also becomes a construction contractor.	
1980s	In 1981, the Chang Phuak branch opens (second store); in 1988, the group's first supermarket opens and a convenience store business begins operations (and later enters into a sub-area license agreement with C.P. Seven Eleven Co., Ltd.).	So Kankha Group opens its first department store in 1982, a second one in 1985, and a third one in 1988; Si Suwan Group opens its department store in 1987 (with a supermarket), and in 1989 announces a plan to construct a commercial complex; in 1988, the PDS Club is established.

Period	Tantraphan Group	Trends in Chiang Mai's Retail and Distribution Industries
1990s	In 1991, the name Rim Ping Supermart Co. is changed to Tantraphan Department Store Co. and its capital increases to make it the core company of the group; in 1992, Tantraphan Airport Plaza opens (as a third department store and shopping center); in 1993, Tantraphan Department Store Co.'s capital increases and investment from outside the family (S&P Co.) is accepted for the first time; in 1994, Tantraphan Supermarket Co. is established and the transfer of the supermarket department is made to the new company; by the end of 1995, the department store and shopping center businesses are sold to the Central Group.	Due to financial deregulation, provincial branches of financial companies rapidly increase in number; Bangkok-based major retailers advance into provincial cities; in 1992, Si Suwan Group enters into conflict with the municipal administration over a construction permit for a commercial complex they had started to build (the project is finally suspended); in 1994, the Si Suwan Group opens a hypermarket; from 1993 onwards, So Kankha Group opens a total of four supermarkets in Chiang Mai city and its suburbs.

SOURCE: Author interviews; Thai-language newspapers.

Tantraphan Store evolved into the first modern department store in Thailand's provinces, but there was a limit to further expansion of the business. One of the reasons for this was that the main customers for high-quality clothes were limited to wealthy individuals and high-ranking officials living in Chiang Mai. Another factor that limited business expansion, as far as daily necessities were concerned, was that the store was unable to cover consumers living in rural areas until the 1960s because of undeveloped road networks.[11] It was around the 1980s, when the consumer market in Chiang Mai gradually grew to such an extent that the Tantraphan Group significantly expanded its department store business. The growth of Chiang Mai's consumer market was directly related to the enforcement of national economic and social development plans, including the provision of infrastructure such as road networks. These development plans catalyzed the socioeconomic changes that directly or indirectly stimulated provincial consumer markets to grow. Other catalytic factors included the development of tourism spurred by the government's promotion policy, the increase of cash income by multiple cropping and the introduction of commercial crops in the agricultural sector, and the successive establishment of educational and governmental facilities, including the opening of Chiang Mai University in 1964 (*Khu Khaeng*, October 1988, 141–65). Benefiting from these new developments, the Tantraphan Group opened the Tantraphan Department

Store's second branch in 1981. The store's floor space was 2,000 square meters at first, but was later expanded to 7,500 square meters. The group also diversified its business into supermarkets and convenience stores in 1988. During the same period, competitors in the local industry, such as So Kankha Group and Si Suwan Group, also opened department stores in rapid succession.

The advance of Central Department Store into provincial cities from the early 1990s brought about a shock to provincial retail industries, which were then enjoying an investment boom. In 1990, Central Department Store announced a plan to open its first provincial store in Chiang Mai, bringing a heightened sense of crisis to Chiang Mai's retail industry as well as those in other provincial cities. For this meant that the Central Group would not only become the supplier for provincial stores, but it would also be an influential competitor to local retail industries, while up until now it had only been an important clothes supplier for provincial department stores. It seems that this new development had a significant impact on Tantraphan Department Store, in particular, which had long been in a close business relationship with Central Department Store. Central Department Store's Chiang Mai branch was a large project with a 16,000-square-meter floor space and tenanted in a large-scale shopping center known as Kad Suan Kaew (44,000 square meters of floor space in total).[12] As a countermeasure, the Tantraphan Group announced its plan to construct Tantraphan Airport Plaza (24,000 square meters of floor space in total and representing Tantraphan Department Store's third branch), using the same shopping center format as Kad Suan Kaew. Tantraphan Department Store (18,000 square meters of floor space) was the core tenant of Tantraphan Airport Plaza. This was an unprecedented large-scale project for provincial retailers. Both shopping centers began doing business in 1992.

The competition for opening new commercial facilities like these was brought about by the growth of provincial cities' consumer markets, as well as the competition among banks' lending practices to commercial and consumer finance sectors in the provinces, in particular, not to mention prior investment of Bangkok-based capital in the provinces. In other words, the large projects established in provincial cities were not always based on real demand. As a result, these projects generally had relatively low profitability in comparison with their investment, causing the deterioration of their financial structures. Tantraphan Group, in particular, made excessive investment that became a financial burden. Although it increased its capital through the allocation of new stocks to a third party,[13] the Tantraphan Group failed to improve the profitability of its main business and finally fell into financial difficulties. According to the company's financial statements, Tantraphan Department Store's ordinary profit was steadily going downhill: a loss of 26 million baht in 1992 (ordinary profit ratio to sales was -2.4 percent), a loss of 203 million baht in 1993 (-15.9 percent), and a further loss of 208 million baht in 1994 (-20.7 percent).

In this critical situation, a proposal for a merger came from CR Co., Ltd. and, by December 1995, Tantraphan Department Store was virtually taken over by the Central Group.[14] Since then, the Tantraphan Group has continued its business by attempting to use differentiation strategies to avoid direct competition with big outside companies, with its remaining supermarket and convenience store chains as its core businesses.

FORMATION AND FAILURE OF THE PDS CLUB

Preceding the advance of Bangkok-based retail capital into the provinces, with the Central Department Store as the first in line, provincial department stores attempted to organize themselves into a horizontal network by founding the PDS Club in 1988. Initially, the club's main activity was to exchange information among its members at their trimestrial meeting.[15] When the large Bangkok-based retailers started a full-scale advance into provincial cities, PDS members began to daringly establish joint enterprises among themselves in opposition to the encroachment. Some examples were CNB Co., Ltd. in the northeast and SC Co., Ltd. in the south, both of which received a sub-area license from C.P. Seven Eleven Co., Ltd. to manage 7-Eleven stores in their respective areas.

The most important joint enterprise among the members of the PDS Club was the TDC (Thai Distribution Center) Co., Ltd. founded in 1992. TDC had two functions. It served as a cooperation buying system as well as a distribution center for PDS Club's members, and was Thailand's first company in this category of business. Its registered share capital was initially 30 million baht (increased to 100 million baht in early 1993), 55 percent of which came from six PDS Club members, and 33 percent of which came from the Australia-based P&O Cold Storage Co., Ltd. (*PJK-RS* March 29, 1993). Two reasons spurred PDS Club's members to establish TDC Co., Ltd. One was that, in reaction to the advance of Bangkok-based retailers into the provinces, provincial department stores drastically expanded their business and also rapidly introduced new retail formats, such as supermarkets and convenience stores, which was accompanied by a sudden increase in the number of items and amount of goods sold. This made it indispensable for PDS members to systematize their inventory management systems, using information technology (*TNSK* August 19, 1993). The second reason for establishing TDC was that provincial department stores were concerned that they could not successfully compete with the large Bangkok-based department stores' provincial branches in point of price and assortment, because Bangkok-based manufacturers sold their products at a lower wholesale price to Bangkok-based companies than it did to provincial companies. The formation of TDC would, theoretically, give provincial companies a competitive edge by allowing them to pool their resources.

The core of TDC's physical distribution system was its distribution center established in Bang Buathong, Nonthaburi Province, northwest of Bangkok. The total sum invested in the company reached 170 million baht, and the center had an 8,000-square-meter floor and storage space of more than 10,000 pallets. Operations began in December 1993. In addition, TDC Co., Ltd. also had a plan to expand its business in the future to frozen food delivery and the development of TDC's house brands. If the distribution center had been operating to its full capacity, the company could have delivered goods within 24 to 48 hours of receiving customer orders from provincial department stores, and this would have made it possible for each customer to drastically reduce its inventory (*PJK-RS* March 29, 1993).

However, TDC Co., Ltd. came to a standstill within one year of its creation. This occurred because PDS Club's members didn't make use of the company's services to the expected extent, so that the distribution center remained at about 40–50 percent net of its capacity (*PJK-RW* October 3, 1994). Moreover, for the company to sufficiently operate the distribution system, suppliers also actually had to use it.[16] Unfortunately, suppliers similarly used it much less than expected.[17] As a result, TDC Co., Ltd. was virtually absorbed by the Central Group. By November 1994, the company was reestablished under the new management of DDT (Davids Distribution [Thailand]) Co., Ltd., a joint enterprise among Central Department Store, Robinson Department Store, and Australia-based Davids Holding Co., Ltd. (*PRCT-TK* November 24, 1994).

The organization of the PDS Club was undermined by the advance of CR Company into the provinces. In order to expand its provincial business, CR had adopted a strategy to affiliate leading local department stores, with the result that PDS Club's members became targets of this expansion strategy. Actually what occurred was that CR approached leading department stores in each region proposing that they become affiliated with CR, with Tantraphan

Department Store being a typical case. Some members turned down CR's proposal, but, nevertheless, PDS Club's activities greatly declined (*PJK-RW* April 20, 1995). In this way, by the mid-1990s, the large Bangkok-based department store groups were replacing provincial department stores as the leaders in the provincial retail industry. Before long, however, a more drastic change occurred throughout the entire consumer market in Thailand.

3

THE FINANCIAL CRISIS AND THE RISE OF NEW RETAIL FORMATS

THE CONSUMER MARKET BEFORE AND AFTER THE CRISIS

CONSUMPTION TRENDS

Real growth rates of GDP (Gross Domestic Product) and consumer spending had remained high in Thailand from the late 1980s until the mid-1990s. However, the real growth rate of GDP began to slow down in the fourth quarter of 1996 as compared to 1995, and fell into negative growth in the second quarter of 1997, just prior to the financial and currency crisis. Similarly, the real growth rate of private consumption expenditures began to slow down in the second quarter of 1997, and fell into negative growth by the third quarter of the same year. After that, the two growth rates remained at very low levels until the end of 1998. Although economic indices began to show signs of recovery beginning in 1999, the Thai economy was still less vigorous than it was during the economic boom. Only in 2000–2001 did growth rates return to their pre-crisis level.

Thailand's total retail sales over the period 1996–2000 mirror, to a great extent, the change of real GDP and real private consumption expenditures (see table 3.1). However, total retail sales fluctuation is much greater than the fluctuations of GDP and private consumption expenditures. This is, partly, because retail sales for all of Thailand are based on nominal (vs. real) terms, and also because retail sales figures have a certain statistical limitation, as a result of how official agencies in Thailand calculate retail sales. The Business Development Department, Ministry of Commerce requires only those retailers with annual sales of 1.2 million baht or more to report their monthly sales figures to the taxation office in their respective districts. Following that, the Ministry of Finance's Revenue Department adds these sales figures together to obtain the total retail sales for the whole country.[1] In other words, many small- and medium-sized retailers, whose annual sales did not reach 1.2 million baht in 1998, due to the economic meltdown following the financial and currency crisis, were not counted for that year. This suggests that the retail sales figures provided by the government are lower than the actual figures in a rapidly shrinking consumer market, while the rate of increase in these same figures rises to higher levels in an expanding market.

TABLE 3.1 Thailand's GDP growth rates, private consumption expenditures, and retail sales, 1996–2006

	GDP (Gross Domestic Product)		Private consumption expenditures		Retail industry sales for the whole country (est.)	
(Year)	at 1988 prices (million baht)	growth rate (%)	at 1988 prices (million baht)	growth rate (%)	at current market prices (million baht)	growth rate (%)
1996	3,115,338	5.9	1,694,443	5.8	983,931	23.5
Q1	766,427	4.7	404,406	2.9	223,786	18.6
Q2	773,668	6.5	430,359	6.8	260,720	38.5
Q3	778,008	7.8	427,632	7.1	259,671	26.8
Q4	797,235	4.6	432,046	6.2	239,754	11.6
1997	3,072,615	-1.4	1,671,178	-1.4	958,029	-2.6
Q1	774,119	1.0	420,784	4.0	238,751	6.7
Q2	769,190	-0.6	438,422	1.9	237,915	-8.7
Q3	765,475	-1.6	416,320	-2.6	246,440	-5.1
Q4	763,831	-4.2	395,652	-8.4	234,923	-2.0
1998	2,749,684	-10.5	1,478,785	-11.5	660,793	-31.0
Q1	719,305	-7.1	384,549	-8.6	212,418	-11.0
Q2	662,415	-13.9	373,663	-14.8	165,700	-30.4
Q3	658,899	-13.9	357,932	-14.0	148,445	-39.8
Q4	709,065	-7.2	362,641	-8.3	134,229	-42.9
1999	2,871,980	4.4	1,542,775	4.3	863,332	30.7
Q1	717,789	-0.2	371,892	-3.3	193,070	-9.1
Q2	685,245	3.4	379,177	1.5	203,430	22.8
Q3	714,340	8.4	388,274	8.5	227,015	52.9
Q4	754,606	6.4	403,432	11.2	239,816	78.7
2000	3,008,401	4.8	1,623,716	5.2	1,066,269	23.5

	GDP (Gross Domestic Product)		Private consumption expenditures		Retail industry sales for the whole country (est.)	
(Year)	at 1988 prices (million baht)	growth rate (%)	at 1988 prices (million baht)	growth rate (%)	at current market prices (million baht)	growth rate (%)
Q1	764,339	6.5	399,389	7.4	249,286	29.1
Q2	727,229	6.1	405,922	7.1	252,697	24.2
Q3	731,689	2.4	402,025	3.5	273,414	20.4
Q4	785,144	4.0	416,380	3.2	290,871	21.3
2001	3,073,601	2.2	1,690,644	4.1	1,213,091	13.8
2002	3,237,042	5.3	1,782,648	5.4	1,399,557	15.4
2003	3,468,166	7.1	1,898,464	6.5	1,648,434	17.8
2004	3,688,189	6.3	2,016,859	6.2	2,009,984	21.9
2005	3,858,019	4.6	2,109,339	4.6	2,248,682	11.9
2006	4,059,645	5.2	2,173,060	3.0	2,364,814	5.2

SOURCE: NESDB, *GDP Statistics*, as of February 2008 (www.nesdb.go.th); for retail industry sales 1996–2000, internal documents from Bank of Thailand (originally Ministry of Finance); for retail industry sales 2001–2006, data was estimated by the author based on Bank of Thailand internal documents, the consumer price index, and the retail sales index at 2002 prices.

NOTE: Growth rate is compared with the same period of the previous year. Since retail industry sales for the entire country was only available for the years 1996 through 2000 from Bank of Thailand internal documents, the author estimated figures from 2001 onwards, as noted above. The calculation method used by the author to obtain these estimated retail sales figures is provided in the appendix.

In any case, it is well known that any of the indices mentioned above will show a sharp decline in a country's economic situation and a shrinkage in its consumption market following a crisis. So, why did the financial and currency crisis so severely impact Thailand's consumption market? Three points can be advanced to explain this. First, as a result of the Thai baht swiftly losing more than half of its value in 1997, many companies were confronted with hefty financial problems, such as foreign exchange loss and an increased debt repayment burden. These problems stemmed from the fact that many large companies had rapidly expanded their business by borrowing foreign currency after Thailand's 1990 financial liberalization, and especially after the establishment of the Bangkok Off-Shore Market (BIBF) in 1993. In addition, local companies borrowed a huge amount of short-term funds, which were flowing into Thailand at the time, from commercial banks and finance companies or through trade credit with their subsidiary and affiliated companies (Mieno, 2000). Even companies that were not facing severe financial problems were struggling as a result of the credit crunch caused by domestic financial institutions holding a huge sum of non-performing loans (NPLs).

Second, many of the companies that experienced significant deterioration in their balance sheets began to carry out both business restructuring and large-scale layoffs, so that unemployment became a serious problem (Suehiro, 1998, 220–22). According to the National Statistical Office's *Labor Force Survey*, the number of unemployed people[2] rapidly increased to 1.42 million in 1998 (the rate of unemployment was 4.4 percent) from 0.5 million in 1997 (1.5 percent unemployment).

Third, the availability of consumer loans, which had stimulated consumption during Thailand's economic boom, rapidly shrank due to many finance companies going out of business. In addition, the Thai government raised the VAT (Value Added Tax) from 7 to 10 percent in August 1997, right after the financial and currency crisis (in March 1999, the government temporarily reduced the rate back to 7 percent). This measure was aimed at securing revenue for a series of institutional and economic reforms as well as for financial retrenchment, which was required as a conditionality attached to an urgent US$17 billion IMF loan granted to Thailand. These changes, which directly influenced individual consumption, caused consumer purchasing to fall to even lower levels.

As a result of these three occurrences, the rapid decrease in individual consumption became both the cause and effect of the deterioration of business performance, creating a vicious circle.

RECONSIDERATION OF THE CONSUMPTION BOOM ARGUMENT

From the end of the 1980s until the mid-1990s, Thailand's consumer market rapidly expanded. Many economists and scholars, as well as the mass media, chose to look only at the bright side of the consumption boom, and seemed to be convinced that Bangkok's middle class had played a leading role in the country's high levels of consumer spending. When such spending later cooled down due to the financial and currency crisis, the tone of these arguments shifted dramatically. Suddenly, pundits were saying that middle-class spending was only one factor that had led to the bubble economy (Endo 1998a). Needless to say, during the consumption boom, Thailand's consumer market had failed to expand evenly across the country and across all income strata. Similarly, the financial and currency crisis impacted geographic areas and income strata differently.

As we know, Thailand's consumer market since the mid-1980s has been characterized by a "mosaic structure," in which major disparities exist among geographical areas and among income strata. This structural characteristic of the consumer market is still evident today (NSO, *Report of the 2007 Household Socio-Economic Survey*). The mosaic structure of Thailand's consumer market is the reason why provincial and Bangkok-based department stores competed to open new stores in provincial cities, which led to excessive competition. This implies that the consumer market for high-quality goods sold by department stores was never large enough to meet the supply of all the new department store openings even during the consumption boom. It, therefore, seems natural that the consumption of shopping goods with a higher income elasticity of demand drastically decreased during and after Thailand's economic meltdown. Following the financial and currency crisis, the middle class, who had increased their private financial assets by means of investing in stock during the investment boom and had been leading the consumption boom, likely restrained themselves from purchasing unnecessary and non-urgent goods, such as high-priced durable and luxury consumer goods, during Thailand's economic downturn.

However, if we look at the country's consumer market from the perspective of convenience goods consumption (daily foods and necessities), it is obvious that rural areas are important markets, as much as urban areas. Daily foods and necessities are indispensable irrespective of income. Moreover, the income-elasticity of demand for these types of goods is low. Even in the mid-1990s, during Thailand's rapid economic growth, the low-income class, earning a monthly household income of less than 8,000 baht, accounted for more than 70 percent of the country's households, most of which were rural inhabitants (see chap. 2, table 2.3). As of 2000, 68.9 percent of the population continued to live in rural areas, more specifically non-municipal areas (NSO, *The 2000 Population and Housing Census*). In short, the purchasing power of rural inhabitants and the low-income stratum for daily foods and necessities is, as a whole, very large, even though per capita income is relatively small. When taking all of this into consideration, it becomes obvious that, with regard to daily necessities, the low-income stratum and rural consumers are prime consumer market targets. In the 1950s, manufacturers and importers of daily foods and necessities had already recognized this, and had begun to expand into provincial areas.

Naturally enough, since the new retail formats, like hypermarkets, that had emerged in the mid-1990s were selling daily foods and necessities at lower prices, they rapidly increased their sales, and later turned the post-crisis recession into a business opportunity. However, in order to determine whether new retail formats have developed to such an extent as to bring a revolutionary change to Thailand's retail and distribution system, it is necessary to consider the following four points. First, it is necessary to observe that while domestic and foreign mass media and current reports mostly highlight the rapid growth of new retail formats in Thailand, they do not back up this claim with sufficient data. Moreover, they do not examine how the new retail formats changed following Thailand's recovery from the financial and currency crisis, nor do they mention the counter-measures that leading retailers in local areas have taken against the rise of these new foreign-led retail formats.

Another factor to consider is that hypermarkets, relying on their "one stop shopping" function to sell goods ranging from daily foods and necessities to durable consumer goods, like home electronics, have grown the most out of all the new retail formats. But are the preconditions, such as progress towards motorization, fully in place that would allow consumers to make full use of hypermarkets' unique function? Also, do supermarkets, which mainly sell food, really have a more competitive advantage than local wet markets (*talat sot*)? Do convenience stores, with their remarkable growth rates, actually have such influential power as to fundamentally change the distribution system associated with them, as happened in Japan?

One other factor to keep in mind is that the rapid growth of new retail formats should have had a significant impact on other formats by turning them into competitors, especially traditional small-scale groceries (*cho huai*). But, is this the actual situation? Can the "thick and short" distribution channels of direct dealings between large consumer-goods manufacturers and new retail formats alone cover the whole country's consumer market, as characterized by its mosaic structure? If these channels alone are insufficient to cover all the geographic regions of Thailand, how have manufacturers that built their own marketing channels by the end of the 1980s changed their marketing strategies with the rise of the new retail formats of the 1990s, so as to increase the market share of their products?

Lastly, what counter-measures has the industry taken and what policies has Thailand's government adopted thus far in confronting the distribution problem brought about by the rise of new retail formats? Have these measures actually restrained the expansion of new retail formats and contributed to the protection and nurturing of the local retail and distribution industry? The remainder of this chapter and the next three chapters respectively will address each of these points.

ADVANCE OF FOREIGN-LED RETAILERS AND THE RISE OF NEW FORMATS

BACKGROUND

In the late 1990s, some of Europe's major retail companies made a full-scale advance into Asian markets. The maturity of the consumption market in Europe and the oligopoly of its retail industry were so strong that European retail companies were struggling to expand their business in their respective domestic markets.[3] This was coupled with retail business regulations throughout Europe that seemed to restrict domestic business expansion. This can be regarded as a push factor into Asian markets. A pull factor into Asia was the region's emerging markets, generally expected to grow at a relatively high rate, thus making it attractive to investors. The European companies that chose to enter Asian markets had medium- and long-range growth strategies, which included expanding their business into Asia at an early stage. As a result, they hoped to be able to secure enough market share in the region to have an advantage over rival companies in the intensifying competition within global markets (Futagami 2000b, 112–14).

This last point is particularly important. One of the reasons major European companies were able to rapidly expand their businesses on a global scale was due to management innovation and the rapid progress of information technology (IT). Prior to this, the retail industry was characterized as a domestic industry, restricted by geographical and cultural factors. IT and the combination of push and pull factors stimulated a rapid transnationalization of the retail business, such that the retail industry is now an integral part of the global marketplace (Yahagi, 2001).

Table 3.2 shows that by 1999 European companies were actively investing in East and Southeast Asian countries, especially in Thailand, where many of Europe's major companies had already established themselves. One of the reasons for this is that Thailand, compared with its neighbors, had substantial consumer market growth as well as political stability. In addition, the lower prices of the stocks and assets of Thailand's retail companies following the financial and currency crisis gave European companies an ideal chance to build a foothold for further expansion of their businesses in Asia.

Table 3.2 also shows that Western companies introduced new retail formats, such as hypermarket stores and supermarkets, most of which predominately

TABLE 3.2 Advance of Western retailers into East and Southeast Asia, as of 1999/2000

			Sales (as of 2000)		Ownership[b] (as of 1999)								
Business group's name	Country of origin	Format[a]	Ranking	Million US$	Thailand	Indonesia	Malaysia	Singapore	China	Hong Kong	Taiwan	Korea	Japan
Wal-Mart Stores	USA	DS/HM	1	191,799		JV/W			JV			Subsidiary	
Carrefour S.A.	France	HM	2	59,895	Subsidiary	Subsidiary	Subsidiary	Subsidiary	Subsidiary	Subsidiary	Subsidiary	Subsidiary	Subsidiary
Royal Ahold	Netherlands	SM	4	48,497	Subsidiary	JV	Subsidiary	S/W	S/W				
Metro AG	Germany	HM	6	43,375					JV				
Tesco	UK	SM/HM	13	30,608	Subsidiary						JV	Subsidiary	
Casino	France	HM	29	17,629	Subsidiary						Subsidiary		
Delhaize "Le Lion"	Belgium	SM	30	16,792	Subsidiary			JV					
Marks & Spencer	UK	SS	42	12,403	Franchise	Franchise	Franchise	Franchise		Subsidiary		Franchise	JV
Boots	UK	SS	59	8,019	JV								Subsidiary
Makro	Netherlands	C&C	–	9,416	Subsidiary	JV	Subsidiary		JV		Subsidiary		

SOURCE: Futagami (2000, 27); Yahagi (2001, 18); companies' annual reports; *Nikkei Ryutsu Simbun* (a Japanese business newspaper), October 4, 2001.

NOTE: Sales ranking and sales figures, as of 2000, were sourced from *Nikkei Ryutsu Simbun*; sales figures originally appeared in Japanese yen and were converted to US dollars using the following exchange rate for the year 2000: US$1=¥116=€1.16. Data for Makro was sourced from the company's annual report since this company was not part of *Nikkei Ryutsu Simbun*'s rankings. The Makro sales figures originally appeared in euros. The dash (–) in the "ranking" column for Makro indicates the company was not ranked by *Nikkei Ryutsu Simbun*.

[a] Codes used in the "Format" column represent the following: DS=discount store, HM=hypermarket, SM=supermarket, SS=specialty store, C&C=cash-and-carry.

[b] Codes used in the "Ownership" column represent the following: JV=joint venture; JV/W=withdrawal from joint venture; S/W=withdrawal from subsidiary.

sold low-priced daily foods and necessities. During the financial crisis in Asian countries, when consumers refrained from buying luxury goods and focused on low-priced daily necessities, there was still ample room for these retail formats to expand. Moreover, these transnational retail corporations had an immense business scale (in some instances, larger than the entire Thai retail industry)[4] and could expand their own chain operations in the country all at one time by taking over local chains.

DEREGULATION OF FOREIGN INVESTMENT

The Thai government's policy to deregulate foreign investment in 1999 spurred the major European retail companies to more actively invest in Thailand during the country's post-crisis period. Previously, Thailand's National Executive Council No. 281, promulgated in 1972, forbid the majority of investment in various industries, including domestic commerce, to be held in foreign capital.[5] Any foreign retail company that wished to advance into the Thai market had to establish a joint venture with a local partner that controlled the majority of investment in local currency. This suggests that the management strategy of the foreign company might sometimes be constrained by the local joint-venture partner.

Under the changing economic environment in Thailand during the investment boom of the late 1980s, the government came to recognize the importance of incorporating deregulation into law. In 1993, the first Chuan government began drafting a bill, but it was not until after the financial and currency crisis that it finally took shape.[6] Following the crisis, many Thai-owned companies were faced with a large amount of debt and foreign exchange loss, and some responded to these financial difficulties by asking their foreign partners to increase their capital investment. At the time, foreign investment regulations made this difficult. Local companies thus pressured the government to hasten deregulation and the enactment of a new law. The Foreign Business Act, B.E. 2542 (1999), was promulgated in November 1999 and the law was enforced in March 2000.[7]

The Foreign Business Act substantially relaxed foreign capital regulations. For example, foreigners could, in principle, make a 100 percent investment, even in a retail business, with the exception of small capital projects under 100 million baht. Despite this, as of December 31, 2000, every major retail company in Thailand with foreign capital investment maintained a Thai majority in its stockholdings ratio of individuals or juridical persons. At first glance, it would thus appear that there was not a great deal of foreign investment in the retail industry even after the financial crisis. However, in this context, the "Thai" majority mostly represented local companies established with foreign capital, and could, therefore, actually be regarded as foreigner-owned companies.

Then, why were foreigners officially minority stockholders in the dummy companies they were establishing even once deregulation was in force? The answer to this question lies in how the Foreign Business Act was written. According to the business act, foreigners are, in principle, allowed to make a 100 percent investment, even in retail businesses. However, the annex to the business act set out a series of reservations that applied to various types of businesses and trade, such as domestic trade of local agricultural products, for example, in which foreign investment was precluded. Since European hypermarkets and supermarkets dealt in agricultural products, they might actually break the law if they were majority stockholders. That is why European companies were careful with their stockholdings ratio. Despite appearances, foreign investment at the time, no doubt, strengthened foreign control over business ownership. Foreign investment also rapidly strengthened foreign control at the top levels of management, including boards of directors and executive committees, such that foreign capital actually had a strong hold over both the ownership and the management of retail companies in Thailand.

The increased presence of foreign capital in Thailand's retail industry was part of the global business development of multinational retail companies. This was not a transient phenomenon accompanying the financial and currency crisis, but rather has become a movement in which there is no turning back.

RISE OF NEW RETAIL FORMATS

Changes in the domestic and international economy helped catalyze European retail companies to advance into the Thai market in the 1990s, especially after the financial and currency crisis. The retail businesses they brought into the Thai market were new retail formats (cash-and-carry stores, hypermarkets, supermarkets, convenience stores, category killers, and specialty stores), most of which originated from local retail business groups that had introduced these formats during the investment boom. The remarkable point is that the change in Thailand's retail industry is not a simple post-crisis phenomenon, but had already begun during the era preceding the crisis. These new retail formats have had a big impact on the retail industry in Thailand, where before the only modern retail businesses had been department stores.

Table 3.3 shows the retail sales for each retail format as well as private consumption expenditures for the whole country from 1993 to 2006. From this table, we can see that the sales percentage of department stores had already begun to decline prior to the financial and currency crisis, while the percentage of general mass merchandisers (cash-and-carry stores and hypermarkets) had been on a sharp rise. In 2000, the general mass merchandisers finally exceeded department stores in total sales.[8]

TABLE 3.3 Thailand's retail sales and private consumption expenditures, 1993–2006

	Department stores		Hypermarkets, Cash-and-Carry		Supermarkets		Convenience stores		Total retail sales for Thailand		Private consumption expenditures	
	sales (million baht)	growth rate (%)	sales (million baht)	growth rate (%)	sales (million baht)	growth rate (%)	sales (million baht)	growth rate (%)	sales (million baht)	growth rate (%)	current market prices (million baht)	growth rate (%)
1993	62,663	–	13,343	–	6,350	–	3,932	–	n/a	–	1,730,519	–
1994	81,668	30.3	22,220	66.5	7,299	14.9	5,760	46.5	n/a	–	1,958,726	13.2
1995	111,912	37.0	35,030	57.7	8,216	12.6	7,923	37.6	796,625	–	2,225,739	13.6
1996	126,400	12.9	52,542	50.0	11,854	44.3	9,923	25.2	983,931	23.5	2,479,828	11.4
1997	114,582	-9.3	69,442	32.2	19,908	67.9	12,333	24.3	958,029	-2.6	2,586,956	4.3
1998[a]	95,000	-17.1	77,258	11.3	20,417	2.6	14,407	16.8	660,793	-31.0	2,505,312	-3.2
1999	97,004	2.1	87,406	13.1	21,033	3.0	16,920	17.4	863,332	30.7	2,595,113	3.6
2000	106,068	9.3	108,725	24.4	20,878	-0.7	20,471	21.0	1,066,269	23.5	2,762,925	6.5
2001	n/a	–	129,418	19.0	21,313	2.1	23,847	16.5	1,213,091	13.8	2,941,012	6.4
2002	n/a	–	146,323	13.1	25,152	18.0	32,445	36.1	1,399,557	15.4	3,119,979	6.1
2003	n/a	–	164,971	12.7	26,327	4.7	43,392	33.7	1,648,434	17.8	3,385,602	8.5
2004	n/a	–	186,736	13.2	26,593	1.0	43,084	-0.7	2,009,984	21.9	3,711,286	9.6
2005	n/a	–	206,775	10.7	27,931	5.0	56,012	30.0	2,248,682	11.9	4,060,414	9.4
2006	n/a	–	229,982	11.2	28,123	0.7	72,126	28.8	2,364,814	5.2	4,376,585	7.8

SOURCE: Internal documents from Bank of Thailand (originally Ministry of Finance) for department stores' sales and growth rate; companies' financial statements for hypermarkets, cash-and-carry stores, supermarkets, and convenice stores' sales and growth rates; author estimates based on Bank of Thailand internal documents for total retail sales for Thailand; NESDB, *GDP Statistics* (www.nesdb.go.th) for private consumption expenditures.

NOTE: Growth rate is compared with the same period of the previous year. "Sales" refers only to sales income (it does not include other income, such as rental income). The total sales for each retail store format was calculated by the author as follows: in the case of a public limited company, consolidated figures were used; among non-listed companies, such as chain stores with the same store name, the sales figures of each store were added together to reach a total sum for such stores. With regard to hypermarkets, cash-and-carry stores, supermarkets, and convenience stores, only the Bangkok-based leading chains are represented in these figures.

[a] Due to limited data, total retail sales for Thailand in 1998 and 1999 might be underestimated.

Convenience stores are much smaller than general mass merchandisers in terms of sales, but often rival them in terms of growth rate. This was the case not only during the post–financial crisis but also in the post-recovery period as well, up until 2006. While supermarkets' sales have been steadily increasing, they have had an inferior growth rate compared to other new formats.[9] However, since the sales volume of general mass merchandisers is extremely large, the overall growth of new retail formats seems remarkable.

Meanwhile, however, retail sales for the entire country increased at a higher rate than private consumption expenditures (at current market prices), though there was a drop both before and after the financial and currency crisis. Changes in the ratio of total sales of these new retail formats to total sales of the retail industry are examined in table 3.4. From this table, we can observe, yet again, that the percentage of department stores had already begun to decline prior to the financial and currency crisis, and the percentage of general mass merchandisers rose rapidly both before and after the crisis.

Contrary to general belief, the percentage of general mass merchandisers was stagnant or even declined from the post-recovery period until 2005. In 2006, when consumption slumped due to a steep rise in oil prices and political instability, the percentage rose to some extent, but not remarkably so. The general mass merchandiser format is growing in absolute value of money, but has not showed much increase as a percentage of total retail sales for the whole country.[10] This is particularly noteworthy because current reports and news, even in Thailand, never actually point out this fact. Needless to say, the sales percentages of convenience stores and supermarkets as a ratio of Thailand's entire retail sales are not yet large either. In short, while it is true that the new retail formats sales, notably that of general mass merchandisers, have rapidly increased, their ratio to the retail industry's total sales is not yet as significant as local newspapers and current analyses by Thai and foreign scholars have emphasized.[11] Although it should be noted that tables 3.3 and 3.4 do not cover all of the new retail formats, the retail sales for the whole country also do not include small-scale retailers whose total sales are under 1.2 million baht. Taking this into consideration, the rise of new retail formats is undeniable, but has most likely been rather overestimated. This point is very important in understanding Thailand's distribution system as a whole, and will be further examined in the next chapter.

TABLE 3.4 Thailand's retail sales as a percentage of modern trade, 1995–2006

Year	Department stores (%)	HM[a] and C&C[b] (%)	SM[c] (%)	CVS[d] (%)	Modern trade[e] (%)	Total Retail sales (%)	HM and C&C sales / private consumption expenditures x100 (%)
1995	14.0	4.4	0.9	1.0	20.4	100.0	1.6
1996	12.8	5.3	1.1	1.0	20.3	100.0	2.1
1997	12.0	7.2	2.1	1.3	22.5	100.0	2.7
1998	14.4	11.7	3.1	2.1	31.3	100.0	3.1
1999	11.2	10.1	2.4	1.9	25.7	100.0	3.4
2000	9.9	10.2	2.0	1.9	24.0	100.0	3.9
2001	n/a	10.7	1.8	1.9	n/a	100.0	4.4
2002	n/a	10.5	1.8	2.3	n/a	100.0	4.7
2003	n/a	10.0	1.6	2.6	n/a	100.0	4.9
2004	n/a	9.3	1.3	2.1	n/a	100.0	5.0
2005	n/a	9.2	1.2	2.5	n/a	100.0	5.1
2006	n/a	9.7	1.2	3.0	n/a	100.0	5.3

SOURCE: Annual reports of listed companies; financial statements of unlisted companies; Bank of Thailand (www.bot.or.th and internal documents); NESDB (www.nesdb.go.th).

NOTE: Sales percentages for HM and C&C, SM, and CVS include only sales data from leading Bangkok-based chain stores. All figures have been rounded up to the nearest decimal place, which acccounts for the total sum of the various retail formats' sales percentages differing slightly from the modern trade total sales percentage.

[a] HM = hypermarkets

[b] C&C = cash-and-carry stores

[c] SM = supermarkets

[d] CVS = convenience stores

[e] Modern trade refers to department stores, HM, C&C, SM, and CVS, collectively, and is used to differentiate between traditional trade, such as wet markets and *cho huai* (small-scale grocery stores).

Let's now focus on some further details regarding the rise of new retail formats before and after the financial and currency crisis. Table 3.5 shows a list of the top thirty retail companies in Thailand based on 1999 sales. In order to compare sales with the pre–financial crisis period, the table also shows a 1996 ranking of the top thirty retail companies as well as the sales percentage increase or decrease between 1996 and 1999 sales.[12]

TABLE 3.5 Thailand's top thirty retailers in sales, 1996 vs. 1999

Ranking[a]		Company/chain store name[b]	Year of establish-ment	Group name (nationality)	Format[c]	1999 sales (million baht)	1996/1999 sales (% change)[d]
1996	1999						
1	1	Siam Makro (Plc)	1988	Makro (Holland)	C&C	34,493	9.0
5	2	Big C Supercenter (Plc)	1994	Casino (France)	HM	22,464	108.8
7	3	Ek-Chai Distribution/ Tesco Lotus	1993	Tesco (UK)	HM	20,924	250.5
6	4	C. P. Seven Eleven	1988	CP	CVS	15,141	71.2
2	5	Central Dept. Store (+)	1974	Central	Dept. S.	12,909	-31.9
4	6	The Mall Group/ The Mall	1980	The Mall	Dept. S.	11,264	3.4
11	7	CRC Ahold (+)/ Tops	1996	Royal Ahold (Holland)	SM	11,032	272.1
20	8	CenCar/ Carrefour	1994	Carrefour (France)	HM	8,367	418.8
3	9	Robinson Dept. Store (Plc)	1983	Central	Dept. S.	6,501	-57.0
–	10	Power Buy	1996	Central	CK	4,453	–
8	11	Siam-Jusco	1984	AEON (Japan)	SM	4,219	8.8
12	12	Foodland Super-market	1972	Foodland	SM	2,751	7.8
–	13	City Mall Group/ The Emporium	1997	The Mall et al.	Dept. S.	2,528	–
9	14	Tang Hua Seng Dept. Store	1976	Tang Hua Seng	Dept. S.	2,517	-22.0
18	15	Isetan (Thailand)	1989	Isetan (Japan)	Dept. S.	1,621	-3.4
–	16	CRC Sports/ Super Sports	1996	Central	CK	1,460	–
–	17	Auchan Chiang Mai (withdrew in 2001)	1996	Auchan (France)	HM	1,159	–
19	18	Pata Dept. Store (+)	1975	Pata	Dept. S.	1,158	-29.3
15	19	Banglumpoo Dept. Store (+)	1978	Banglumpoo	Dept. S.	1,103	-43.5
–	20	Boots	1996	Boots (UK)	SS	1,059	–
24	21	Klang Plaza (+)	1975	Klang Plaza	Dept. S.	1,049	-2.1

Ranking[a]		Company/chain store name[b]	Year of establish-ment	Group name (nationality)	Format[c]	1999 sales (million baht)	1996/1999 sales (% change)[d]
1996	1999						
–	22	Bel-Thai Supermarket/ Food Lion	1996	Delhaize (Belgium)	SM	911	–
NL	23	Villa Market JP	1988	Phusanakhom family	SM	886	41.8
23	24	Bangkok-Tokyu Dept. Store	1983	Tokyu (Japan)	Dept. S.	833	-27.5
22	25	Sogo (Thailand) (+)	1983	Sogo (Japan)	Dept. S.	749	-42.6
NL	26	Siam FamilyMart	1992	FamilyMart (Japan)	CVS	725	418.0
14	27	Merry Kings Dept. Store (+)	1977	Merry Kings	Dept. S.	686	-72.5
21	28	Topland Plaza (+)	1989	Top Land	Dept. S.	684	-49.8
27	29	Diana Dept. Store (plc)	1995	Phithanphanit family	Dept. S.	633	-19.1
NL	30	Ngee Soon Superstore	1960	Wirarattanarot family	W/SM	617	85.4

SOURCE: Annual reports of listed companies; financial statements of unlisted companies.

NOTE: Retail-cum-wholesalers are included in the list of companies/chain stores, while automobile and motorcycle dealers are excluded. "Sales" refers to sales income only (it does not include other income, such as rental income). The sales for all formats were calculated by the author as follows: in the case of a public limited company, consolidated figures were used; among non-listed companies that maintain chain stores with the same store name, the sales figures of each store were added together to reach a single total sum.

[a] The dash (–) in the "ranking" column indicates the company had not yet been established as of 1996, while "NL" indicates that the company was not listed as one of the top thirty stores in 1996.

[b] The code "(+)" in the "company/chain store" column indicates a non-listed company with chain stores that have the same store name.

[c] Codes used in the "format" column represent the following: C&C=cash-and-carry store; Dept. S=department store; HM=hypermarket; SM=supermarket; SS=specialty store; W/SM=wholesaler-cum-supermarket

[d] The dash (–) in the last column indicates that the company was not yet established as of 1996; as a result, a comparison against 1999 sales cannot be made.

From this table, three main points can be observed. First, European retail companies made a remarkable progress during the period. Concrete examples were Holland-based Makro, France-based Casino Group (Big C), and UK-based Tesco, which ranked first to third. In the same way, Holland-based Royal Ahold, France-based Carrefour, France-based Auchan, UK-based Boots, and Belgium-based Delhaize (Food Lion) respectively ranked seventh, eighth, seventeenth, twentieth, and twenty-second in 1999. Moreover, these were all new retail formats and the growth rates in sales compared to 1996 were relatively high.

The second point to observe is that Thailand's local major department stores were in a hard fight. Robinson Department Store, in particular, saw its sales decrease by nearly 60 percent compared to 1996, and its ranking drop sharply from third to ninth. Central Department Store, the top chain in Thailand's department store industry, experienced a drop in its sales and ranking as well. However, with the amalgamation of the groups in 1995, Central Department Store and Robinson Department Store separated their home electronics and sporting goods departments from the body of the department store, and transferred these two departments to the newly established category killer companies Power Buy Co., Ltd. (10th in 1999) and CRC Sports Co., Ltd. (16th in 1999), respectively. This should, therefore, be taken into consideration when evaluating the reduced sales of the two department store chains from 1996 to 1999. Nevertheless, both Central and Robinson lost their leader's status. The Mall Department Store, however, which had ranked third in Thailand's department store industry for a long time, seemed to be putting up a relatively good fight. As for The Emporium (13th in 1999), an upper-class department store established on Sukhumvit Road in Bangkok, it succeeded in winning popularity among foreign residents and Thai upper-middle and upper-class consumers.

The third point to observe from table 3.5 is that the local middle-class department stores were more seriously damaged than the major department stores. For example, Tang Hua Seng Department Store saw its sales decrease by a little more than 20 percent in 1999 compared to 1996 and its ranking dropped from ninth to fourteenth. Merry Kings Department Store's sales decreased by more than 70 percent and its ranking plummeted from fourteenth to twenty-seventh, while Imperial Department Store, which ranked tenth in 1996, was out of the top thirty in 1999 due to the post-crisis closure of its stores. Other small- and medium-scale department stores experienced drastic decreases in sales and ranking in a similar way. Table 3.6 illustrates these three points more clearly.

In comparing 1996 and 1999, the sales concentration ratio of high-ranking companies increased, especially the top five and top ten. In comparing business groups, the weight of The Mall Group rose a little, while the weight of both the Central Group and CP Group sharply declined. Therefore, the weight of these three local leading groups as a whole was drastically reduced. In comparing the data by nationality, foreign companies that were in Thailand's top thirty ranked companies surpassed Thai companies in sales. As regards type of retail format, general mass merchandisers rose remarkably in contrast to the declining position of department stores, which up until 1996 had been the predominant format in Thailand's modern trade sector.

TABLE 3.6 Thailand's top thirty retailers as a percentage of total retail sales, 1996 vs.1999

	1996		1999	
	million baht	Percentage of total retail sales	million baht	Percentage of total retail sales
Cumulative sales				
Top 5 companies	86,422	8.8	105,931	12.3
Top 10 companies	111,214	11.3	147,548	17.1
Top 20 companies	131,895	13.4	167,123	19.4
Total top 30 companies	141,358	14.4	174,896	20.3
By business group				
Central Group	48,279	4.9	25,323	2.9
CP Group	47,250	4.8	15,141	1.8
The Mall Group	10,895	1.1	13,792	1.6
By nationality				
Thai	97,596	9.9	66,341	7.7
Foreign	43,762	4.4	108,555	12.6
By format				
Department stores	69,218	7.0	44,235	5.1
General mass merchandisers	53,289	5.4	87,406	10.1
Supermarkets	10,005	1.0	19,799	2.3
Convenience stores	8,846	0.9	15,866	1.8
Other[a]	0	0.0	7,590	0.9
Total for the whole country	983,931	100.0	863,332	100.0

SOURCE: Same as table 3.5 regarding sales of each company; same as table 3.1 regarding total sales of the retail industry for the whole of Thailand.

NOTE: "Sales" refers to sales income only (it does not include other income, such as rental income). Business group and nationality are determined based on the major stockholders and who controls the management of the company.

[a] "Other" includes category killers and specialty stores.

DOMESTIC COMPANIES' RESPONSE

REORGANIZATION OF DOMESTIC BUSINESS GROUPS

In contrast with the rise of foreign-led new retail formats following the financial and currency crisis, some local retail companies reduced the size of their business and others closed down their stores. Central Group and CP Group, both of which diversified their retail business activities during the investment and consumption boom, were no exceptions.

As shown in table 3.7, Central Group virtually withdrew from many of its retail businesses by the end of 1999, while firmly maintaining ownership and management of department stores that had been the group's core business since the mid-1950s. The group became a minor shareholder of Big C Supercenter and Siam FamilyMart, and sold all of CenCar (Carrefour) and CRC Ahold (Tops) stocks to France-based Carrefour Group and Holland-based Royal Ahold Group, respectively.[13] At the same time, European companies strengthened their financial structures by drastically increasing capital.

As a result, the ownership structure of the Central Group changed as well. It greatly changed in two respects. First, Central sold its stocks in general mass merchandiser businesses (i.e., hypermarkets) to foreign companies. It sold all its stocks in CenCar and was thus no longer affiliated with Carrefour, and it reduced its registered capital in Big C from 39.8 percent to 13.4 percent, such that Robinson Department Store and CRC no longer had a direct capital relationship with Big C. Second, the Central Group's founding family drastically increased its registered capital from 800 million baht to 3,300 million baht in the Harng Central Department Store Co., Ltd. (HCDS), in which it held 100 percent of the stocks. HCDS was then placed as the holding company of the Central Group's entire retail business (see table 3.7; chap. 2, fig. 2.1).

Central's purpose for doing this was to reorganize the group's ownership structure, which had been complicated by its diversification. HCDS had already, at the end of 1996, held as much as 82.5 percent of stock in CRC, a holding company of both Central and Robinson, and was virtually playing a role as another holding company as well as running a department store. After the financial and currency crisis, HCDS came to supervise not only the Central Group's retail business but also its consumer goods manufacturing and wholesale business, while withdrawing from running a department store by transferring it to Central Department Store Co., Ltd. (CDS).[14] In addition, CRC came to control the Central Group's entire department store business under

TABLE 3.7 Major stockholders of the Central and CP Groups, 1996 vs. 1999

Format/ company name	Year of establish-ment	Chain store name	Total registered capital: At the end of 1996 capital (million baht) stockholder	ownership (%)	Total registered capital: At the end of 1999 capital (million baht) stockholder	ownership (%)	Remarks[a]
Central Group							
Department stores							
Harng Central Department Store [HCDS]	1968	Central	800		3,300		A
			Jirathiwat family	100.0	Jirathiwat family	100.0	
Central Department Store [CDS]	1974	Central	3,335		3,335		A
			CRC[b]	99.9	CRC	99.9	
Robinson Department Store Plc	1983	Robinson	1,870		1,481		A
			CRC	51.7	CRC	47.6	
			Securities Depositary Center	24.3	Securities Depositary Center	33.2	
CR (Thailand)	1995	Robinson	501		501		A
			Robinson Dept. Store Plc	99.9	Robinson Dept. Store Plc	99.9	
Hypermarkets (HM)							
Big C Supercenter Plc[c]	1994	Big C	2,700		8,000		B
			Jirathiwat family	35.8	Jirathiwat family	13.4	
			Robinson Dept. Store Plc	14.0	Saowanee Holdings[d]	27.0	
					Casino (France)	41.0	
CenCar	1994	Carrefour	800		6,200		C
			Carrefour (France)	40.0	Carrefour (France)	40.0	
			SSCP (Thailand)[e]	20.0	SSCP (Thailand)	59.9	
			CRC	40.0	–		
Supermarkets (SM)							
CRC Ahold[f]	1996	Tops	306		1,529		C
			CRC	n/a	Nawak (Thailand)	50.9	
			Robinson Dept. Store Plc	32.2	Ahold (Holland)	49.0	

Format/ company name	Year of establish-ment	Chain store name	Total registered capital: At the end of 1996 capital (million baht) stockholder	ownership (%)	At the end of 1999 capital (million baht) stockholder	ownership (%)	Remarks[a]
Convenience Stores (CVS)							
Siam FamilyMart	1992	FamilyMart	100		600		B
			Robinson Dept. Store Plc	40.0	Robinson Dept. Store Plc	13.3	
			FamilyMart (Japan)	30.0	FamilyMart (Japan)	43.0	
			SP (Saha Group)	10.0	SP (Saha Group)	8.3	
			ICC (Saha Group)	10.0	ICC (Saha Group)	8.3	
			Itochu (Japan)[g]	10.0	Itochu (Japan)	6.0	
			–		SFM Holding	21.0	
CP Group[h]							
Cash-and-carry (C&C)							
Siam Makro Plc[i]	1988	Makro	2,400		2,400		B
			Makro Holding (Thailand)	37.5	Makro Holding (Thailand)	37.5	
			Makro (Holland)	20.9	Makro (Holland)	22.5	
			Holms Green	7.7	Holms Green	7.7	
			CP Group	9.7	–		
Hypermarkets (HM)							
Ek-Chai Distribution System	1993	(Tesco) Lotus	6,000 (as of Apr. 1997)		22,000		B
			CP Group	100.0	CP Group	6.8	
			–		Tesco (Thailand)[j]	93.2	
Supermarkets (SM)							
Sunny's Supermarket	1990	Sunny's	5		Sold to the Delhaize Group (Belgium)[k]		C
			Jiarawanon family	100.0			
Convenience Stores (CVS)							
C. P. Seven Eleven	1988	7-Eleven	2,000		2,000		A
			CP Group	42.2	CP Group	32.5	
			Other (CP Group)[l]	38.9	Other (CP Group)	38.9	
			Other foreign companies	11.3	Other foreign companies	25.1	

SOURCE: Annual reports of public limited companies; company documents (Baep 56-1) submitted to the Stock Exchange of Thailand; financial statements of non-listed companies.

NOTES: A dash (–) indicates that the stakeholder held no shares during that particular time period.

[a] Codes in the "Remarks" column refer to the following: "A"=as of the end of 1999, the group controlled management and held a majority of the stock'; "B"=as of the end of 1999, the group had given up control of management and held a minority of the stock; "C"=as of the end of 1999, the group withdrew from the business and sold all of its stock.

[b] CRC (Central Retail Corporation) became operative in August 1996. Its forerunner was the Rainbow Global Holding Co., Ltd. Harng Central Department Store Co., Ltd., the Central Group's virtual holding company, held 82.5% of CRC stock.

[c] Big C Supercenter Plc became operative in June 1996. Its forerunner was S. K. Garment Co., Ltd., a subsidiary of the Robinson Group.

[d] Saowanee Holdings was the Casino Group's affiliated company in Thailand. The Casino Group held 49% of Saowanee stock.

[e] Details of SSCP (Thailand) Co., Ltd. are not clear, but since the board members of the company overlap with those of CenCar Co., Ltd., it is considered to be a subsidiary of the Carrefour Group.

[f] In 1996, the ownership and management of Save One Co., Ltd., a subsidiary of the Robinson group, were transferred to the Jirathiwat family, the owner family of the Central Group, and the company name was changed to CRC Ahold Co., Ltd. As of the end of 1996, besides Robinson Department Store Plc, CRC was thought to hold a considerable part of CRC Ahold stock, but data is not available. As of the end of 1999, the Holland-based Royal Ahold Group was thought to virtually hold 99.9% of CRC Ahold stock.

[g] Itochu (Japan) includes the headquarters of Itochu in Japan, as well as Itochu (Asia) Co., Ltd. in Singapore and Itochu (Thailand).

[h] CP Group refers to Charoen Pokphand Group Co., Ltd., as well as CP Merchandising Co., Ltd., C. P. Seven Eleven Co., Ltd., Charoen Pokphand Petrochemi Co., Ltd., etc. The CP Group held a majority (51%) of stock in both Makro Holding and Holms Green, as of the end of 1996 and 1999.

[ii] Of the major stockholders of Siam Makro Plc, Makro Holding (Thailand) and Holms Green were joint ventures between the Makro Group (Holland) and the CP Group.

[j] Tesco (Thailand) was a joint venture established mainly by the UK-based Tesco Group in 1998.

[k] The Belgium-based Delhaize Group established Bel-Thai Supermarket Co., Ltd. as a subsidiary in 1996 in the form of a joint venture between Delhaize "Le Lion" Netherlands Co., Ltd. (49%) and Food Lion (Thailand) Inc. (51%) and operated a supermarket chain (Food Lion) in Thailand.

[l] "Other (CP Group)" includes the group's other affiliated companies and the Jiarawanon family, which owns the CP Group.

the supervision of HCDS. It is worth mentioning here that the Central Group's founding family gradually increased its presence and, therefore, its weight in CRC's board of directors after two persons from the Robinson Group's founding families resigned from their posts in July 1998.[15]

With HCDS and CRC as its core, the Central Group restructured itself in order to overcome its post-crisis difficulties. This suggests that all the Robinson Group-led retail businesses were restructured with CRC as their core, including Robinson Department Store with its post-crisis excess debt and non-profitable affiliated provincial department stores.

In the same way, the CP Group drastically reduced its retail business division after the financial and currency crisis (see table 3.7). For example, the group sold most of its stock in the hypermarket business (Lotus) to the UK-based Tesco Group, the leading supermarket chain in the UK, thus becoming a minor stockholder without administrative authority. Although the CP Group remained one of the major stockholders of the cash-and-carry business (Makro), the group virtually gave up its administrative authority. In 1999, the CP Group sold its supermarket business (Sunny's) to the Belgium-based Delhaize Group, which soon thereafter began operating the Food Lion supermarket chain in Bangkok and its vicinity. As a result, the CP Group's retail and distribution business division came to concentrate its managerial resources on the convenience store business (7-Eleven stores).[16]

BIPOLARIZATION OF DOMESTIC DEPARTMENT STORES

The two major local business groups, which had been leading Thailand's retail industry by promoting diversification prior to the financial and currency crisis, sold non-core businesses to foreign companies in order to concentrate managerial resources in their core businesses and to overcome the post-crisis difficulties. As for the CP Group, however, reorganizing its distribution business was only part of the group's business, because the group had always been a conglomerate centered around agribusiness and entered the distribution industry at the end of the 1980s, later than its rivals. In addition, convenience stores, which the CP Group selected as core businesses in its distribution business division, were a promising format, and C. P. Seven Eleven Co., Ltd. actually succeeded in listing stocks on the Stock Exchange of Thailand in 2003. Meanwhile, the Central Group had been consistently developing retail businesses as its core since its foundation in 1947, and the restructuring of its retail business, therefore, was a critical issue for the future of the group.[17] In addition, the Central Group chose to keep its department store business despite the format's declining prominence in the retail industry. Table 3.8 provides a snap shot of the performance of the department store business crucial to Central Group since the financial crisis and compares it with The Mall Group's department store business.

TABLE 3.8 Department store business of the Central and The Mall Groups, 1990–2006

	Central Group						The Mall Group			
	HCDS[a]		CDS[b]		Robinson Plc		The Mall Group[c]		City Mall Group[d]	
Year	million baht	growth rate (%)	million baht	growth rate (%)	million baht	growth rate (%)	million baht	growth rate (%)	million baht	growth rate (%)
					Sales					
1990	5,499	16.5	2,190	72.4	–	–	3,916	–	–	–
1991	6,669	21.3	2,545	16.2	–	–	3,596	-8.2	–	–
1992	5,890	-11.7	2,919	14.7	7,400	–	4,844	34.7	–	–
1993	6,776	15.0	3,555	21.8	8,184	10.6	7,154	47.7	–	–
1994	9,265	36.7	4,725	32.9	9,656	18.0	9,040	26.4	–	–
1995	5,914	-36.2	8,451	78.9	12,218	26.5	10,603	17.3	–	–
1996	1,200	-79.7	7,854	-7.1[e]	15,116	23.7	10,895	2.8	–	–
1997	1,032	-14.0	7,502	-4.5	8,820	-41.7	11,339	4.1	710	–
1998	–	–	7,496	-0.1	6,246	-29.2	10,281	-9.3	2,071	191.6
1999	–	–	11,605	54.8	6,501	4.1	11,264	9.6	2,528	22.1
2000	–	–	12,928	11.4	7,000	7.7	12,251	8.8	3,188	26.1
2001	–	–	13,987	8.2	7,558	8.0	13,678	11.6	3,751	17.7
2002	–	–	16,134	15.4	7,615	0.8	14,721	7.6	4,196	11.9
2003	–	–	18,662	15.7	7,765	2.0	15,086	2.5	4,476	6.7
2004	–	–	20,972	12.4	8,835	13.8	16,226	7.6	4,979	11.2
2005	–	–	23,120	10.2	9,817	11.1	16,806	3.6	4,683	-5.9
2006	–	–	22,645	-2.1	10,812	10.1	16,583	-1.3	4,202	-10.3
					Ordinary profit					
1990	112	180.0	113	66.2	–	–	94	–	–	–
1991	264	135.7	170	50.4	–	–	42	-55.3	–	–
1992	93	-64.8	63	-62.9	330	–	68	61.9	–	–
1993	578	521.5	59	-6.3	296	-10.3	71	4.4	–	–
1994	302	-47.8	91	54.2	527	78.0	55	-22.5	–	–
1995	165	-45.4	313	244.0	358	-32.1	69	25.5	–	–
1996	25	-84.8	254	-18.8	445	24.3	56	-18.8	–	–

	Central Group						The Mall Group			
	HCDS[a]		CDS[b]		Robinson Plc		The Mall Group[c]		City Mall Group[d]	
Year	million baht	growth rate (%)	million baht	growth rate (%)	million baht	growth rate (%)	million baht	growth rate (%)	million baht	growth rate (%)
1997	-343	–	156	-38.6	-1,130	–	88	57.1	-7	–
1998	–	–	-171	–	-2,263	–	150	70.5	12	–
1999	–	–	294	–	-5,034	–	446	197.3	149	1,141.7
2000	–	–	1,017	245.9	-1,965	–	531	19.1	169	13.4
2001	–	–	976	-4.0	-421	–	631	18.8	176	4.1
2002	–	–	1,748	79.1	489	–	697	10.5	186	5.7
2003	–	–	1,562	-10.6	543	11.0	677	-2.9	332	78.5
2004	–	–	2,482	58.9	751	38.3	651	-3.8	213	-35.8
2005	–	–	3,011	21.3	867	15.4	753	15.7	126	-40.8
2006	–	–	2,833	-5.9	685	-21.0	842	11.8	127	0.8

SOURCE: Companies' financial statements.

NOTE: Growth rate is compared with the same period of the previous year. "Sales" refers only to sales income (it does not include other income, such as rental income). All figures for listed companies represent consolidated data. All data represent a January to December fiscal year, except for HCDS, whose fiscal year ran from September to August for the years 1990 and 1991 only, and The The Mall Group whose fiscal year ran from April 1990 to March 1991 for the year 1990 only.

[a] HCDS refers to Harng Central Department Store Co., Ltd. Since 1998, it has basically become a holding company.

[b] CDS refers to Central Department Store Co., Ltd. (previously, Chidlom Department Store).

[c] The Mall Group Co., Ltd. runs The Mall Department Store.

[d] City Mall Group Co., Ltd. runs The Emporium.

[e] On November 22, 1995, a fire broke out in Central Department Store (CDS), Chidlom branch, the main store of the Central Group, which caused the company an extraordinary loss of 187 million baht in the statement of accounts for the year, and most likely is one of the factors that accounts for the significant drop in the company's 1996 growth rate.

Table 3.8 shows the changes in sales and ordinary profit of the two leading local department store groups—Central Group and The Mall Group—from the period of the consumption boom beginning in 1990, through 1997 and the financial crisis, and up until 2006. For the Central Group, we selected HCDS, CDS, and Robinson Department Store, which were the three major department store companies of the group. However, some of points discussed earlier need be taken into consideration. One is that HCDS transformed itself into a holding company by transferring its department store business to CDS around 1995. Another is that the Central Group separated the supermarket departments of Central Department Store and Robinson Department Store to establish CRC

Ahold (Tops) in 1996, and then proceeded to separate the home electronics and sporting goods departments to establish Power Buy and CRC Sports, respectively, in 1997. The ratio of ordinary profit to net sales is calculated in table 3.9, based on data in table 3.8.

TABLE 3.9 Profitability of department stores in Thailand, 1990–2006

	Ordinary profit ratio to sales (%)				
	Central Group			The Mall Group	
Year	HCDS[a]	CDS[b]	Robinson Plc	The Mall Group	City Mall Group
1990	2.0	5.2	–	2.4	–
1991	4.0	6.7	–	1.2	–
1992	1.6	2.2	4.5	1.4	–
1993	8.5	1.7	3.6	1.0	–
1994	3.3	1.9	5.5	0.6	–
1995	2.8	3.7	2.9	0.6	–
1996	2.1	3.2	2.9	0.5	–
1997	-33.2	2.1	-12.8	0.8	-0.9
1998	–	-2.3	-36.2	1.5	0.6
1999	–	2.5	-77.4	4.0	5.9
2000	–	7.9	-28.1	4.3	5.3
2001	–	7.0	-5.6	4.6	4.7
2002	–	10.8	6.4	4.7	4.4
2003	–	8.4	7.0	4.5	7.4
2004	–	11.8	8.5	4.0	4.3
2005	–	13.0	8.8	4.5	2.7
2006	–	12.5	6.3	5.1	3.0

SOURCE: Companies' financial statements.

[a] HCDS refers to Harng Central Department Store Co., Ltd. Since 1998, HCDS has basically become a holding company and it has not been regarded as a department store, therefore, no data is shown for the years 1998–2006.

[b] CDS refers to Central Department Store Co., Ltd. (previously, Chidlom Department Store).

[c] Robinson's consolidated data prior to 1991 is not available.

[d] The City Mall Group, which operates The Emporium, was established in 1997, which is why no data is available from 1990–1996.

As tables 3.8 and 3.9 demonstrate, neither Central Department Store nor The Mall Department Store showed much growth in ordinary profit during the consumption boom of the early 1990s. Both of their ratios of ordinary profit to sales, percentage-wise, had been decreasing or showed a downward tendency, despite the fact that during this period, they both achieved a rapid growth in sales volume by actively multiplying department stores and diversifying retail businesses. Yet the profitability of their department store business, or core business, was deteriorating. In the case of the Central Group, this was partly because it had dispersed managerial resources with the rapid expansion of its business (Endo 2002, 281–300). In other words, the groups' deteriorated business performances should not be attributed only to external factors, such as the financial crisis, but also to internal factors such as managerial problems dating back to the consumption boom period.

In 1997–98, when confronted with the financial crisis, the growth rates in sales of Central (CDS), Robinson, and The Mall remained stagnant or fell into negative figures. However, there was a big differential between companies in the department store industry. Robinson Department Store suffered a sharper decrease in sales during this period and remained in a slump for a longer period of time. This becomes clearer when comparing the ordinary profit and the ordinary profit ratio to sales among those department store companies. In spite of heavier dependence on foreign currency debt from the very beginning, Robinson Department Store had not taken sufficient measures against exchange risk, which caused the department store to suffer serious damage from the financial and currency crisis.[18] In addition to the decrease in sales during the economic recession, the department store had to face a drastic increase in the amount of interest it had to pay due to the sudden drop in the exchange rate. As a result, Robinson showed an ordinary loss as high as 1.1 billion baht in 1997. Not reflected in tables 3.8 and 3.9 is that the Robinson showed a large sum of currency exchange loss amounting to approximately 6.5 billion baht, representing an extraordinary loss for that year. In this way, the department store fell into excessive debt in 1997, and the Company Resuscitation Law was finally applied to the department store in May 2000.[19]

By contrast, Central Department Store and The Mall Department Store experienced shorter-term and less severe drops in sales. Since 1999, the two department stores satisfactorily increased sales, at a time when Thailand's business environment overall showed signs of recovery. As for Central Department Store, its growth was partly a result of gradually integrating affiliated companies into CDS. Considering the substantial increase of ordinary profit and ordinary profit ratio to sales in the same period of time, it appears that the department store succeeded in improving not only growth but also profitability. The Mall Department Store improved profitability as well.

Various factors enabled these two groups to improve their business performance, one of which was the implementation of thorough inventory control.[20] For example, Central Department Store established an exclusive distribution center in Bang Phlat, a suburb of Bangkok, and was able to realize an efficient physical distribution system by applying foreign retailers' know-how (*PJK-RW* March 5, 2001). As a result, its inventory turnover (cost of goods sold/final inventories) rapidly increased from 3.6 in 1995 to 7.8 in 2006.[21] In the same way, The Mall Group's inventory turnover increased from 3.9 to 12.6 in the same period.[22] Moreover, the City Mall Group Co. Ltd., running The Emporium department store, saw its ordinary profit return to the black in 1998, and has shown an almost stable positive performance since then, despite opening its business at the worst time possible, on July 27, 1997, immediately after the financial and currency crisis. As for the Robinson Department Store, its ordinary profit returned to the black as late as 2002 and has achieved significant profits since then.[23]

Thai mass media as well as Asian and Western researchers often highlight the decline of department stores following the financial and currency crisis, and contrast it with the rise of new retail formats, with hypermarkets being a typical one. Many medium-scale department stores had to reduce or withdraw their business under the post-crisis reorganization of the retail industry. Yet, Central and The Mall managed to substantially improve their growth and profitability, and have maintained profitable business performances until the present time. Robinson has also managed to overcome its financial difficulties. What caused department stores throughout the retail industry to reach such contrasting results?

One reason lies in the fact that large-scale department stores have an advantage in their ability to purchase the latest, trend-setting goods, such as big-name apparel brands. Small- and medium-sized department stores, on the other hand, are often at a disadvantage in that they cannot showcase enough of the latest trends in various consumer goods because suppliers give them less priority, given their smaller size. Another reason for such contrasting results in department stores' sales is that department stores in Thailand are divided into two categories: popular and upper-class stores. The popularization of department stores led by the middle-class occurred just as new retail formats entered Thailand's consumer market. It is only natural that there would be differences in the types and assortment of goods and customers between department stores and general mass merchandisers, for instance. What is unexpected is that they have become direct competitors due to the popularization of department stores. This can be seen from the author's analysis of nine middle-class department store companies in Bangkok, which had to close down or sharply reduce their business after the financial and currency crisis. Prior to that, as of 1996 (one year before the crisis), these stores had an average gross profit ratio to sales of only 9.3 percent (the simple mean value of the nine companies).[24]

This gross profit ratio is lower than the three big hypermarkets' gross profit ratio for the same year (simple average of 11.9 percent), which demonstrates that medium-sized department stores adopted a popularization strategy based on a narrow profit margin. By contrast, Central Department Store, which adopted a differentiation strategy that focused on upper-class stores as opposed to general mass merchandising stores, realized a higher gross profit ratio during the recovery term, up to 27.1 percent in 2006.

Substantial income differences exist among the urban middle class, which suggests that certain income strata are not always satisfied with hypermarkets. Moreover, there is every reason to believe that consumers choose particular retail formats and particular stores based on the type of goods they wish to purchase, which can be divided into "convenience goods" and "shopping goods." Convenience goods are widely distributed and relatively inexpensive goods that are purchased frequently and with minimum effort, such as grocery items. Shopping goods, on the other hand, are higher-end products that are bought occasionally and usually compared for their appropriateness, quality, cost, and particular features before a purchase occurs. In any case, with a "mosaic structured" consumer market as the backdrop, some department stores have chosen to target specific customers to differentiate themselves from hypermarkets. This enables them to have an original market positioning and to stay away from popularization. In this context, it is easy to understand why an upper-class department store like The Mall Group's Emporium succeeded.[25]

NEW TRENDS IN THE RETAIL INDUSTRY

Thailand's retail industry changed yet again between the post-crisis and post-recovery periods. Tables 3.10 and 3.11, which show 2006 figures, allow for a comparison with tables 3.5 and 3.6, which show 1999 figures. First of all, a comparison of table 3.5 with table 3.10 shows that the top ten companies in 1999 were still among the top ten companies in 2006, even if their ranking changed slightly. New retail formats such as Tesco Lotus, Big C, and Carrefour in the hypermarket category, Makro in the cash-and-carry category, and 7-Eleven in the convenience store category further increased their sales, while the two major department stores, Central and The Mall, were also doing well. Robinson Department Store, which benefited from the Company Resuscitation Law following the financial and currency crisis, had since recovered and maintained its position in the top ten, as of 2006. The companies ranked eleventh and below, however, have undergone some noteworthy changes, as the tables demonstrate. Bangkok-based medium-sized department stores (Pata, Banglumpoo, and Merry Kings) and provincial department stores (Klang Plaza, Topland Plaza, and Diana) dropped out of the top thirty or closed down their business, while some new retail formats, such as specialty stores (Watson and B2S) and home centers (Home Works) entered the top thirty.

TABLE 3.10 Thailand's top thirty retailers in sales, 1999 vs. 2006

Ranking[a]		Company/chain store name[b]	Year of establish-ment	Group name (nationality)	Format[c]	2006 sales (million baht)	1999/2006 sales (% change)[d]
1999	2006						
3	1	Ek-Chai Distribution/Tesco Lotus	1993	Tesco (UK)	HM	93,922	348.9
4	2	C. P. Seven Eleven (CP All) (Plc)	1988	CP	CVS	66,055	336.3
2	3	Big C Supercenter (Plc)	1994	Casino (France)	HM	58,033	158.3
1	4	Siam Makro (Plc)	1988	Makro (Holland)	C&C	55,531	61.0
5	5	Central Dept. Store	1974	Central	Dept. S	22,645	75.4
8	6	CenCar/Carrefour	1994	Carrefour (France)	HM	22,496	168.9
7	7	Central Food Retail (+)/Tops	1996	Central	SM	20,104	82.2
6	8	The Mall Group (+) /The Mall	1980	The Mall	Dept. S	18,360	63.0
9	9	Robinson Dept. Store (Plc)	1983	Central	Dept. S	10,812	66.3
10	10	Power Buy	1996	Central	CK	9,958	123.6

Ranking[a] 1999	2006	Company/chain store name[b]	Year of establishment	Group name (nationality)	Format[c]	2006 sales (million baht)	1999/2006 sales (% change)[d]
27	11	Siam FamilyMart	1992	FamilyMart (Japan)	CVS	6,071	737.4
–	12	Siam Paragon Retail/ Siam Paragon	2001	The Mall et al.	Dept. S	5,909	–
NL	13	Central Watson/ Watson	1996	Central et al.	SS	4,748	283.2
13	14	City Mall Group/ The Emporium	1997	The Mall et al.	Dept. S	4,202	66.2
NL	15	Super Cheap	1995	Anantajarunwong family	W/SM	3,664	441.2
12	16	Foodland Supermarket	1972	Foodland	SM	3,610	31.2
16	17	CRC Sports/ Super Sports	1996	Central	CK	3,222	120.7
NI	18	B2S	1995	Central	SS	2,759	–
20	19	Boots	1996	Boots (UK)	SS	2,624	147.8
14	20	Tang Hua Seng Dept. Store	1976	Tang Hua Seng	Dept. S	1,927	-23.4
11	21	AEON [Thailand]/ Siam-Jusco	1984	AEON (Japan)	SM	1,864	-55.8
30	22	Tang Ngee Soon Superstore	2000	Wirarattanrot family	W/SM	1,836	197.6
23	23	Villa Market JP	1988	Phusanakhom family	SM	1,817	105.1
24	24	Bangkok-Tokyu Dept. Store	1983	Tokyu (Japan)	Dept. S	1,652	98.3
–	25	CRC Power Retail/ Home Works	2001	Central	HC	1,641	–
NL	26	Choice Mini Store/ 7-Eleven[f]	1988	Tantraphan	CVS	1,551	431.2
15	27	Isetan (Thailand)	1989	Isetan (Japan)	Dept. S	1,275	-23.6
NL	28	Yongsanguan Group	1994	Yongsanguan	W/SM	1,223	399.2
–	29	Big A Trading	2000	Netsamanon family	W/SM	987	–
NL	30	Chiang Mai Siam TV	1981	Ploemphithakkun family	CK	930	340.8

SOURCE: Annual reports of listed companies; financial statements of unlisted companies.
NOTE: Retail-cum-wholesalers are included in the list of companies/chain stores, while automobile and motorcycle dealers are excluded. "Sales" refers to sales income only (it does not include other income, such as rental income). The sales for all formats were calculated by the author as follows: in the case of a public limited company, consolidated figures were used; among non-listed companies with chain stores that have the same store name, which are designated by (+), the sales figures of each store were added together for a single total. As for C. P. Seven Eleven Plc, the figures are based on company data (not consolidate figures) from their annual reports, because the company operates subsidiary hypermarkets in China, representing approx. 30 percent of consolidated sales. The sales figures for The Mall Department Store, Nakhon Ratchasima Branch (The Mall Ratchasima), founded in 1997, were added to the sales figures of The Mall Group Company. Due to data limitations, the growth rate of Super Cheap is compared with 1998 figures. As for Tang Ngee Soon Superstore, the company was previously known as the Ngee Soon Superstore, and as a result the growth rate for both companies was treated as a single company.

[a] The dash (–) in the "ranking" column indicates the company had not yet been established as of 1999, while "NL" indicates that the company was not listed as one of the top thirty companies for 1999.

[b] The code "(+)" in the "company/chain store" column indicates a non-listed company with chain stores that have the same store name.

[c] Codes used in the "format" column represent the following: C&C=cash-and-carry store; CK=category killer; CVS=convenience store; Dept. S=department store; HC=home center; HM=hypermarket; SM=supermarket; SS=specialty store; W/SM=wholesaler-cum-supermarket.

[d] The dash (–) in the last column indicates that the company was not yet established as of 1999; as a result, a comparison against 2006 sales cannot be made.

[e] In 2004, the Central Group repurchased a supermarket business (Tops) from Holland-based Royal Ahold and changed the company's name to Central Food Retail Co., Ltd.

[f] Choice Mini Store runs a 7-Eleven in northern Thailand with a sub-area license granted by C. P. Seven Eleven (C. P. All) Plc. Similarly, Ngan Nung runs a 7-Eleven in the south also through a sub-area license.

Another noteworthy aspect of this ranking is that six provincial traders, including newcomers, ranked among Thailand's top thirty retail companies. Among these six companies, Choice Mini Store (26th) of the Chiang Mai-based Tantraphan Group is running 7-Elevens in the three northern provinces of Chiang Mai, Lamphun, and Mae Hong Son, with sub-area licenses from CP All Plc (formerly, C. P. Seven Eleven Plc). As of October 28, 2006, there were 101 branches (*PRCT-TK* November 6, 2006). With a withdrawal from the department store business at the end of 1995, the Tantraphan Group lost its leading position in the local retail industry, but concentrated its managerial resources into the convenience store and supermarket businesses in an effort to survive. The group also changed the direction of the supermarket business by using a niche strategy of targeting the upper-income strata, including foreign residents.[26] As a result, the group found its way back to growth.[27]

Other interesting companies are Super Cheap (15th), Tang Ngee Soon Superstore (22nd), Yongsanguan Group (28th), and Big A Trading (29th). These mass merchandisers based in provincial cities are mainly selling daily foods and necessities and are a combination between cash-and-carry wholesalers and supermarkets. Super Cheap, in particular, not only sells daily foods (both fresh and processed) and necessities, but also high-priced goods like furniture and home electronics in a large warehouse style one-storied building. It is the top store in Phuket. According to a consumer goods manufacturer, Super Cheap sales exceeded that of each branch of Tesco Lotus, Big C, and Makro in this locality.[28] The store sells in bulk to small-scale retailers and restaurants and also in retail for general consumers; its customers come from neighboring provinces as well. The inside of the store is not air-conditioned, except for the glass meat counter that is separated from the rest of the store. In addition, stock goods are piled up in their unopened delivery cardboard boxes on the upper part of the display racks. The company is characterized by a thorough low-cost operation, including a narrow profit margin and large sales volume. Tang Ngee Soon Superstore, a long-established store based in Udon Thani, saw its 2006 sales exceeding 1,800 million baht. Although it only sells daily processed foods and necessities, it holds the top store position in this province.[29] It has the same characteristics of a low-cost operation such as Super Cheap, including a narrow profit margin and a large sales volume. Many other provincial stores share a similar format, though they all rank below the top thirty stores.[30]

This change, observed at an individual company level, is next considered at a group level by examining the sales volume according to business group, nationality, and format (type of operation). If we compare table 3.11 with table 3.6, we can see that the sales concentration ratio among high-ranking companies has either settled down or decreased. Foreign companies had reduced their market share more substantially than Thai companies. This is partly due to the Central Group repurchasing a supermarket business (Tops) from the Holland-based Royal Ahold in 2004. Yet even without taking into account the influence of this event, the trend would still be the same. Although the dominance of foreign capital in Thailand's retail industry is a feature often discussed in Thailand's mass media and industry reports, contrary to general belief, foreign investment has surprisingly not increased its share in the retail industry since 1999. Another characteristic of Thailand's retail industry is that the total share of general mass merchandisers ranking first, third, fourth, and sixth in 2006 as a part of retail sales for all of Thailand decreased slightly from 10.1 percent in 1999 down to 9.7 percent in 2006.[31] Convenience stores have satisfactorily increased in weight, but not yet enough as to lead the retail industry.

TABLE 3.11 Thailand's top thirty retailers as a percentage of total retail sales, 2006

	2006	
	million baht	Percentage of total retail sales
Cumulative sales		
Top 5 companies	296,186	12.5
Top 10 companies	377,916	16.0
Top 20 companies	416,652	17.6
Total top 30 companies	431,428	18.2
By business group		
Central Group	75,889	3.2
CP Group	66,055	2.8
The Mall Group	28,471	1.2
By nationality		
Thai	187,960	7.9
Foreign	243,468	10.3
By format		
Department stores	66,782	2.8
General mass merchandisers	229,982	9.7
Supermarkets	27,395	1.2
Convenience stores	73,677	3.1
Provincial wholesaler-cum-supermarkets	7,710	0.3
Other[a]	25,882	1.1
Total for the whole country	2,364,814	100.0

SOURCE: Same as table 3.5 regarding sales of each company; same as table 3.1 regarding total sales of the retail industry for the whole of Thailand.

NOTE: "Sales" refers only to sales income (it does not include other income, such as rental income). Business group and nationality are determined based on the major stockholders and who controls the management of the company.

[a] "Other" includes category killers, specialty stores, and home centers.

When looking at the retail market by business group, local groups have started to regain their strength. The recent rise of the Central Group comes from the repurchase of a supermarket business (Tops) as well as the revival of the department store business and the growth of new retail formats (i.e., category killers and specialty stores). From table 3.11, The Mall Group's share seems to have decreased but, in December 2005, it also established Siam Paragon, an immense, upper-class shopping center with a luxury department store of the same name as its core tenant located opposite Siam Square.[32] It is one of the largest shopping centers in Asia. The group will very likely increase its share again in the near future.

Foreign capital-led new retail formats, which rapidly rose before and after the financial and currency crisis, saw their share as a percentage of the retail sales for the whole country decrease following recovery from the financial crisis, though in terms of absolute value, these foreign capital-led formats have increased their sales. The next chapter examines the fluctuating growth of new retail formats and provides an in-depth analysis of the unique traits of these types of retailing operations.

4

HAVE NEW RETAIL FORMATS REALLY BROUGHT A DISTRIBUTION REVOLUTION?

CHARACTERISTICS OF NEW RETAIL FORMATS

Until the mid-1980s, Thailand's retail industry was characterized by a dual structure, consisting of only a few modern retailers, such as department stores, and many small-scale groceries. Of all the new retail formats that caused a change in the traditional industrial structure, cash-and-carry (Makro) and convenience stores (7-Eleven) emerged first. They both opened their first stores in 1989. Since then, other new retail formats, such as hypermarkets, supermarkets, category killers, specialty stores, and so on, have emerged one after another. Although there are a variety of new retail formats, all have in common a chain operation system.

Department stores in Thailand, unlike the new retail formats, do not operate under the chain store system. Instead, they have adopted the trade practice of consignment and use sales representatives ("sales reps") provided by the manufacturer/supplier for selling their major retail commodities, such as apparel.[1] Consignment is a practice widely found in the department store industry that consists of placing goods in the hands of another, but retaining ownership until the goods are sold. This is a favorable practice for department stores, since they are not required to bear inventory costs and the risk of unsold goods. Moreover, owing to the use of suppliers' sales reps, which are dispatched to stores selling their products, department stores can shift sales personnel expenses onto suppliers, such as apparel makers.[2] However, this sales system is not completely favorable to department stores because the transfer of sales data and price decision-making to suppliers leads to the decline of department stores' merchandising power, as it relates to purchasing, merchandise assortment, merchandise control, and sales. Actually, quite a few local department stores can be regarded as retail property developers rather than retailers.

In contrast to department stores' trade practices, new retail formats like hypermarkets and cash-and-carry stores favor normal purchasing over consignment. These formats make efforts to rapidly develop their chain operation system and increase the amount of goods bought from manufacturers in order to raise their bargaining power to set prices. Simultaneously, they promote direct dealings with manufacturers by bypassing wholesalers.

As a result, they have succeeded in sharply decreasing the cost of sales, also known as "cost of goods sold" (COGS).

In addition, they centralize company data by placing each branch's data under the head office's control to achieve optimum inventory and purchase orders utilizing online electronic data processing (EDP) in the head office's EDP center. Moreover, hypermarkets and cash-and-carry stores strategically establish their distribution centers in order to deliver goods to multiple stores as efficiently as possible. In short, they build a logistics system based on advanced information technology that allows them to keep prices low. Other new retail formats, such as supermarkets and convenience stores, have implemented similar systems. In other words, new retail formats strive to build an efficient supply chain system, in which sales data goes upstream to the distribution channels from the stores to consumer goods manufacturers. This new system is exactly the opposite of the traditional retail system in Thailand, in which manufacturers produce goods based on estimated sales projections and thus force manufactured goods downstream to the stores. This is the very reason why views emphasizing that Thailand is experiencing a distribution revolution, with new retail formats at the helm, are widely accepted at present.

Among the characteristics of the new retail formats, three points are especially important to note: direct dealings with manufacturers, new commercial practices, and the building of logistics systems. To better understand Thailand's direct dealings with manufacturers it may be useful to compare this with the experience of Japan during its own rapid economic growth period from the mid-1950s to the early 1970s. In Japan, supermarkets rapidly grew during that time, but direct dealings between major consumer goods manufacturers and large-scale retailers did not similarly grow, contrary to the expectation of those who interpreted the event as a "distribution revolution." The traditional distribution system, in which wholesalers played an important role, remained predominant. This was because large-scale retailers had no choice but to depend on wholesalers for inventory management and delivery functions, since they concentrated most of their managerial resources on enlarging and multiplying stores and could not afford to build a new distribution system. Moreover, wholesalers expanded their businesses by creating a wider branch network over several provinces and merging with smaller wholesalers, thus building an efficient distribution system. Contrary to the case of Japan, Thailand's new retail formats did not make use of wholesalers, but instead established central distribution centers at an early stage of business development, where they had manufacturers directly deliver the goods. It is natural that Western capital-led new retail formats preferred to transplant a business system already standardized in their home countries rather than spending a lot of time and costs building long-term business connections with local wholesalers. From the very beginning, new retail formats developed more rapidly in Thailand than in Japan, so that local wholesalers had very little time to cope with the change.

The commercial practices introduced by new retail formats were unfamiliar to Thailand's retail and distribution industry. New retail formats, having increased their bargaining power owing to their enormous buying power, began asking manufacturers for entrance fees, rebates, planogram fees, advertising costs, sales promotion costs, distribution center fees, and so on (Endo 2005). Hypermarkets, for example, could, in the end, make a net profit by adding such non-operating revenue to their profit structure, even though their operating profit was reduced due to their use of low price structures.

Regarding logistics, including a physical distribution system, the head office of new retail formats is connected on-line with their distribution centers and with each store. In this information network, the head office's EDP center analyzes the point-of-sales (POS) data transferred by each store, and then sends the collected sales and purchase order data to both the distribution center and suppliers/manufacturers. Upon receiving the orders, suppliers deliver the goods directly to the distribution center.[3] Then, as the delivery data is recorded in the stock lists of the distribution center and the EDP center, bar codes are automatically issued and put on each good. Goods are divided into two groups, one for stock at the distribution center and the other for cross-docking. Cross-docking is a logistics practice that consists in unloading goods from an incoming truck and loading them directly onto outbound trucks with little or no storage period in between, which effectively reduces inventories. In this case, delivered goods are immediately subdivided to deliver to each store. To better understand this logistics system it may be useful to look at the operations of the hypermarket Tesco Lotus as an example. Figure 4.1 shows the ordering of daily foods and necessities and the delivery system of Tesco's chain stores.[4]

FIGURE 4.1 Chain operation of a hypermarket: The case of Tesco Lotus

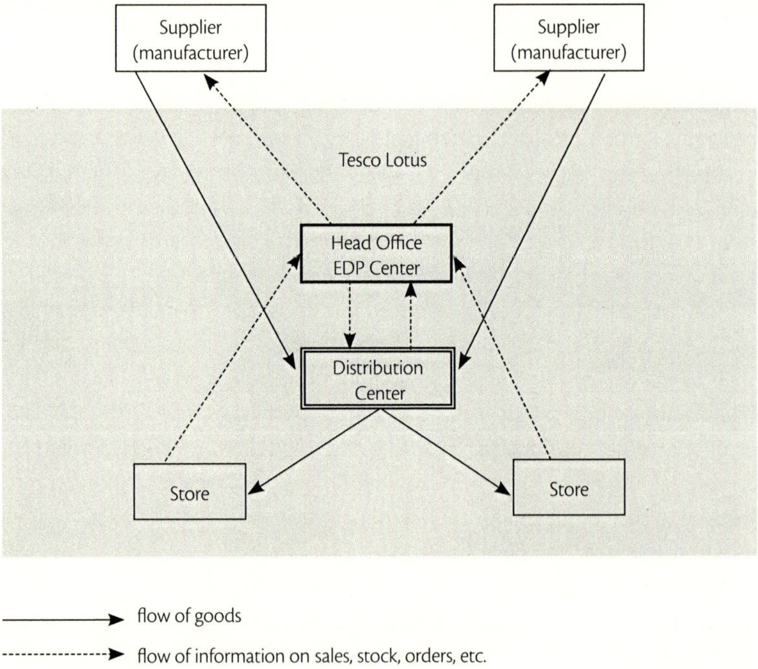

SOURCE: Author interview with Ek-Chai Distribution System Co., Ltd.
NOTE: EDP refers to electronic data processing.

The central distribution center of Tesco Lotus is located in the Wang Noi district of Ayutthaya, about 50 kilometers north of Bangkok, in a very convenient place for truck transportation along Phahonyothin Road (National Highway Route 1). The floor space of the center has been enlarged in accordance with the increase in the number of Tesco stores. As of 2003, the 24-hour operating distribution center had a total floor space of 75,000 square meters, among which

44,500 square meters was set at a normal temperature, 15,500 square meters were allotted to cross-docking, and 10,000 square meters to perishable foods. This distribution center receives an extensive amount of goods, ranging from five to seven hundred truck loads per day (max. 800,000 cases of goods), and dispatches 150 to 170 container trailers to the stores (Arun 2004, 86–103). Once the goods are delivered to the stores, the trailers receive goods from local manufacturers and agricultural producers to transport back to the distribution center. This practice is known as a backhauling system, with which the company strives to achieve an efficient physical distribution (Arun 2002b, 22–32). Basically, all goods (including perishable foods) are first delivered to the central distribution center,[5] where the quality of the goods is inspected. The company entrusts this inspection to SGS, an internationally renowned, quality certification company, which certifies that the quality of goods meets Food and Drug Administration (FDA) standards.[6]

Both Big C and Carrefour have built a similar system as well. In the case of Carrefour, which has fewer stores than Tesco Lotus, deliveries from the distribution center in Yannawa, in the south of Bangkok, to each store are outsourced to non-affiliated transport companies, unlike the case of Tesco Lotus.[7] Similarly, Big C has entrusted all its physical distribution to an affiliated joint venture company with foreign investment. As of 2006, 120,000 cases of goods were delivered daily by 250 trucks from Big C's central distribution center (total floor space of 50,000 sq m), also located in the Wang Noi district of Ayutthaya, in the same area as Tesco Lotus' distribution center (Big C Supercenter Plc 2007, 73–74).[8]

Contrary to hypermarkets, the cash-and-carry Makro had not established a central distribution center until 2008. Major manufacturers deliver goods directly to each Makro store, while small- and medium-sized manufacturers, not having their own physical distribution system, deliver goods through the cross-docking centers of third party logistics providers (3PL).[9] Supermarkets and convenience stores also have similar physical distribution and logistics system as hypermarkets, but there are a few differences that reflect each retail format's special characteristics, e.g., the sales of perishable foods as core goods, in the case of supermarkets. The systems specific to supermarkets and convenience stores will be discussed in greater detail later in this chapter. We will now turn to comparing the business performances of the various retail formats to uncover how well these systems have actually been working.

CASH-AND-CARRY STORES AND HYPERMARKETS

DISTINCTION BETWEEN FORMATS

Of all the new retail formats, cash-and-carry stores and hypermarkets have had the strongest impact on Thailand's retail industry. They are namely, Makro (Siam Makro Plc), Tesco Lotus (Ek-Chai Distribution System Co., Ltd.), Big C (Big C Supercenter Plc), and Carrefour (CenCar Co., Ltd.). At one time, other local and foreign companies were running similar general mass merchandising businesses, among them Big Kings (Merry Kings Department Store Group), Savco Wholesale (Welco Department Store Group), and Auchan (France), but all of them have now closed down or withdrawn from the business.

One similarity between cash-and-carry and hypermarket formats lies in the characteristics of the standard store for each chain. In both cases, the standard store is a low-rise, warehouse-style building, with a floor store space of around 10,000 square meters and a large parking area (700–900 car capacity). Both formats also have an extensive range of goods, including daily foods (perishable and processed) and necessities, clothes, bedding, furniture, home electronics, and so on, with a low price structure. Customers place goods they wish to purchase in a large-sized shopping cart and pay in one lump sum at the checkout counter. Hypermarkets often have some floor space for small-scale specialty store tenants and restaurants as well as the main floor for themselves.

Although these two formats have many common points and are both often regarded as general mass merchandisers, cash-and-carry stores were originally membership wholesale clubs, while hypermarkets have always been large-scale retailers that combine discount stores and supermarkets. Nominally, the cash-and-carry stores concentrate mainly on selling in bulk to small-scale grocery stores and restaurants, while hypermarkets are literally a retail business targeting general consumers. However, shortly after its business had opened, Makro noticed that its customers were not only grocery stores but also general consumers without proper membership credentials, and, therefore, reduced the sale-lot of goods in some categories, adapting its format to conduct a kind of simultaneous retail business (Sombun 2002, 91–92). Hypermarkets, on the other hand, established a corner in their stores dedicated to daily processed foods and necessities in relatively large lots, so that many customers, such as small-scale grocery stores for example, started to use hypermarkets as a cash-and-carry wholesaler.[10] Consequently, the distinction between the two formats became unclear and they came to compete directly with each other. As a result, Makro redefined its position in the distribution industry starting around 2000, and strove to carry out a differentiation strategy against hypermarkets by highlighting itself as a membership-based wholesaler (Siam Makro Plc 2002, 9; 20–23).[11]

The differences between the two formats do not stop here. Makro puts more effort than hypermarkets into reducing operating costs. This is reflected in the way goods are stocked in their original delivery cardboard boxes on the upper shelving of display racks, rather than stored in a separate area, as well as by a floor space that is more dimly lit and also less air-conditioned, and so on. Although there are similarities between cash-and-carry stores and hypermarkets in terms of the variety of goods they carry, Makro limits goods to a fewer number of national brands, concentrating on intermediate-quality goods. As a result, Makro offers approximately 20,000 stock keeping units (SKUs), much fewer than hypermarkets, which offer approximately 50,000 SKUs.[12] In addition, Makro puts relatively more emphasis on lower-priced, private label products, and less emphasis on the sale of non-foods. For instance, in 2003, Makro's product ratio was divided as follows: 10 percent for perishable foods, 65 percent for processed foods, and 25 percent for non-foods,[13] while Big C's product ratio was 9 percent for perishable foods, 48 percent for processed foods, and 43 percent for non-foods (Big C Supercenter Plc 2003, 24–25). The percentage of perishable foods sold in both chain operations is substantially lower than that of supermarkets.

BUSINESS DEVELOPMENT AND PROFITABILITY STRUCTURE

Table 4.1 outlines the business development of cash-and-carry and hypermarket formats of Makro, Tesco Lotus, Big C, and Carrefour. Of these four large general mass merchandisers, Makro emerged first in Thailand, and was established in 1988. The other three companies were established later, all in the mid-1990s. Nevertheless, in a mere ten years after opening for business, they all managed to rapidly increase their sales, so much so as to become the front-runners in Thailand's retail industry. The infusion of foreign investment and the transfer of ownership into foreign hands during the post-crisis era accelerated the expansion of theses businesses. When considering the sales per store between 1996 and 2006, as table 4.1 suggests, the increase in sales during this ten-year period was most likely resultant on an increased number of stores or an extensive enlargement of store floor space, rather than on increased sales efficiency.[14] This is true of both cash-and-carry stores (Makro) and hypermarkets (Tesco, Big C, and Carrefour).

TABLE 4.1 Development of general mass merchandisers in Thailand

Company name	Chain store name	Format[a]	Year of establishment	Ownership 2006	Total sales (million baht) / Number of stores (as of year end) / Average sales per store (million baht) 1996	1999	2002	2006
Siam Makro Plc	Makro	C&C	1988	Makro (Holland)	31,655	32,707	35,732	55,531
					14	17	21	29
					2,261	1,924	1,702	1,915
Ek-Chai Distribution System	Tesco Lotus[b]	HM	1994	Tesco (UK)	5,970	20,924	54,341	93,922
					6	17	46	75
					995	1231	1181	1252
Big C Supercenter Plc	Big C	HM	1994	Casino (France)	10,761	22,464	38,214	58,033
					11	20	32	49
					978	1,123	1,194	1,184
CenCar	Carrefour	HM	1996	Carrefour (France)	1,613	8,367	15,936	22,496
					2	9	17	24
					806	930	937	937

SOURCE: Financial statements, annual reports, websites, and stockholder lists of each company; Thai-language newspapers.

[a] Codes used in the "format" column represent the following: C&C=cash-and-carry stores; HM=hypermarkets.

[b] Tesco Lotus, as of 2006, included nineteen Lotus Value stores (Lotus Khum Kha), which are medium-sized stores (floor space approx. 6,000 sq m).

TABLE 4.2 Profitability of general mass merchandisers in Thailand, 1995–2006

	Hypermarkets			Cash-and-Carry
	Tesco Lotus	Big C	Carrefour[a]	Makro
Gross profit ratio to sales (%)				
1995	11.5	19.3	–	7.9
1996	11.5	14.8	9.5	8.2
1997	12.5	12.6	11.3	8.1
1998	11.1	11.1	12.6	8.0
1999	13.8	11.0	14.0	7.7
2000	15.1	11.4	15.4	8.1
2001	15.9	11.1	15.9	7.3
2002	16.0	10.3	16.5	6.2

	Hypermarkets			Cash-and-Carry
	Tesco Lotus	Big C	Carrefour[a]	Makro
2003	16.6	9.8	16.7	5.7
2004	16.9	10.0	16.9	5.9
2005	19.3	9.6	16.0	5.4
2006	20.2	9.4	17.4	5.4
Ordinary profit ratio to sales (%)				
1995	-2.9	1.3	–	3.6
1996	0.4	1.4	-9.7	3.2
1997	0.2	-1.2	-8.4	2.4
1998	-20.1	-4.1	-9.2	2.6
1999	-2.9	-1.7	0.1	2.6
2000	0.9	3.9	-0.1	3.8
2001	2.6	3.8	3.2	3.7
2002	3.8	4.0	3.8	3.4
2003	3.2	4.1	1.3	3.1
2004	3.3	4.8	1.4	3.4
2005	4.5	5.1	0.0	3.1
2006	4.1	5.4	1.3	3.1
"Other revenue" ratio to sales (%)				
1995	n/a	n/a	–	n/a
1996	n/a	n/a	1.7	n/a
1997	n/a	n/a	2.2	n/a
1998	n/a	2.9	1.6	n/a
1999	2.4	3.5	1.6	n/a
2000	2.4	4.3	2.7	n/a
2001	3.0	5.5	7.1	n/a
2002	3.9	7.0	7.9	n/a
2003	4.2	7.7	4.6	3.4
2004	4.6	7.2	4.6	3.6
2005	3.9	8.1	4.7	3.8
2006	4.1	9.0	5.3	3.4

SOURCE: Companies' financial statements.

NOTE: "Other revenue" refers to non-operating revenue, such as investment revenue from subsidiary and affiliated companies plus interest revenue; it primarily consists of rebates, sales-promotion revenue, distribution center fees, and so on. "n/a" means that data was not provided in the company's financial statements.

[a] Carrefour was established in1994, but it did not begin to operate until 1996. This explains why there are no sales figures for 1995.

Regarding each company's profitability and sales efficiency, we can see from tables 4.2 and 4.3, respectively, the differences between cash-and-carry stores and hypermarkets. It is true that hypermarkets have shown low gross profit ratios (i.e., ratio of gross profit percentage to net sales) and low ratios of selling, general, and administrative expenses to sales (SG&A cost ratio).[15] But Makro's gross profit ratio and SG&A cost ratio have been still lower and its inventory turnover higher than hypermarkets. In short, as a membership wholesale club, Makro has adopted and implemented a clearer policy of low-cost operations and a narrower profit margin and larger sales volume than hypermarkets.

TABLE 4.3 Efficiency of hypermarkets and cash-and-carry stores in Thailand, 1995–2006

	Hypermarkets			Cash-and-Carry
	Tesco Lotus	Big C	Carrefour[a]	Makro
SG&A cost ratio[b]				
1995	18.6	19.6	–	6.3
1996	14.0	15.3	17.9	6.9
1997	13.6	15.5	18.8	8.1
1998	30.0	16.1	20.8	8.6
1999	16.7	14.1	16.2	8.1
2000	16.2	14.1	18.0	8.0
2001	16.3	15.3	19.6	7.9
2002	16.5	16.1	20.5	7.3
2003	16.9	16.3	19.9	6.7
2004	17.7	16.2	20.0	6.6
2005	18.5	16.3	20.6	6.6
2006	19.3	17.0	21.3	6.2
Inventory turnover (cost of goods sold/inventories)				
1995	3.1	4.0	–	11.6
1996	3.2	4.7	7.8	10.1
1997	5.8	5.4	8.9	11.9
1998	6.9	8.5	11.4	12.8
1999	7.3	8.8	7.5	11.8
2000	7.3	8.2	9.1	12.5
2001	8.3	7.3	6.4	12.5
2002	8.1	7.7	8.1	12.3
2003	8.2	9.4	8.0	11.2
2004	8.9	9.8	8.1	10.9
2005	8.4	10.5	9.2	12.2
2006	9.7	10.9	9.5	13.0

SOURCE: Companies' financial statements.

[a] Carrefour was established in1994, but it did not begin to operate until 1996. This explains why there are no sales figures for 1995.

[b] SG&A cost ratio=ratio of selling, general, and administrative expenses to sales

Now, let us compare the indexes among companies by focusing on hypermarkets. The ordinary profit ratio to sales indicates that Tesco Lotus and Big C have succeeded in increasing profitability since the recovery from the economic slump of the financial and currency crisis. However, attention should be paid to Big C's remarkably low gross profit ratio. Since the company's "other revenue" ratio to sales is higher than Tesco and Carrefour by 3 to 4 percent, Big C might be including some revenue, which should be primarily added to the sales, in "other revenue" (a part of non-operating revenue). Even with this possibility taken into consideration, we cannot, however, deny that Big C's gross profit ratio was relatively low between 1995 and 2006. Nevertheless, Big C's ordinary profit ratio was relatively good during that same period, because, on the one hand, the company succeeded in reducing its SG&A cost ratio compared to its competitors, and, on the other hand, it also improved sales efficiency by increasing its inventory turnover. By contrast, Carrefour showed unstable profitability. From the very beginning, Carrefour expanded its chain in Thailand at a slower pace than its rivals. Plus, Carrefour had smaller sales per store (see table 4.1) and a relatively high SG&A cost ratio. This combination of factors reduced Carrefour's ordinary profit.

Although the differences between Big C, Tesco, and Carrefour are not small despite belonging to the same retail format, a high ratio of "other revenue" is common to all three companies. This is true for the cash-and-carry Makro as well. "Other revenue" is determined by deducting investment income from subsidiary and affiliated companies, and interest income from non-operating revenue, and consists mainly of various fees and charges paid by suppliers on turnover, such as rebates, sales promotion revenue, and distribution center fees. These are new commercial practices brought about by the new retail formats. By using these practices, each new retail format that has a low price policy can supplement their operating profit shortage to achieve ordinary profit.[16] Table 4.2 gives a snapshot of the actual weight of "other revenue" for each company.

General mass merchandisers (i.e., cash-and-carry stores and hypermarkets) have rapidly increased their sales since the financial and currency crisis, while they have not shown much increase as a percentage of total retail sales for the whole country during the economic recovery period of the late 1990s and early 2000s. One possible reason for this is that there are some differences between these remarkably growing general mass merchandisers. For example if we compare the sales growth rates of the cash-and-carry format and the hypermarket format, we see that Makro's sales growth rate between 1999 and

2006 was 69.8 percent, while the three hypermarkets' sales growth rate during the same period reached a total of 237.1 percent. Even among hypermarkets, important differentials in their sales growth rates can be found between companies during the same period of time. For instance, Tesco Lotus grew from 5,970 million baht in 1996 to 93,922 million baht in 2006 (representing a 348.9 percent sales growth), Big C grew in that same period from 10,761 to 58,033 million baht (158.3 percent sales growth), and Carrefour grew from 1,613 to 22,496 million baht (168.9 percent sales growth), as seen in table 4.1. The differentials between companies are also one of the reasons why general mass merchandisers have not dramatically increased their weight compared to retail sales for the whole country, contrary to the impression that hypermarkets, Tesco Lotus in particular, are rapidly growing. More important is that even companies that have achieved solid business performances actually have problems with their growth strategies. As shown in table 4.1, Tesco Lotus did not dramatically increase its per-store sales during the rapid business expansion period beginning in 1999. Considering the high rates of increase in the consumer price index (CPI) and in the retail sales for the entire country, we can go as far as to say that Tesco Lotus's per store sales have virtually decreased.

The increase in general mass merchandisers' sales was dependent on the increase in the total number of stores rather than in per store sales. Therefore, the strategy of opening new stores can be regarded as a key to company growth in this specific retail format.

STRATEGIES FOR OPENING NEW STORES

Makro (cash-and-carry) is basically a wholesaler, characterized by a wider trading area per store than a hypermarket. This is also suggested by the fact that its per store sales are considerably larger than that of the three hypermarkets, as shown in table 4.1. After the establishment of its first store in Lat Phrao, east of Bangkok, in August 1989, Makro successively opened a second store in Chaeng Watthana, north of Bangkok, in March 1990, a third store in Si Nakharin, southeast of Bangkok, in November 1990, as well as a fourth store in Bang Bon, southwest of Bangkok, in December 1990. Soon after that, Makro started to advance into the provinces, with a fifth store in Chonburi, eastern Thailand, in February 1993, a sixth store in Chiang Mai, northern Thailand, in August 1993, and a seventh store in Nakhon Ratchasima, northeastern Thailand, in January 1994. As time went on, Makro continued to actively advance into the provinces, opening eight new stores in provincial cities between 2002 and 2005. It is worth mentioning that the locations of these eight stores include relatively small and intermediate provincial cities such as Sakon Nakhon and Roi Et in northeastern Thailand, Trang in southern Thailand, and Sa Kaeo in eastern Thailand. This suggests that there is not much room for Makro to further open new stores in major provincial cities, and even less so in the Bangkok metropolitan area. The fact that Makro has been showing a slower rate of increase in both sales and the number of stores than the three hypermarket companies is also supporting evidence for this.[17]

By contrast, hypermarkets, especially Tesco Lotus and Big C, seem to have satisfactorily increased sales in accordance with the active opening of new stores. Beginning around 2002, however, the three hypermarket companies began to change their strategies for opening new stores by more actively advancing into the provinces and establishing small and medium-sized stores, similar to Makro's strategy. Ek-Chai Distribution System Co., Ltd., which runs Tesco Lotus, has been particularly active in this regard. In addition to the Tesco Lotus hypermarket format (approx. 10,000 sq m floor space), the company has developed a new medium-sized hypermarket format, known as Lotus Khum Kha (Lotus Value) (4,000 sq m floor space), a supermarket format, Talad Lotus (800 sq m floor space), and Lotus Express, a new format combining supermarket and convenience store formats (300 sq m floor space). Tesco Lotus began to shift its business weight to these new retail formats starting around 2004 (*TNSK*, January 21, 2006). Big C also began to open medium-sized hypermarkets as well as the small-size, hard-discount store Leader Price (800 to 1,000 sq m floor space), which mainly offers its private label goods at low prices.

However, one may wonder why Ek-Chai Distribution System felt the need to develop small- and medium-sized Tesco stores, as the company was the fastest growing of all the hypermarkets and ranked first in the industry. It is true that, from 2002 on, the regulations regarding large-scale retail stores and their location caused retail companies to change their strategies for opening new stores (Endo 2005). But actually, the company had already begun to develop small- and medium-sized stores and to shift its business strategy even before these regulations were instituted. This fact suggests that, even before the introduction of the new regulations by the Thai government, the intensifying competition within the industry had gradually brought about saturation in the market and that there was already very little room to open new stores, especially in the Bangkok metropolitan area. This caused hypermarket companies to engage in diversification into small- and medium-sized stores. One of the strong points of the hypermarket format is its centralized management system that includes store standardization. Yet with the diversification of store formats, it was only natural that problems would arise related to the management of hypermarkets' various store formats.

We also cannot overlook the problems connected with the expansion of chain stores into the provinces. It is true that hypermarkets have wider room to open new stores in the provinces than department stores because there's a larger market for lower priced goods. However, when the structural characteristics of Thailand's consumer market are taken into consideration, the potential number of stores per area is actually rather limited. Each hypermarket company has one or two stores per province at the most. For this reason, the physical distribution costs become comparatively high in the case of hypermarkets that need to deliver goods to stores dispersed throughout the country via a central distribution center. In this respect, hypermarket companies are at a disadvantage compared to leading provincial distributors, such as Super Cheap and Tang Ngee Soon, which constitute a new retail format that combines a cash-and-carry wholesaler with a supermarket.[18]

It should be further pointed out that motorization, which is a precondition for hypermarket growth, has not yet sufficiently progressed in Thailand. According to NSO's *Household Socio-Economic Survey*, the household automobile ownership rate for the entire kingdom still remains at a low level, though it did increase from 5.9 percent in 1994 to 9.9 percent in 2004. In some cases, Thais, especially in the provinces, purchase a pick-up truck as an automobile substitute due to a commodity tax that favors pick-up trucks. If household ownership rates of pick-up trucks were added to automobile rates, household "car" ownership rates would have reached 25.2 percent in 2004.[19] However, this also means that, without car, at least three-fourths of Thai households, as of 2004, did not have easy access to hypermarkets, which are often located along highways far from the residential areas. This is a significant issue, especially in the provinces where public transportation is still underdeveloped, as of 2012.[20]

Due to slow motorization rates and the structural characteristics of Thailand's consumer market, cash-and-carry stores and hypermarkets have not sufficiently expanded into the provincial consumer market. This means it is likely that there is still substantial room for traditional retailers and wholesalers to continue to develop. However, whether traditional distributors actually have sufficient room to exist and expand depends on the extent to which other new retail formats, such as supermarkets and convenience stores, have developed.

SUPERMARKETS

BUSINESS DEVELOPMENT AND PROFITABILITY STRUCTURE

While supermarkets are a new retail format, they have not managed to achieve remarkable growth. Table 4.4 shows the development of the four major supermarket chains in Thailand: Tops, Jusco, Foodland, and Villa. Of these chains, Foodland founded in 1972 has the longest history.[21] However, it only had three stores until the mid-1980s, so its presence was small in the Thai retail industry. Other supermarkets in the early days were small-sized chain stores as well, or have already gone out of business. That is why this study regards supermarkets as one of the new retail formats that have appeared since the end of 1980s.

TABLE 4.4 Development of supermarkets in Thailand

Company name	Chain store name	Format	Year of establishment	Ownership as of 2006	Sales (million baht) / Number of stores (as of year end) 1996	1999	2002	2006
Central Food Retail (formerly, CRC Ahold)	Tops[a]	SM[b]	1996	Central Group[c]	2,965	11,032	14,523	20,104
					22	33	44	96
AEON (Thailand) (formerly, Siam-Jusco)	Jusco	SM	1984	AEON (Japan)	3,879	4,219	4,031	1,864
					9	14	10	6
Foodland Supermarket	Foodland	SM	1972	Foodland	2,553	2,751	2,717	3,610
					7	7	8	11
Villa Market JP	Villa	SM	1988	Phusanakhom family	625	886	1,176	1,817
					5	7	n/a	9

SOURCE: Financial statements, annual reports, websites, and stockholder lists of each company; Thai-language newspapers.

[a] Tops is not a listed company and, therefore, consolidated figures are not available. Sales figures for Tops were thus derived by adding up each subsidiary company's sales figures to reach a sum total.

[b] SM=supermarket

[c] The Central Group purchased twenty Food Lion chain stores from the Belgium-based Delhaize Group in 2004, which was when Delhaize withdrew from Thailand. It refurbished these stores as Tops Supermarkets. This accounts for the substantial increase in the number of its stores between 2002 and 2006.

The typical supermarket as a new retail format is Central Group's Tops Supermarket (Central Food Retail Co., Ltd.). During the post-crisis period, Tops was a subsidiary of Holland-based Royal Ahold, but in April 2004 the Central Group repurchased it as a 100-percent subsidiary. The Central Group also purchased twenty promising Food Lion stores from the Belgium-based Delhaize Group, which decided to withdraw from Thailand's supermarket business.[22] Central refurbished these stores as Tops Supermarkets. In this way, Tops has become by far the largest chain among Thailand's supermarkets, both in number of stores and in sales volume. Of the four major supermarket chains in table 4.4, only Tops is a national chain that has expanded throughout the country, while the others are Bangkok-based local chains. Japan-based Jusco (AEON [Thailand] Co., Ltd., formerly Siam-Jusco Co., Ltd.) established its first store in 1985 and has developed both a supermarket format and a general merchandise store format. Since 2001, Jusco has had to restructure its business, closing down and selling unprofitable stores, thus reducing its business scale.[23] The local supermarket chain Villa (Villa Market JP Co., Ltd.) occupies a unique position in that it targets the upper-income strata and foreigners in Bangkok. In addition to these chains, there are many other supermarkets in Bangkok and provincial cities that operate with local capital. As of 2006, local capital took the lead in the supermarket format in Thailand in contrast to general mass merchandisers.

Tables 4.5 and 4.6 allow us to compare the profitability and efficiency between Thailand's four major supermarket companies. The supermarket retail format is based on a self-service system and that sale of consumer goods, primarily food, with a low profit margin and high turnover. The two tables demonstrate that the four supermarkets actually have a gross profit ratio and SG&A cost ratio as low as hypermarkets, but a higher inventory turnover than them. However, they have relatively lower ordinary profit ratios than hypermarkets, and Tops and Jusco, in particular, had a loss of ordinary profit almost every year between 1996 and 2004.

Operating profits, which are not shown in tables 4.5 and 4.5, were even worse. Tops experienced operating losses from at least 1996 to 2006 and Jusco from 1994 to 2006, according to their respective financial statements. One of the reasons for such low profitability is that both companies had a higher SG&A cost ratio than other supermarket companies. Tops' SG&A cost ratio, in particular, was very high from 1998 to 2000 because Royal Ahold Group, which purchased Tops in 1998, invested a large amount of money in building a new physical distribution system.[24] This ratio, however, remained relatively high until recently. Jusco has made efforts to improve its profitability by restructuring its business beginning in 2001, because the company was not only up against stiff competition with other supermarkets and other retail formats but also had to deal with the deterioration of its business performance due to the financial and currency crisis. Finally in 2006, the Business Rehabilitation Law was applied to Jusco as well.[25] Compared with these two companies, Foodland and Villa have shown more stable profitability, though still not at particularly high levels.

TABLE 4.5 Profitability of major supermarkets in Thailand, 1995–2006

	Tops[a]	Jusco	Foodland	Villa
Gross profit ratio to sales (%)				
1995	–	15.2	13.2	9.4
1996	14.0	15.6	13.3	9.9
1997	12.3	n/a	12.3	9.5
1998	15.0	n/a	11.7	11.3
1999	16.0	14.3	11.5	11.7
2000	16.3	14.8	12.1	8.1
2001	14.1	14.9	12.6	9.1
2002	13.0	14.6	12.8	9.5
2003	12.9	14.5	12.8	9.6
2004	12.7	14.0	13.6	11.7
2005	13.1	15.2	13.6	11.5
2006	14.1	15.8	13.6	12.7
Ordinary profit ratio to sales (%)				
1995	–	7.5	4.6	0.3
1996	-2.4	-2.3	4.4	0.8
1997	-3.2	n/a	2.5	0.8
1998	-7.7	n/a	2.4	1.0
1999	-9.3	-3.8	2.3	1.1
2000	-3.0	-2.3	2.4	1.2
2001	2.9	-0.4	1.9	1.2
2002	-3.5	-0.6	1.8	1.1
2003	-1.7	-3.8	1.9	1.0
2004	-0.6	-1.2	1.9	1.0
2005	3.8	5.0	2.2	1.2
2006	1.8	5.8	2.3	1.4

SOURCE: Companies' financial statements.

[a] Figures for Tops are only those of its head office, Central Food Retail Co., Ltd. The supermarket was not established until 1996, which is why there are no sales figures for 1995.

TABLE 4.6 Efficiency of major supermarkets in Thailand, 1995–2006

	Tops[a]	Jusco	Foodland	Villa
SG&A cost ratio[b]				
1995	–	18.4	10.4	9.7
1996	17.2	20.8	10.4	10.6
1997	20.9	n/a	11.7	11.3
1998	30.5	n/a	11.5	12.4
1999	27.4	19.9	11.2	12.3
2000	28.0	17.8	12.1	9.5
2001	20.3	19.7	13.3	11.0
2002	23.3	19.3	13.7	10.9
2003	21.9	19.9	14.1	11.5
2004	21.2	20.2	14.5	13.8
2005	19.2	19.8	14.6	13.8
2006	22.1	23.5	14.7	14.8
Inventory turnover (cost of goods sold/inventories)				
1995	–	12.3	13.5	12.3
1996	3.5	13.9	11.9	20.4
1997	12.0	n/a.	12.6	14.6
1998	19.7	n/a.	11.1	17.2
1999	26.3	11.7	15.6	16.3
2000	21.8	10.8	11.0	15.2
2001	20.7	9.6	11.4	11.5
2002	10.9	10.3	11.2	10.1
2003	12.8	11.5	9.7	8.9
2004	11.7	15.2	11.4	8.4
2005	11.4	11.5	10.9	7.4
2006	10.2	12.6	11.3	8.1

SOURCE: Companies' financial statements.

[a] Figures for Tops are only those of its head office, Central Food Retail Co., Ltd. Tops was not established until 1996, which is why there are no sales figures for 1995.

[b] SG&A cost ratio=ratio of selling, general, and administrative expenses to sales.

As tables 4.5 and 4.6 illustrate, Tops, which is, at present, the only national chain in Thailand's supermarket industry, has high operating costs and unstable profitability. Jusco, the only foreign chain of the four major supermarket chains, came to a near standstill in 2001 in terms of its profitability, and had to undergo a major restructuring of its business and its strategies for opening new stores. As for Foodland and Villa, these two supermarket chains have managed to steadily boost their business performances but have expanded at a slow pace. The supermarket format has thus not shown as much growth as expected.

Yet, several important questions remain. Why does Tops, by far the largest supermarket chain in Thailand, have such low profitability? Why did Jusco's general merchandise store business fail in Thailand, while it had at least one successful run in Japan? Why do the relatively successful Foodland and Villa supermarkets only expand their business gradually? Such questions suggest that there are some problems not only at the company level but also specific to the supermarket format.

BUYING AND LOGISTICS

Supermarkets must out of necessity compete with other new retail formats, such as hypermarkets and convenience stores, because the goods they sell are primarily foods and daily necessities. However, supermarkets differ from other new retail formats in such respects as floor space and their assortment of goods. Supermarkets' floor space is generally between 1,000 and 2,000 square meters, which is smaller than a hypermarket (approx. 10,000 sq m) but larger than a convenience store (approx. 100 sq m). The number of items in a supermarket greatly differs according to each store, e.g., Foodland maintains approximately 13,000 SKUs per store, and Tops has about 50,000 SKUs per store. This once again places supermarkets in an intermediate position between hypermarkets and convenience stores. The percentage of a supermarket's perishable goods (in terms of sales) is between 30 percent (Tops) and 50 percent (Foodland), each of which is much higher than hypermarkets and convenience stores. For this very reason, supermarkets are also in direct competition with traditional wet markets (*talat sot*, or simply *talat*, in Thai).

Supermarket companies buy a portion of their perishable foods—their primary commodity—directly from producers. With regard to meat, in particular, each company has direct dealings with a small number of major food manufacturers, such as Betagro and Charoen Pokphand Foods Plc (CPF), the CP Group's food-processing and sales company. Direct dealings enable supermarket companies to put their purchasing policies into practice more easily. For example, Tops is striving to differentiate itself from its competitors by contracting with food manufacturers to procure meat from livestock raised without chemicals. As for fruits and vegetables, Tops and other major supermarkets contract with farmers to buy high-quality goods, such as organic produce. However, there are a significant number of cases in which independent brokers intermediate between producers and supermarkets because supermarket buyers often do not have the requisite skills to correctly purchase and merchandise specific products.

The fact that supermarkets need brokers' intermediation suggests that they may have difficulties with their competitors in respect to commodity differentiation. Since supermarkets buy a portion of their perishable foods from producers and another portion from independent brokers, who serve as intermediaries between producers and various supermarkets and hypermarkets, supermarket companies cannot differentiate themselves from their competitiors in their assortment of perishable goods.

Supermarkets also buy a portion of their fruits and vegetables as well as marine food products from wholesale markets. Wholesale markets, in this case, are not always clearly divided from wet markets, but the market traders often sell in retail or wholesale according to customers' needs.[26] Talat Thai and Talat Si Mumu Muang are at present de facto central wholesale markets for fruits and vegetables, and Talat Thale Thai for marine food products. These wholesale markets are located in the provinces surrounding Bangkok. In this case, as well, supermarket buyers do not buy the products at the wholesale markets themselves, but instead, generally depend on independent brokers for procurement. This method of purchasing perishable goods can be problematic, resulting in, for instance, a decrease in merchandizing ability and an ineffectively differentiated assortment of goods.

The physical distribution system thus becomes extremely important in relation to purchasing perishable goods. It is basically the same system as that of hypermarkets; however, as supermarkets sell more perishable goods, freshness control becomes a critical issue and each supermarket chain has developed its unique way to deal with this. For instance, Tops, up until 1998, had asked producers and brokers to deliver fruits and vegetables to each of their stores because the company lacked a sufficient physical distribution system. After the chain was purchased by Holland-based Ahold in 1998, Tops built a logistics system with a distribution center as its core. Following the repurchase of Tops supermarkets by the Central Group in 2004, the logistics system and distribution center continued to be used.[27]

Tops actually has two types of distribution centers: one for daily processed foods and necessities (in Bang Bua Thong, Nonthaburi) and another one for perishable foods (in Mahachai, Samut Sakhon), both of which are located in the suburbs of Bangkok. At the present time, Tops entrusts the management of the Bang Bua Thong center to DHL Co., Ltd., while Tops manages the Mahachai center itself by renting warehouses from a local company. The Mahachai center manages its perishable goods by dividing and storing them into five temperature categories, ranging from refrigerated to frozen. Ninety-five percent of Tops' perishable foods are delivered from this center to each store throughout the country. An outside company specializing in the field implements a quality control system for Tops' distribution center,[28] while a foreign-run refrigerated transport company is entrusted with delivery from the distribution center to the stores to ensure thorough freshness control in the storage and transportation of all goods. As a result, in 2001, Tops received a Good Manufacturing Practice (GMP) certificate from MASCI, a certification institute under the jurisdiction of the Thai government, and the HACCP food safety certificate from TQCSI Co., Ltd.[29]

The other major supermarket chains, although on a smaller scale than Tops national chain, are also making efforts to control the freshness of perishable foods. For example, Foodland set up a quality inspection room in each of its stores rather than building a distribution center for perishable foods. It implements a thorough inventory control using information technology to minimize the number of goods left unsold (Arun 2002a, 38–42). Jusco has its suppliers deliver temperature-controlled products (e.g., milk, meat, fish, delicatessen foods, and most fruits and vegetables) directly to each store. It, too, does not have a distribution center because of the small number of its stores.[30] Instead of a distribution center, Jusco established a perishable food-processing center and a central packaging system attached to its Sukhaphiban branch to make efforts to ensure freshness control and the standardization of goods. Villa Supermarket, which targets the upper-income strata and foreign residents in Bangkok, has adopted a consignment system for goods such as beef, and entrusts outside experts with most of its merchandising activities, ranging from the purchase of goods to inventory control.[31]

POSITION IN THE RETAIL INDUSTRY

The major supermarket companies all attach importance to the physical distribution and freshness control of perishable foods, but differ in the way they achieve them: shouldering it by themselves or outsourcing it. However, this doesn't always result in giving them a competitive advantage against other retail formats. As far as perishable foods sales in Thailand are concerned, wet markets are probably the most powerful rivals to supermarkets. Quite a few newspapers have reported that wet markets have been heavily damaged by the new retail formats,[32] but even major supermarkets still regard them as tough competitors.[33] The fact that the supermarket format has not grown as fast as expected suggests that many wet markets are still only partially influenced by the rise of new retail formats, though some markets are actually suffering a decrease in sales caused by the increasing number of new retail formats.[34]

Wet markets indeed have many strong points. For instance, shoppers have room to bargain with vendors. Sellers and buyers know each other by sight, so that a visit to the market often turns into an enjoyable moment. In some cases, shoppers are also allowed to buy on credit. The most important point, however, is that perishable food prices are generally cheaper in wet markets than in supermarkets. Although supermarkets have more bargaining power against suppliers because of bulk buying, the large investments they make to construct a quality and freshness control system and a physical distribution system for perishable foods ends up weighing on sales prices, which thus become relatively expensive. Conversely, wet markets do business on very low gross profits, with very low SGA expenses as well. In addition, wet markets are not necessarily inferior to supermarkets in terms of freshness. Even though they are unable to implement sufficient temperature controls, the freshness of the goods is ensured by a high turnover rate, and stock is usually sold out for the day.[35] Judging from the mosaic structure of Thailand's consumer market, supermarkets' differentiation strategies related to chemical-free and organic vegetables would, for example, appeal only to a limited number of consumers.[36] Although Tops sells high-quality chicken in cooperation with CPF Company, other kinds of CPF chicken are often sold in wet markets as well,[37] and most consumers pay little attention to the difference in quality between them.

One additional item to be noted is that Thai people make a practice of buying just enough food for each day because perishable foods rot quickly in Thailand's high temperatures and humid climate. The household refrigerator ownership rate for the country, which is indispensable when buying large quantities of perishable foods, was only 49 percent in 1994 during the height of the consumption boom (NSO, *Household Socio-Economic Survey*). Although the ownership rate rose to about 80 percent in 2004, many of these refrigerators are small-sized, especially in rural areas, which suggests that the Thai consumer market is not yet sufficiently equipped to buy perishable foods in large quantities, and, as previously mentioned the household automobile ownership rate remains at a low level as well. Needless to say, it takes quite a long time to change shopping practices. Thus, the supermarket format has not yet become a threat to the existence of wet markets.

With regard to processed foods and daily necessities, supermarkets are in an inferior position to hypermarkets because supermarkets sell fewer items and have too limited a buying power to compete with hypermarkets in the pricing of the same items. This is reflected in the fact that Jusco changed its development strategy after failing at its general merchandising business and decided to focus exclusively on the supermarket business. The reason for this is that general merchandise stores compete more directly with hypermarkets in terms of the assortment of their goods than do supermarkets, which mainly sell food.[38]

While hypermarkets have adapted to weekend shoppers, who buy a large quantity of goods at one time, they are rather inconvenient for daily shopping since their floor spaces and parking areas are too large. In this respect, supermarkets should have an advantage over hypermarkets, but many major supermarkets in Thailand (especially, the largest chain Tops) are located in department stores or shopping centers and are not always easily accessible. Regarding timesaving convenience, supermarkets are, therefore, inferior to convenience stores.

Supermarkets have not always succeeded in differentiating themselves from wet markets. In addition, they have failed to sufficiently display their advantage over hypermarkets and convenience stores. There are, however, some successful supermarkets. Two examples are Foodland and Villa. Foodland steadily expanded its business as a local chain in Bangkok, while Villa targeted the upper-income strata and foreign residents in Bangkok.[39] However, the development of these supermarket chains remains localized.[40] When the structural characteristics of Thailand's consumer market are considered, it is clear that supermarkets' limited niche strategy will necessarily confront difficulties when trying to drastically expand their business. Even the largest supermarket chain, Tops, has recently changed its strategy of opening new stores by sub-dividing its stores into four types of stores that range from upper-class stores to popular stores according to the store location, in order to adapt more thoroughly to the eclectic consumer market. These four types of stores include: Central Food Hall, which is a high-end supermarket (one store in Central Department Store, Chidlom Branch and one in Central World Plaza, each with a floor space of 4,000–9,000 sq m; Tops Market, which is geared towards the upper-middle class income strata (1,000-4,000 sq m floor space); Tops Super, which targets general consumers (1,000-4,000 sq m floor space); and Tops Daily, which is a small-sized store (300 sq m floor space).[41] However, it is not yet clear whether this strategy will succeed, because it will complicate the head office management, just as it did in the case of hypermarkets when they changed their strategies regarding the opening of new stores.

CONVENIENCE STORES

BUSINESS DEVELOPMENT AND PROFITABILITY STRUCTURE

Convenience stores as a whole are much smaller in sales but have higher growth rates than general mass merchandisers. Of the convenience store chains in Thailand, two major chains, 7-Eleven (CP All Plc [formerly, C. P. Seven Eleven Plc][42]) and FamilyMart (Siam FamilyMart Co., Ltd.) occupy a prominent position in the industry. There are other chains, such as V Shop (Mini Mart Express Co., Ltd.), Fresh Mart (Fresh Mart International Co., Ltd.), and some others attached to gas stations, but each of them only has a small number of stores or the details of their business are unknown.[43] For these reasons, this section will only focus on the two major convenience store chains.

Table 4.7 shows the development of 7-Eleven and FamilyMart over the ten-year period 1996 to 2006. Of these two convenience store chains, 7-Eleven has an overwhelmingly larger number of stores and thus higher sales. Since 2001, FamilyMart has been actively opening new stores (*PRCT-TK*, January 22, 2001), and it accelerated the pace of its store openings after inviting Kanok Wongtrangan to serve as CEO in 2003. Kanok had previously contributed greatly to the reconstruction of Robinson Department Store.[44] Despite this, at the end of 2005, the number of Siam FamilyMart stores was still only one-sixth of that of 7-Eleven stores.

In considering the development of convenience stores in Thailand, a few points need to be addressed. First of all, when comparing data between 7-Eleven and FamilyMart stores, the number of stores represents that of each chain store operation, while sales data accounts only for that of each company's head office because total sales figures of the entire chain are not available. This means that both 7-Eleven and FamilyMart's sales data does not include franchisees and sub-area license holders.[45] The percentage of corporate stores in both chains is, nevertheless, much higher than in Japan, where convenience store chains are mainly based on a franchise system. As of 2006, the number of corporate stores in Thailand amounted to 60 percent of the entire 7-Eleven chain (C. P. Seven Eleven 2007, 33), and 90 percent of the FamilyMart chain.[46] All of this suggests that the company's head office data is substantially important to roughly understand each chain's business performance. If one were to estimate each chain store's total sales, this would only make the prominence of 7-Eleven in Thailand even clearer.

TABLE 4.7 The development of convenience stores in Thailand

Company name of head office	Chain store name	Format	Year of establish-ment	Ownership as of 2006	Total sales (million baht) / Number of stores (as of year end) / Average sales per store (million baht)			
					1996	1999	2002	2006
CP All Plc[a] (formerly, C. P. Seven Eleven Plc)	7-Eleven	CVS[b]	1988	CP Group	8,846	15,141	30,165	66,055
					682	1,324	2,042	3,784
					13	11	15	17
Siam FamilyMart[c]	FamilyMart	CVS	1992	FamilyMart (Japan)	140	725	2,280	6,071
					15	106	292	536
					9	7	8	11

SOURCE: Financial statements, annual reports, websites, and stockholder lists of each company; Thai-language newspapers.

NOTE: In addition to 7-Eleven and FamilyMart, Thailand has other local convenience store chains, such as V Shop, Fresh Mart, and 108 Shop. These, however, have been omitted from this table because their scales of operation are much smaller.

[a] Sales figures for CP All Plc are based on sales figures for the company stores only, while the number of stores includes corporate and franchise stores as well as sub-area license stores located in the provinces. Since CP All operates hypermarkets in China, representing approximately 30 percent of its sales, it was not possible to use consolidated sales figures.

[b] CVS=convenience stores

[c] The 1999, 2002, and 2006 figures for the number of FamilyMart stores are based on figures as of the end of 2000, 2003, and February 2006, respectively.

Differences between the two convenience store chains are also apparent with regard to profitability. Table 4.8 compares the financial data of both chains on the basis of the companies' head office figures only. From this table, we can see that 7-Eleven's gross profit ratio steadily increased between 2000 and 2006, while that of FamilyMart decreased during the same period, for the most part. As a result, the difference between them has widened by around 10 percent. One of the reasons why FamilyMart's gross profit ratio has been in a slump is thought to have originated in its smaller sales volume per store. Another possible reason is that the purchase price of goods per unit is relatively higher than 7-Eleven, due to the company's weak buying power caused by its small number of stores. Table 4.7 showed that FamilyMart's sales per store reached only 60 percent of that of 7-Eleven.[47] Since 7-Eleven's sales per store are underestimated due to the higher percentage of franchisees, the differential between the two chains is actually thought to be even larger. In any case, the low gross profit ratio is one of the reasons why FamilyMart has suffered an extensive ordinary profit loss, even after accelerating the opening of new stores in 2001. By contrast, 7-Eleven's ordinary profit ratio has been stable at a relatively high rate of almost 5 percent, as shown in table 4.8.

TABLE 4.8 Profitability of major convenience stores in Thailand, 1995–2006

	7-Eleven	FamilyMart
Gross profit ratio to sales (%)		
1995	16.9	14.5
1996	15.5	17.1
1997	16.0	15.9
1998	17.1	16.0
1999	18.6	17.2
2000	19.8	17.4
2001	21.0	17.4
2002	21.2	14.3
2003	20.8	13.1
2004	24.4	14.0
2005	23.7	14.1
2006	24.2	15.1
Ordinary profit ratio to sales (%)		
1995	1.7	-32.4
1996	3.2	-23.2
1997	2.9	-13.6
1998	3.0	-21.6
1999	3.2	-19.8
2000	4.6	-17.1
2001	5.4	-11.5
2002	4.3	-8.6
2003	4.4	-5.6
2004	5.5	-6.6
2005	4.1	-6.5
2006	3.0	-6.6
"Other revenue" ratio to sales (%)[a]		
1995	n/a	1.1
1996	n/a	3.9
1997	n/a	5.3
1998	n/a	2.0

	7-Eleven	FamilyMart
1999	n/a	6.8
2000	4.7	3.8
2001	5.6	4.1
2002	4.6	3.6
2003	4.3	3.7
2004	6.9	4.4
2005	6.9	5.2
2006	4.6	7.7

SOURCE: Companies' financial statements.

[a] "Other revenue" refers to non-operating revenue, such as franchise royalties, rebates, sales-promotion revenue, distribution center fees, and so on.

A franchise system using external managerial resources is usually considered a more reasonable option than a corporate-store system in terms of minimizing management costs and expenses for new store openings.[48] One may then wonder why Siam FamilyMart has mainly opened corporate stores and 7-Eleven, as well, has significantly more corporate stores than franchisees. In contrast with 7-Eleven in Japan, where the first store was established as a franchisee, table 4.9 shows that 7-Eleven in Thailand only opened corporate stores during the first stages of its operations and that the percentage of franchisees was only 9.5 percent even at the end of 1992, when the total number of stores reached 130 stores (the percentage of corporate stores was 82.3 percent). After that, the percentage of franchisees increased rapidly, but decreased sharply again during the financial and currency crisis. Beginning around 2003, the percentage of franchisees started to increase again, but even by the end of 2006 the percentage of corporate stores was higher than that of franchise stores. Overall, the absolute number of corporate stores is still increasing. This is an important issue to bear in mind when examining the convenience store format.

FRANCHISE CHAIN SYSTEM

In November 1988, at the time of its foundation, C. P. Seven Eleven Co., Ltd. (currently CP All Plc) purchased an exclusive area franchise for the Thai domestic market from US-based Southland Corporation (currently Seven Eleven Inc.). Then in June 1989, it established its first store on Patpong Road in Bangkok, in the form of a corporate store. This store is located in a central business district, a busy pedestrian area in the daytime and the famous red-light district visited by foreign tourists at nighttime. Whereas, in Japan, the first 7-Eleven store was established as a franchisee in a Tokyo residential area. This demonstrates that Thailand's policy for opening new stores was to focus on commercial rather than residential areas, and to target foreigners as well as local Thais. After the opening of its first store, C. P. Seven Eleven continued to open new stores in Thailand, as shown in table 4.9.

TABLE 4.9 Number of 7-Eleven stores in Thailand

	Corporate stores		Franchise stores		Sub-area license stores		Total	
Year	No. of stores	%	No. of stores	%	No. of stores	%	No. of stores	%
1989	7	100.0	0	–	0	–	7	100.0
1990	27	100.0	0	–	0	–	27	100.0
1991	60	85.7	6	8.6	4	5.7	70	100.0
1992	130	82.3	15	9.5	13	8.2	158	100.0
1993	202	74.5	36	13.3	33	12.2	271	100.0
1994	254	63.7	87	21.8	58	14.5	399	100.0
1995	288	51.9	179	32.3	88	15.9	555	100.0
1996	348	51.0	234	34.3	100	14.7	682	100.0
1997	n/a	–	n/a	–	n/a	–	902	100.0
1998	n/a	–	n/a	–	n/a	–	1,104	100.0
1999	n/a	–	n/a	–	n/a	–	1,324	100.0
2000	1,137	74.8	303	19.9	81	5.3	1,521	100.0
2001	1,278	74.2	355	20.6	89	5.2	1,722	100.0
2002	1,503	73.6	437	21.4	102	5.0	2,042	100.0
2003	1,608	67.1	662	27.6	127	5.3	2,397	100.0
2004	1,782	62.3	923	32.3	156	5.5	2,861	100.0
2005	1,931	58.3	1,191	36.0	189	5.7	3,311	100.0
2006	2,119	56.0	1,449	38.3	216	5.7	3,784	100.0

SOURCE: GM Business (August 1997); Somprarotna et al. (2000, 89); Thot (2005, 135); annual reports of CP All (C. P. Seven Eleven) Plc.

The reason why C. P. Seven Eleven put such emphasis on the corporate store format during initial stages of its operations was that it considered it necessary to expand the chain as quickly as possible in order to acquire the suppliers' understanding of this new retail format and to garner their cooperation, which is indispensable for the development of a convenience store business. C. P.

Seven Eleven also preferred the corporate store format to the franchise system because the company had made it a rule to open new stores by purchasing property and then building a store on it, or by entering into long-term leases, in anticipation of future increases in the value of its fixed assets (Suriya et al. 1997, 73–81). Incidentally, if C. P. Seven Eleven had been able to accurately anticipate future increases in the value of its fixed assets, it should have stuck to buying property. However, the company ended up leasing stores as much as buying property, probably because of difficulties in purchase negotiations. This is because many owners of existing grocery stores (*cho huai*), which are targets for convenience store development, are generally aging people who are not interested in selling their well-located stores and property because of their high asset value, especially since Thailand has virtually no inheritance tax.[49]

In this way, C. P. Seven Eleven strove to accelerate the pace of its store openings, mainly in the form of corporate stores. However, the CP Group, to which C. P. Seven Eleven belongs, was initially unable, in the first few years, to sufficiently invest in the convenience store business due to its heavy involvement in the telecommunication business (Telecom Asia Corp. Plc), causing a slower than expected pace of store expansion (Suriya et al. 1997, 89–95). It is possible to imagine that the investment burden, whether the purchase or long-term lease of property, had accumulated to unbearable level, given that, at the time, land prices were soaring in the middle of the investment and property development booms. 7-Eleven's business performance was actually quite bad during the first few years, according to the financial statements of the company, which showed ordinary profit ratio figures in the red, at -12.9 percent in 1990 and -4.6 percent in 1991. It was in 1991 that the company decided to concentrate on opening new stores, including franchise and sub-area license stores as well as corporate stores. After that, as was shown in table 4.9, the percentages of franchises and sub-area license stores to the whole 7-Eleven chain in Thailand rapidly increased, and in 1996, the year before the financial and currency crisis, the percentage of franchise stores reached 34.3 percent and sub-area license stores hit 14.7 percent. The total number of franchises and sub-area license stores combined thus drew close to the total number of corporate stores.[50]

It seemed that C. P. Seven Eleven would continue to expand its business by shifting its focus to the franchise system, but with the 1997 financial and currency crisis, the company sharply reduced the pace of its franchise store openings, which further increased the proportion of its corporate stores again. Soon after that, C. P. Seven Eleven revised the requirements of the preexisting franchise system in order to ease the opening of new stores. It increased the percentage of franchise stores to 38.3 percent as of the end of 2006 (see table 4.9). This, however, didn't change the fact that corporate stores still represented the majority (56 percent) of the chain's stores. Compared with Japan's 7-Eleven, in which the percentage of franchise stores is nearly 100 percent, the percentage of franchise stores in Thailand's 7-Eleven remained very low as of 2006. Why is this? What kind of problems did the former franchisee system have that precluded Thailand's 7-Eleven from rapidly increasing the number of franchise stores? And, in what ways did the company change this system? Table 4.10 compares the former franchise system (Type A) and the new franchise system (Type B) of C. P. Seven Eleven.

TABLE 4.10 Franchise system of CP All Plc (formerly, C. P. Seven Eleven)

Former Franchise System (Type A)	New Franchise System (Type B)
Requirements for franchisee • Ownership of store or long-term lease of eight years or more. • Busy traffic location, e.g., near bus stops, wet markets (*talat*), intersections, etc. (examined by the head office). • Floor space of more than 100 sq m. • Width of store building more than 7 m.	Characteristics compared with the old system • Head office leases the stores. • Head office selects the location and establishes the stores for the franchisees. • Start-up costs for the franchisee are lower, and head office now borrows money from banks for the franchisees. • Franchisee targets are the younger generation. • Independence of the employees in the head office is also encouraged.
Total start-up costs: 4.5 million baht • Franchisee invests 3 million baht, allocated as follows: 1.2 million baht for opening inventory costs; 0.9 million baht for interior finishing; 0.7 million baht as compensation for potential damages; and 0.2 million baht for management fees. • Head office invests 1.5 million baht.	Total start-up costs: 4.5 million baht • Franchisee invests 1.5 million baht, allotted as follows: 1 million baht for security deposit; 0.35 million baht for franchise fees; 0.1 million baht for store transfer fees; and 0.05 million baht for other fees. • Head office invests 3 million baht.
Profit division ratio • Franchisee: 65% of gross profit • Head office: 35% of gross profit	Profit division ratio • Initial income of each franchisee: 0.02 million baht per month. • Increases according to any rise in the gross profit.

Former Franchise System (Type A)	New Franchise System (Type B)
New store openings • Franchisees prepare store openings themselves, including everything from finding a proper location to interior finishing, in cooperation with the head office. Store furniture and equipment are leased by the head office (franchisees are responsible for any repair expenses).	New store openings • The head office establishes new stores and manages them for more than six months until sales reach a fixed amount and then they are transfered to franchisees. In addition, corporate stores are sometimes converted to franchise chain stores.
Inventory • Each franchisee invests 1–1.2 million baht.	Inventory • The head office is responsible for inventory investment and management.

SOURCE: Suriya et al. (1997, 76–81, 214–15); Sompratthana et al. (2000, 102–17); Phirawut (2004, 61–63, 75–76); Thot (2005, 48–51, 135–37).

This table demonstrates that the company previously imposed some relatively tough requirements when recruiting franchisees (Type A). For example, franchisee applicants had to own their store or hold a right for a long-term lease (at least eight years or more), and the said-store had to have a certain floor space (100 sq m) as well as an appropriate location (near a heavily trafficked area). In addition, franchisees had to put up 3 million baht in start up costs for opening the store, and received only 65 percent of the gross profit, and the remaining 35 percent went to the head office to cover various fees, including a "loyalty" fee. If we use Japan as a point of comparison, a franchisee in Japan pays the equivalent of about 1 million baht for starting up a new store (as of April 2008, based on 7-Eleven, Japan's website). Taking into account the difference in the income categories between both countries (Japan is a high income economy, while Thailand is a lower middle income economy), the costs of starting a 7-Eleven franchise store in Thailand are substantially higher compared to Japan. To cover the excessively heavy start-up costs for opening a store, franchisee applicants in Thailand needed to borrow money from a bank, but they tended to have such a low personal credit rating that they faced difficulties when requesting bank loans (Sompratthana et al. 2000, 112). When banks became reluctant to lend money, most notably during the financial and currency crisis, franchisee applicants had an even harder time raising the money they needed. As a result, the head office appears to have turned franchise stores that were facing financial difficulties into corporate stores.[51]

C. P. Seven Eleven subsequently decided to establish new requirements for opening franchise stores, sometime in 2004 (based on information from the company's annual reports) in which the head office was now in charge of all the start-up procedures for new store openings on behalf of franchisees, from the selection of store locations to the construction of the store buildings (Type B). It would then manage the new stores for more than six months until sales reached a certain level before leasing them to the franchisees (see table 4.10).[52] Under this new Type B system, franchisees only have to invest 1.5 million baht of the 4.5 million baht required to open a franchise store, while the head office provides the remaining 3 million baht. The head office is also responsible for inventory investment and management. This new system enables franchisees to reduce the amount of investment needed at the time of a store opening. In addition, the head office takes charge of bank loan details on behalf of the franchisees, in return for a deposit of 1 million baht, which franchisees are required to make.

The backing of C. P. Seven Eleven Company allows franchisees with low financial credit ratings to borrow money from banks. The head office opens and manages the new stores for more than six months until they get off the ground, and then converts them into franchise stores. With this new system, the company can recruit new franchisees among the younger generation, who are willing to manage a convenience store but have neither property nor funds to do so. According to the company website, Siam FamilyMart Company introduced a very similar system as well.[53] C. P. Seven Eleven has also adopted a policy to give ambitious employees the chance to run their own store by transferring to them the management of existing corporate stores.

In this way, C. P. Seven Eleven currently raised the proportion of franchise stores, mainly Type B ones, in which the head office leases the stores to franchisees. However, some problems associated with the new franchise system cannot be overlooked. One such problem is that, in the case of a Type B franchise store, the head office cannot help investing more money than in a Type A franchise store, though less than in the case of a corporate store. One of the merits of the franchise system is that the head office can reduce managerial resources by utilizing certain external resources. Taking this into consideration, the expansion of chain operations mainly in the form of Type B franchise stores would increase the investment burden of the head office, that is, C. P. Seven Eleven, and could reduce the merit of the franchise system by half. More problematic is that in the case of Type B franchise stores, the owners or franchisees have only limited authority to manage the stores, while the head office conducts most of the business activities, ranging from the opening of new stores to construction and fund-raising and finally to inventory investment.

Type B franchise stores do not have sufficient incentive mechanisms, inherent in other franchise systems, by which franchisees are expected to work harder than head office employees to increase business performance.

In addition, the company was having difficulties, as of 2007, finding well-qualified persons even as "salaried storekeepers" of Type B franchise stores. 7-Eleven in Thailand is, therefore, at a critical turning point, as to whether it will maintain the chain system mainly in the form of corporate stores (and thereby again realize the merits of corporate stores that can implement the policies of the head office down to the lowest level of management) or whether it will focus its efforts on increasing the weight of Type B franchise stores (or Type C stores, which are similar to Type B stores but have a longer term contract).[54] In short, it remains unclear whether the company will continue to actively open new stores, either in the form of franchise stores or corporate stores.[55]

STORE CHARACTERISTICS[56]

As of the end of 2006, Thailand had a total of 3,784 7-Eleven stores, which includes both franchise and corporate stores. This singular fact raises the same kinds of questions as were raised in the case of hypermarkets discussed earlier. That is, in what ways does the company manage the physical distribution and logistics for its rapidly expanding chain stores? What business connections does the company have with suppliers, given its enormous buying power?

From around 2003, C. P. Seven Eleven Company started to operate four distribution centers and implemented almost the same distribution system as hypermarkets. The four distribution centers included a central distribution center (mainly for processed foods and daily necessities) located in Bang Bua Thong, Nonthaburi Province, in the northwest suburbs of Bangkok; a distribution center dedicated exclusively to perishable foods located next to the central distribution center; a distribution center dedicated exclusively to printed matters in Chokchai Ruammit, Bangkok; and another distribution center dedicated exclusively to perishable foods located in Khon Kaen Province, northeastern Thailand.[57] It is reported that the establishment of the central distribution center, in particular the expansion of its facilities several times over, combined with its IT system contributed to the reduction of store inventories by half. As of 2007, the four distribution centers were enough for the company to deliver goods to its chain stores, according to C. P. Seven Eleven.[58] However, in calculating the SG&A cost ratio and inventory turnover, based on the company's financial statements, the SG&A cost ratio deteriorated from 20.6 percent in 1995 to 25.1 percent in 2006 and inventory turnover only slightly improved from 12.8 to 13.1 times during the same time period. Although these business indices do not directly demonstrate the efficiency of physical distribution, there is no denying that C. P. Seven Eleven's expansion of chain stores throughout the country is likely causing increased difficulties in physical distribution and logistics.[59]

Yet, even if 7-Eleven's distribution system was inefficient, its chain store expansion would certainly increase its bargaining power over suppliers. If we look at the use rate of the 7-Eleven distribution centers, that is the percentage of total goods (in terms of money) that suppliers deliver to the 7-Eleven's distribution centers as opposed to each store, it appears that the distribution centers' net working rate has been steadily increasing from 64 percent in 2000, to 78 percent in 2001, to 87 percent in 2002, and as high as 90 percent as of the end of June 2003. With the exception of bread and some other perishable items,[60] most goods are first delivered to 7-Eleven's distribution centers, where they are then subdivided to be delivered to each store. C. P. Seven Eleven, in the same way as hypermarkets, has suppliers pay various fees, such as distribution center fees, entrance fees, rebates, and sales promotion expenses. Because of 7-Eleven's huge selling power, suppliers have no other choice but to meet these demands. In fact, suppliers came to double the frequency of their deliveries in accordance with the "low sales volume of a wide variety of goods" characteristic of convenience stores. This is because a convenience store has a very small floor space of 100 sq m and with scarcely any space for stock. Nevertheless, a convenience store makes efforts to display as many kinds of goods as possible (approximately 2,500 items). Therefore, the volume of each item on the shelf of a store is very small. This is why frequent deliveries are critical to convenience stores.

Keen competition is taking place even among major consumer goods manufacturers to be selected as an "exclusive brand" for 7-Eleven.[61] Some products are excluded from the 7-Eleven's display racks because the manufacturers refused to pay the entrance fee. Small- and medium-sized manufacturers with relatively weak brand power have to accept, quite submissively, the various demands from C. P. Seven Eleven, since the success of their business depends on whether they can trade with 7-Eleven, and therefore benefit from its large sales network throughout the country.

However, compared with 7-Eleven in Japan, which has built an innovative system where convenience stores play a leading role by involving suppliers, e.g., wholesalers and manufacturers (Yahagi 1994), the impact of 7-Eleven upon the retail and distribution industry in Thailand is quite different in two respects.[62] One of the differences is that Thailand's 7-Eleven head office deals directly with consumer goods manufacturers and has them deliver their products in bulk to 7-Eleven distribution centers (with a few exceptions). The head office then delivers goods from the distribution centers to each store.[63] As for Japan's 7-Eleven distribution system, it needed to be drastically changed and did so by concentrating physical distribution affairs into the hands of a few representative wholesalers and entrusting them with the delivery to each store. 7-Eleven in Thailand, on the other hand, does not ask its existing suppliers to drastically change their commercial practices and business connections. In other words, Thailand's 7-Eleven has brought a new distribution channel into the country by having almost directly nothing to do with the country's existing intermediate distribution and physical distribution systems.

Another difference between Japan and Thailand 7-Eleven stores has to do with the assortment of goods for sales. Like Japan, 7-Eleven in Thailand sells 2,000–2,500 items (SKUs) in each store, with a floor space of around 100 square meters. However, it is decisively different from Japan in that the proportion of ready-to-eat foods (e.g., fast foods) to the total sales of each store is very low.[64] This difference is caused by the food culture and purchasing behavior specific to Thailand. For example, people in Thailand generally prefer eating out, at food wagons, for example, and scarcely regard convenience stores as the destinations to buy ready-to-eat foods for lunch or dinner.[65] This is why Thailand's 7-Eleven delivers goods from the distribution centers to its chain stores only once a day, at midnight to avoid daytime high temperatures and traffic congestion.[66] This suggests that convenience stores in Thailand give more priority to the convenience of the head office rather than to that of their customers, which is also different from convenience stores in Japan. Convenience store chains in Japan, by contrast, attach greater importance to ready-to-eat foods because their gross profit rate is high and these are strategic goods that allow a convenience store chain to differentiate itself from the competition. Thus the proportion of ready-to-eat foods to the total sales of each store is high. Considering the high, inherent risk of spoilage to ready-to-eat foods, Japanese convenience store companies "postpone" the production and distribution activities more than they generally would, in order to bring those activities as close as possible to the actual demand in terms of time and place. Although this forces suppliers to shorten their lead-time and deliver goods frequently (three times a day), which causes managerial difficulties, suppliers overcame these difficulties through strategic alliances with convenience store chains (Yahagi 1994).

In this way, the comparison between convenience stores in Japan and Thailand makes the characteristics of convenience stores in Thailand clearer. The small proportion of ready-to-eat foods in Thailand's 7-Eleven chain means that the company does not necessarily have to build close business connections with suppliers, in contrast to convenience store chains in Japan. In short, it can be said that Thailand still lacks the preconditions for the construction of a "convenience store *system*" in the sense Yahagi (1994) discussed.

NOT A REVOLUTION . . . YET

The characteristics of new retail formats differ from that of traditional formats in several ways, including, as we have seen, through their direct dealings with manufacturers, increased bargaining power due to expanding chain operations, and construction of efficient physical distribution and logistics systems, which involve heavy investment in information technology systems to support these systems. Given these characteristics, new retail formats strive to build efficient supply chains, starting from accurately recording sales data at each store. Based on this system, new retail format companies adopted a new commercial practice of requesting suppliers to pay various fees. For this reason, it is generally said that the growth of new retail formats has fundamentally impacted traditional retailers and wholesalers, as well as manufacturers.

However, even the new retail formats in Thailand that seem to prosper are in reality experiencing hindrance to their growth as well as managerial problems. Hypermarkets and cash-and-carry stores, which are the biggest players at present in Thailand's retail and distribution industry, have realized increases in sales only by multiplying the number of stores, but there is now less and less room to open new stores. This is why hypermarkets and cash-and-carry companies have made efforts to change their strategies for opening new stores based on active expansion into the provinces and the development of small- and medium-sized stores. This change in strategy, however, has increased the cost of physical distribution and caused managerial problems in connection with the control and operation of various types of stores. Due to the structural characteristics of Thailand's consumer market and the slow rate of motorization, hypermarkets have not sufficiently incorporated provincial consumer markets into their trading areas.

Supermarkets that sell mainly food have made less progress than other new retail formats. Tops Supermarket, run by the Central Group, is the only national chain in the supermarket business in Thailand, and is suffering managerial problems such as low profitability and high operating costs. Some local chains are doing relatively well, but they adopt a kind of niche market strategy by targeting specific types of customers, such as the upper-class and foreign residents, and, as a result, expand their chain stores at a slow pace. Moreover, supermarkets must compete with wet markets (*talat*) in the sale of perishable foods, as well as with hypermarkets in the sale of processed foods and daily necessities. To date, supermarkets have not yet succeeded in establishing a competitive advantage in Thailand's retail industry.

Convenience stores have been showing remarkable growth rates as a new retail format, but differ greatly in scale among the various convenience store companies. Even CP Group's 7-Eleven, the top chain in the convenience store industry, has various problems in comparison with Japan's 7-Eleven. For example, Thailand's 7-Eleven has such a high percentage of corporate stores and a low percentage of franchise stores that the head office must bear large managerial expenses. Although Thailand's 7-Eleven has recently adopted another kind of franchise system, the new system is inferior to the original franchise one in such respects as the managerial resources saved by the head office and the effect of the incentive mechanisms on franchise stores. In addition, the proportion of strategic goods, like ready-to-eat foods, is so low that Thailand's 7-Eleven has not yet reached a stage in which it can build as strong business connections with suppliers as in Japan. In short, convenience stores in Thailand, at the present time, compared with those in Japan, have not yet sufficiently established themselves as an important retail format and have not had as big an impact on the retail and distribution industry as was initially expected.

New retail formats in present-day Thailand have not brought about as revolutionary a change to the distribution system as local newspapers and current reports tend to highlight. Or, perhaps, the distribution revolution was cut short before it could fully develop. The next chapter discusses the vertical relations within the distribution system, that is, the business connections between consumer goods manufacturers and wholesale and retail distributors.

5

THE REORGANIZATION OF MARKETING CHANNELS AND THE ROLE OF WHOLESALERS

POINTS AT ISSUE

In order to determine what points need further consideration, let us briefly summarize the results of the previous chapters' analyses. First, modern retail businesses, especially new retail formats, rapidly grew under the post-crisis depression in the late 1990s and have become the main players in Thailand's retail and distribution industry. However, their growth rate has slowed since recovery from the crisis. Accordingly, hypermarket companies, for example, have had to reconsider their strategies for opening new stores, notably by expanding into the provinces and developing small- and medium-sized stores. Supermarkets have not yet succeeded in establishing advantageous positions in their competition with other retail formats, including traditional wet markets. Even convenience stores, which show a remarkably high growth rate, have not reached a sufficient business growth level in such respects as the maturity of their franchise chain system and their involvement with suppliers, at least as compared with convenience stores in Japan. The point we need to address here is whether these new retail formats have actually changed the traditional distribution system in Thailand, at the present time, in such a "revolutionary" manner as emphasized by earlier research and current reports.

Second, while traditional retailers, including small-scale grocery stores (*cho huai*), have been affected by the rise of new retail formats, they remain integral to the retail industry. By examining some individual cases, it becomes clear that the business expansion of new retail formats has had a significant impact on small- and medium-sized traditional distributors, but what kind of impact and the extent to which it may have hurt traditional retail formats remains unexamined.

Third, some traditional distributors in provincial cities have grown to become leaders in their respective localities by introducing the systems and know-how of new retail formats into their own businesses. Traditional wholesalers (*yi pua*) have played an important role at the provincial level for a long time. In order to approach the vertical relations in the distribution system, that is, the business connections between consumer goods manufacturers and distributors, we should, therefore, pay more attention to the relationship between manufacturers and traditional wholesalers and small-scale retailers as well as to the relationship between manufacturers and large-scale retailers. This is a point that most earlier studies, for the most part, have overlooked.

Fourth, Thailand's consumer market has been experiencing high economic growth especially since the end of the 1980s, but it also faces wide geographic and income disparities, representing, what the author refers to as, a "mosaic structure." This is important as contextual background to the three points already mentioned, though it has been overlooked by earlier analyses of Thailand's consumer market, which tend to overestimate the weight of the urban middle class. Reconsidering Thailand's consumer market from the viewpoint of convenience goods (daily foods and necessities, in particular), it becomes clear that rural areas and the lower classes are equally important consumer markets.

Finally, the scope covered by chain stores associated with new retail formats is still limited, which contributes to the coexistence of both traditional and modern retailers and distribution channels. The opening of small-sized stores by these new retail formats has been in a few provincial cities only, and it is still unknown to what extent the chains will geographically expand in the future.

Given the above, this chapter aims to describe the entire structure of traditional retail and wholesale industries in Thailand, based primarily on government statistics. It then considers the vertical relationships within the distribution system, that is, the business connections between manufacturers and distributors. Although business connections can be approached in many different ways, this chapter analyzes business connections between manufacturers and traditional distributors by focusing on the marketing channel strategies of manufacturers. The reason for this is that it enables us to consider vertical relationships within both the traditional and modern retail and distribution industry.

Specific points that will be addressed are as follows: (i) the commercial practices introduced into Thailand by new retail formats and their influence on manufacturers; (ii) the ways in which manufacturers have adapted their marketing channels when trading with both modern retailers (new retail formats) and traditional distributors (small-sized retailers and wholesalers); (iii) the differences in marketing channel policies among manufacturers; and (iv) how various manufacturers are adapting to a "mosaic structure" consumer market.

IS THE TRADITIONAL DISTRIBUTION INDUSTRY REALLY DECLINING?

In order to provide an overview of the entire structure of Thailand's traditional distribution industry, it may be helpful to compare it with the case of Japan. Table 5.1 shows the number of retailers and wholesalers in Thailand by firm size. As shown in the table, the percentage of small-scale retail stores (1–4 employees) to the total number of retailers was as high as 90.1 percent in 1987, and rose even higher to 95.5 percent in 2002. Even compared with Japan, which is characterized by small retail businesses, the prevalence of small-scale stores in Thailand is remarkable.[1] Regarding the wholesale industry as well, the percentage of small-scale wholesale stores (1–4 employees) in Thailand was 51.7 percent in 1987 and 67.3 percent in 2002. In Japan, it was 47.1 percent in 1988 and 45.7 percent in 2002, according to official statistics,[2] thus showing an even clearer tendency in Thailand toward small businesses.

While this data shows the prevalence of small-scale stores in Thailand, it cannot fully demonstrate whether the number of retailers and wholesalers is excessive or to what extent multistage distribution is present in Thailand. For example, compared to the number of retailers in Thailand as of 2002 (approx. 0.6 million), there were about 1.3 million retail stores in Japan, roughly twice as much in Thailand. Since this ratio corresponds almost exactly to the population ratio between the two countries, it appears that the number of retail stores in Thailand is almost at the same level as in Japan. However, it is difficult to accurately compare the wholesale industry between the two countries, because Thailand's commercial census is mainly intended for consumer goods, while Japan's commercial census focuses equally on both consumer goods and capital goods. It is also difficult to judge whether Thailand's distribution system is characterized by "multistage distribution" to the same extent as Japan because the wholesale-retail trade ratio cannot be calculated due to a lack of data on the total sales of the wholesale industry in Thailand. In short, we can only conclude that the Thai and Japanese distribution systems are characterized by similar small-size retail and wholesale businesses, and an extensive number of retail stores.

TABLE 5.1 Number of retailers and wholesalers in Thailand by firm size

	Number of employees						
	Total (%)	1–4 (%)	5–9 (%)	10–19 (%)	20–49 (%)	50–99 (%)	≧100 (%)
Retailers							
1987 (total)	360,030	324,419	28,963	4,369	1,635	442	204
	(100.0)	(90.1)	(8.0)	(1.2)	(0.5)	(0.1)	(0.1)
1996 (municipal areas)	259,310	234,106	17,799	5,067	1,623	434	281
	(100.0)	(90.3)	(6.9)	(2.0)	(0.6)	(0.2)	(0.1)
2002 (total)	598,087	571,431	18,891	5,270	1,747	384	339
	(100.0)	(95.5)	(3.2)	(0.9)	(0.3)	(0.1)	(0.1)
(municipal areas)	288,877	267,822	14,966	4,131	1,371	295	267
	(100.0)	(92.7)	(5.2)	(1.4)	(0.5)	(0.1)	(0.1)
(non-municipal areas)	309,210	303,609	3,925	1,139	376	89	72
	(100.0)	(98.2)	(1.3)	(0.4)	(0.1)	(0.0)	(0.0)
Wholesalers							
1987 (total)	16,740	8,651	4,822	2,075	824	215	153
	(100.0)	(51.7)	(28.8)	(12.4)	(4.9)	(1.3)	(0.9)
1996 (municipal areas)	27,116	14,873	6,923	3,114	1,472	439	295
	(100.0)	(54.8)	(25.5)	(11.5)	(5.4)	(1.6)	(1.1)
2002 (total)	49,817	33,528	9,170	4,080	2,170	569	299
	(100.0)	(67.3)	(18.4)	(8.2)	(4.4)	(1.1)	(0.6)
(municipal areas)	33,428	20,583	7,077	3,250	1,801	465	251
	(100.0)	(61.6)	(21.2)	(9.7)	(5.4)	(1.4)	(0.8)
(non-municipal areas)	16,389	12,945	2,093	830	369	104	48
	(100.0)	(79.0)	(12.8)	(5.1)	(2.3)	(0.6)	(0.3)
	Number of employees						
	Total (%)	1–5 (%)	6–10 (%)	11–20 (%)	21–50 (%)	51–100 (%)	≧101 (%)
Retailers							
2007 (total)	772,511	744,478	17,654	6,488	2,394	788	709
	(100.0)	(96.4)	(2.3)	(0.8)	(0.3)	(0.1)	(0.1)
(municipal areas)	376,239	354,729	14,061	5,002	1,694	382	371
	(100.0)	(94.3)	(3.7)	(1.3)	(0.5)	(0.1)	(0.1)

(non-municipal areas)	396,272	389,749	3,593	1,486	700	406	338
	(100.0)	(98.4)	(0.9)	(0.4)	(0.2)	(0.1)	(0.1)
Wholesalers							
2007 (total)	74,578	55,285	9,830	4,978	3,104	859	522
	(100.0)	(74.1)	(13.2)	(6.7)	(4.2)	(1.2)	(0.7)
(municipal areas)	43,135	28,454	7,248	3,849	2,478	674	432
	(100.0)	(66.0)	(16.8)	(8.9)	(5.7)	(1.6)	(1.0)
(non-municipal areas)	31,443	26,831	2,582	1,129	626	185	90
	(100.0)	(85.3)	(8.2)	(3.6)	(2.0)	(0.6)	(0.3)

SOURCE: National Statistical Office, Business Trade and Services Census for 1987 and 2002 data; National Statistical Office, Industrial Census for 1996 and 2007 data.

NOTE: "Municipal areas" as of 1996 included sanitary districts; as of 1999 sanitary districts were abolished and changed to municipalities. Retail data for 2002 and 2007 excludes automobile and motorcycle businesses and durable consumer goods repair businesses. Wholesale data for 2002 and 2007 excludes automobile and motorcycle businesses. In 2002, twenty-five retail businesses and one wholesale business did not participate in the NSO census. Retail data for every year excludes tenants of shopping centers and wet markets.

Now that such characteristics have been underlined, let's discuss to what extent the Thai retail and wholesale industries have actually been affected by the rise of new retail formats. Small-scale retail and wholesale stores in Thailand have generally been estimated to suffer the most from the introduction of new retail formats. Referring to table 5.1 again, let's look at the number of small-scale retail and wholesale establishments. Contrary to general belief, it appears that both small-scale retail and wholesale stores (1–4 employees) increased in number from 1987 to 1996 (urban areas only) and then again in 2002. During this period, the general number of stores increased, while the percentage increase of small-scale stores was even higher. However, there is a problem in statistical continuity between Thailand's 1987 and 2002 commercial censuses.[3] As shown in the table, the total number of retail stores country-wide was about 360,000 in 1987, which sharply increased to nearly 600,000 in 2002, according to the census.[4] During the same period of time, the number of wholesale stores also drastically increased from approximately 17,000 to 50,000, that is, almost three times as many as before. Such a remarkable change in the total number of stores is so unnatural that we should be careful in comparing statistical figures between these two points in time.[5] However, even if we ignore the 1987 figures for now, based on their questionable reliability in terms of statistical continuity, it appears that the numbers of both retail and wholesale stores have shown a tendency to consistently increase up until the latest 2007 industrial census.

In addition to government statistics, various organizations and institutes in Thailand have each been estimating the change in the number of retailers, especially small-scale grocery stores (*cho huai*) over time. For example, the Opposition to Multinational Business Union, which opposes the rapid development of foreign retailing businesses in Thailand, argues that the rise of foreign retailers has caused the number of local small-scale grocery stores to sharply decrease from more than 400,000 down to less than 200,000 in 2006 (*TNSK*, September 17, 2006). At a panel discussion held on October 16, 2006, sponsored by the Law Faculty of Chulalongkorn University, researchers presented information showing the difficulties faced by traditional grocery stores. For example, it was reported that 43,706 small-scale retail stores disappeared between 2001 and 2002, which corresponds to 15 percent of about 300,000 stores throughout the country (*The Nation*, October 17, 2006). According to a survey by AC Nielsen, the world's leading marketing research firm, the number of small-scale grocery stores in Thailand was about 280,000 to 300,000 as of 2006, 5 to 15 percent of which closed down every year (*TNSK*, November 2, 2006).[6] By contrast, the Thai Retailers Association objects to the view that the number of small-scale grocery stores in Thailand has been decreasing drastically of late, saying that it is, in fact, increasing.[7] Generally, though, an overwhelming majority agrees that the number of small-scale retailers in Thailand has dropped, and this has become the commonly accepted view.

Between the author's analysis based on governmental statistics and the common view mentioned above, not only is there an important gap in the number of retail stores in Thailand, but even the conclusion as to whether the number of stores has been decreasing or not differs. Although it is difficult to conclude which of the two views is correct based on currently available data, we can, at least, say that the analyses based on government statistics never supports the view that there has been a sharp decrease in the number of retail stores in Thailand. On the other hand, government statistics lack reliable data regarding the sales of retail and wholesale industries. As for industrial associations, they seldom release business performance data, such as the total sales of the industry.[8] Due to this lack of data, some researchers have, for example, estimated the percentage of new retail formats' sales to the total retail sales of the whole country to be approximately 60–70 percent,[9] but exact figures are unknown.

According to the author's estimates, the sales revenue of new retail formats has been steadily increasing as has the total sales revenue of Thailand's retail industry, but the number of new formats as a percentage of the country's entire retail trade has not always increased as sharply (see chap. 3, tables 3.3, 3.4). However, it is also true that a considerable portion of retail sales in Thailand comes from new retail formats. In other words, even when taking into consideration that the total sales volume in the retail industry is increasing, traditional retailers' share has been decreasing to some extent.

Therefore, we can never say that small-scale grocery stores have not been hurt by the rise of new retail formats. As Somchai Phonrattanajaroen, president of the Thai Wholesale and Retail Association, argues, small-scale grocery stores located in the vicinity of new retail format stores would certainly face serious difficulties.[10] In short, any hurt inflicted on the traditional retail and distribution industry by new retail formats is, at present, concentrated locally,[11] as evidence by the fact that a significant number of retailers and wholesalers have had no other choice but to reduce or close their businesses.

On the other hand, however, some small- and medium-scale wholesalers and retailers are making use of general mass merchandisers as a kind of cash-and-carry wholesaler, while others have barely felt any repercussions from the new retail formats. It appears that some provincial wholesalers have succeeded in transforming themselves into a new type of distributor, by converting the advance of new retail formats into a business opportunity. The expansion of general mass merchandiser chains and new developments among provincial wholesalers have given small-scale retailers more channels to buy goods, which could make it easier to start a new business. Although government statistics only provide the net number of stores, it can be interpreted from the gross number of stores that while many stores did close down, enough stores opened to largely offset the loss. Thus, it seems that the impact of new retail formats varies. Here again, although the rapid growth of new retail formats and its negative impact upon the traditional retail and distribution industry are undeniable, the author wishes to point out the tendency to overestimate the effects of the rise of new retail formats.

The retail and wholesale industry is the second largest industry in Thailand's national economy in terms of its constituent ratio of GDP and its constituent ratio of the employed population.[12] In addition, as mentioned earlier, the number of small-scale retail and wholesale stores has been overwhelmingly higher than larger-scale stores. For this reason, the retail and distribution question has naturally become a significant political issue in Thailand, and one that has spread to consumer goods manufacturers, notably processed foods and daily necessities suppliers. This is because the decline of small- and medium-scale retailers and wholesalers can bring instability to traditional marketing channels led by major manufacturers. The increased buying power of the new retail formats in accordance with their business expansion can cause manufacturers/suppliers to fall into a relatively disadvantaged position. Thus, the present changes in the Thai distribution industry can lead to structural changes, not only at the industry level but also throughout the entire distribution system.

THE TRANSACTION RELATIONSHIP BETWEEN MANUFACTURERS AND NEW RETAIL FORMATS

NEW COMMERCIAL PRACTICES

Modern retail businesses, especially new retail formats, can become an important marketing channel for consumer goods manufacturers in two respects. One is that, with the development of national chain stores, new retail formats have achieved considerable sales volume and a widespread sales network. The expansion of new retail format chains means the extension of channels for manufacturers' products, which ought to be favorably received by the manufacturers. Major consumer goods manufacturers actually regard new retail formats' chains as important business partners.[13] In addition, new retail formats collect sales data through a point-of-sales (POS) system, which is very important for manufacturers in order to build an efficient supply chain and raise profitability. Putting aside the question of what extent these two respects are actually working for consumer goods manufacturers, for the present, it is certain that the new retail format chains have become principal channels for them.

As a result, each manufacturer agrees to direct transactions, as requested by new retail format companies, rather than using traditional wholesalers, which are generally small-scale and cannot accommodate the larger production orders of the new retail formats, such as hypermarkets in particular.[14] Each manufacturer establishes a department that focuses exclusively on trade with new retail formats. This department is separate from the department in charge of trade with traditional retailers.

Many manufacturers have accepted new commercial practices introduced by new retail formats, even though they have not always been in favor of these new practices. Most major manufacturers generally regard the new practices as ordinary commercial practices,[15] but small- and medium-scale manufacturers, having less bargaining power, criticize these practices, accusing major retailers of abusing their dominant bargaining position (for further details, see chap. 6). These new commercial practices include, for example, entrance fees, rebates, advertising expenses, sales promotion expenses, and distribution center fees. Requests to pay for planogram (shelving allocation) fees and the development of private label goods are also included in these practices.[16]

Among these new practices, entrance fees are what a large-scale retailer requests a manufacturer to pay when the manufacturer introduces a new good into the retail marketplace. Retailers charge this fee not only on new products, but also on any previous products with a change in size or volume, justifying the fee by the cost involved in modifying their programs (*TNSK*, July 20, 2006). Furthermore, an entrance fee is charged at each store, so that the fee proportionally rises as new retail formats expand their chains (*TNSK*, September 1, 2006).

Rebate, in this study, refers to a partial reduction, return, or refund on products already sold that is paid by a manufacturer to a distributor (retailer or wholesaler), who has met previously fixed conditions in terms of the volume of product sales. Although it is a type of sales promotion that manufacturers use primarily as an incentive to sell their products, distributors often convert it into a source for price discounts. Even though distributors sell goods at discounted prices (in extreme cases, below cost) to attract their customers, distributors can compensate for the loss with rebates provided by manufacturers. Manufacturers are not in favor of this practice, however, because a rebate is supposed to be used as an incentive to sell manufacturers' products. Nevertheless, distributors abuse rebates, using them as a source for price discounts, which, in turn, causes manufacturers to earn less profit. Another negative effect of rebates is that excessive discounts hurt the manufacturers' brand images. This negative effect on manufacturers becomes more serious as large-scale retailers increase their bargaining power and request manufacturers to raise the price of rebates. In extreme cases, rebates can cause a distributor to sell below cost. Many manufacturers have criticized the practice of large-scale retailers raising the price of rebates (*KTTK-RW*, September 24, 2002). In the case of rising oil prices, for instance, large-scale retailers have requested manufacturers to increase rebates in order to compensate for the rise of operating costs (*PRCT-TK*, June 29, 2006), and have used rebates to shift the cost burden onto manufacturers. This is another case in which large-scale retailers abuse rebates to compensate for losses due to the rise in oil prices.

Advertising expenses are another burden that large-scale retailers demand manufacturers to bear, on the grounds that retailers actually share the expenses that manufacturers should primarily bear. It is critical for small- and medium-sized manufacturers, in particular, to have dealings with the large-scale retailers expanding throughout the country and to be entitled to display their products at chain stores.[17] Even unknown brands can appeal to consumers without advertising, if these brands are sold at stores highly trusted by consumers.

Sales promotion expenses are also a burden that large-scale retailers demand manufacturers to bear under a similar logic. For example, C.P. Seven Eleven Co., Ltd. spends 1.5 percent of its sales revenue on sales promotion expenses, bearing 0.7 percent itself, while suppliers bear the remaining 0.8 percent (Sompratthana et al. 2000, 81). The collection of a distribution center fee is also based on similar reasoning, such that manufacturers can save some costs on delivery to each store by delivering their products in bulk to the distribution center from which large-scale retailers deliver the goods to their chain stores.

These commercial practices, with the exception of rebates, can be regarded as a kind of corporate strategy, wherein new retail formats enlarge their profit-making domain by internalizing intermediate distribution functions. New retail format companies actually consider all these collection fees to be non-operating income, as a way to realize increases in ordinary profit. If the use of new retail format channels enabled manufacturers to enlarge the market for their products and increase their sales, manufacturers would be willing to accept these commercial practices. Moreover, the development of private label goods and planograms (shelving allocations) could potentially create a collaborative relationship between manufacturers and retailers, or the so-called "producer-retailer alliance." However, it could also possibly create diverse interests between retailers and manufacturers. In this respect, these two practices—the development of private label goods and planograms—are different from the commercial practices described above, and, therefore, are discussed in greater detail in the section below.

THE PRODUCER-RETAILER ALLIANCE

New retail formats, especially hypermarket companies emphasizing sales discounts, have been making efforts to develop private label goods.[18] Private label goods are those manufactured or provided by a manufacturer for offer under a large-scale retailer's brand. The retailer, with its immense selling power, plans and develops goods jointly with the manufacturer. In general, private label goods are daily necessities goods, with no decisive quality difference between brands. Consequently, no manufacturer has more brand power than another, and consumers do not necessarily stay with a specific brand. A key selling point of private labels is that their price is usually lower than manufacturers' brands (national brands). For example, Tesco Lotus's private label goods (Tesco and Khum Kha), in the category of daily foods and necessities, have prices set lower than manufacturers' brand goods by 10 to 15 percent and 20 to 30 percent, respectively (*TNSK*, September 10, 2006). The ability to set low prices comes from the fact that large-scale retailers' chains are well known and widely trusted by consumers, thus eliminating the need to spend a lot on advertising for private label goods. It also comes from the fact that large orders enable the company to offer the goods at a lower price. Unlike manufacturers' brand goods, private label goods are exempt from entrance and planogram fees (ibid.). Private label goods are also useful for manufacturers because purchasing contracts for a fixed number of products enable them to have a stable income stream.

According to a Thai-language business magazine, the three major hypermarket chains, Tesco Lotus, Big C, and Carrefour, were providing the following private label goods: Tesco (1,000 items) and Khum Kha (300 items), Leader Price (1,200 items), Carrefour and Number One (700 items in total), as of July 2005 (Sombun 2005a, 64–65). Private label goods characterized by sales discounts remained popular during the consumption slump of 2006 to 2009 caused by the rise in oil prices and political turmoil, so much so that the number of items and categories have actually increased. The sales percentage of private label goods to each chain's total sales amounts to approximately 10 percent for Tesco Lotus (700 categories and 2,200 items) (*TNSK*, May 28, 2006), 5–10 percent for Big C (1,600 items) (*PRCT-TK*, September 21, 2006), and about 10 percent for Carrefour (3,000 items) (*TNSK*, May 1, 2008).[19]

Tesco Lotus has also established a research and development center for private label goods attached to its main store (Sukhaphiban branch) and regularly conducts consumer research (e.g., customers' opinions on private label goods). The company is also striving to implement into the Thai market the advanced methods, standards, and know-how of the UK head office, which has a great deal of experience in developing private label goods. To do so, Tesco Lotus has established a product evaluation center in Bang Kapi, a Bangkok suburb. (*The Nation*, January 26, 2007).

In this way, hypermarket companies have been putting great efforts into private label development. Major manufacturers, in some cases, agree to manufacture private label goods for large-scale retailers (*PRCT-TK*, September 21, 2006), while small- and medium-sized manufacturers produce private label goods in other cases (*TNSK*, May 1, 2008). Irrelevant of the manufacturer's size, the relationship between retailers who order private label goods and manufacturers who accept these orders is not always reciprocal. For example, retailers sometimes return private label goods that they ordered against manufacturers' wishes, thus abusing their dominant position (*TNSK*, September 10, 2006).[20] In some other cases, large-scale retailers use labels and packaging for their private label goods that imitate big-name brands, and consequently cause harm to the manufacturers.[21] For manufacturers who do not produce private label goods, private label goods compete with their own products. Although the percentage of private label goods in Thailand still remains relatively low, there is a possibility that in the future such goods will lead to a conflict between manufacturers and retailers.

Planograms (shelving allocation) are another commercial practice that affects the relationship between retailers and manufacturers. A planogram is, in short, a diagram showing what goods should be displayed on store shelves and how they should be displayed. Planograms, thus, greatly influence the sales performance of a store. That is why suppliers (manufacturers) ask retailers to secure the largest and best position possible for their products and also why, conversely, retailers use planograms as a bargaining tool with manufacturers. For example, hypermarket companies might decide that their planogram fees should be increased, or decreased, according to the strength, or weakness, of products' brands, and the advantages and disadvantages of that position on their shelves (*PRCT-TK*, February 1, 2007). As a result, manufacturers of weak brand products have no other choice but to accept disadvantageous positions on store shelves (*PRCT-TK*, August 21, 2006). An even more severe problem for manufacturers that are in a disadvantageous position is that hypermarket companies basically only stock goods from the top three selling brands in each category as well as some private label goods.[22]

On the other hand, certain influential big-name brand manufacturers have begun to implement category management (planogram proposals) for new retail formats chains. Category management is a kind of merchandising activity in which retailers and manufacturers cooperate in the planning of goods assortment, pricing, sales promotions, and planograms in order to maximize value for consumers.[23] The products sold by the retailer are broken down into discrete groups of related products, called product categories. Each category is run as a business unit with its own set of profitability targets and strategies. Retailers and manufacturers cooperate with each other when the two parties share various closed data, including point-of-sale (POS) data.

As part of category management, or in connection with it, strong brand manufacturers are undertaking various producer-retailer alliances. For example, Unilever Thai Trading Co., Ltd. (hereafter Thai Unilever) makes efforts to share data on consumers' retail purchases, and has also constructed a retail link with Tops supermarket (Sombun 2006c, 71–72). It also practices joint sales promotions and consumer research with various chain stores, such as Tops supermarket and Watson's drug store. The big three hypermarket companies as of 2010, Tesco Lotus, Big C, and Carrefour, were likewise conducting joint sales promotions and consumer research (*PRCT-TK*, July 17, 2006; *PJK-RW*, July 27, 2006). Thai Kao Sales has introduced an efficient consumer response (ECR) strategy based on the POS system in cooperation with new retail format chains in order to meet the rapidly changing consumer market (Hirai 2003, 109–11).

Theoretically, the main purpose of category management is to increase sales and inventory turnover of the good's category as a whole, and not just the sales of individual products. However, a manufacturer entrusted with planogram management can obviously make a proposal that would be more favorable to itself (and conversely, less favorable to its competitors). From the very beginning, category management has often been entrusted to Western manufacturers familiar with this method, especially well-known brand manufacturers in each good's category. This has forced lower-ranking brands and small- and medium-sized manufacturers into more disadvantageous positions. An individual, who once headed the marketing divisions for a local and a foreign consumer goods manufacturer and has chosen to remain anonymous, reported that a rival company's category management not only gradually reduced the display space of his company's products but also caused the display to be relegated to an unfavorable location on the store shelves (Mr. Re-tell 2002, 141–45). In short, category management can, on one hand, develop into a producer-retailer alliance between new retail format companies and big-name brand manufacturers, while on the other hand it can cause weak brand manufacturers to lose sales opportunities, thereby reducing their overall sales.

When new retail formats (hypermarkets, in particular) increase their bargaining power in accordance with the expansion of their chains, consumer goods manufacturers are forced to accept some unfavorable transaction conditions. Even a small number of big-name brand manufacturers may be deprived channel leadership by retailers, who engage in planogram business practices. That is why manufacturers have taken cooperative means by establishing alliances with retailers, as well as implementing countermeasures against tough retailers. These countermeasures are essentially attempts to maintain the balance between modern and traditional distribution channels by refocusing their dealings with traditional retailers and wholesalers, in order to prevent new retail format companies from excessively increasing their bargaining power (Sombun 2006c, 68–72). New retail format chain stores have yet to cover the entire country's consumer market, and they have yet to build a sufficient marketing system that would enable them to share their sales data with manufacturers. Manufacturers, therefore, also focus their attention on traditional marketing and distribution channels, which they make efforts, in some cases, to reorganize.

THE REORGANIZATION OF MARKETING CHANNELS FOR DAILY FOODS AND NECESSITIES

REEVALUATING THE TRADITIONAL DISTRIBUTION INDUSTRY

Traditional wholesalers have been playing an important role in the distribution industry for a long time, especially at the provincial level, and traditional retailers still occupy a large part of Thailand's retail industry, though their importance is decreasing as a result of the rapid growth of new retail formats. Many of the present consumer goods manufacturers interviewed for this study unanimously emphasized the important role of traditional retailers and wholesale distributors.

Table 5.2 shows the major consumer goods manufacturers in Thailand, particularly those selling daily necessities and processed foods, as well as the sales ratio of their distribution channels. As this table demonstrates, as of 2006, the sales ratio of traditional distribution channels is generally larger than that of modern distribution channels. Moreover, except for those commodities characterized by a strong infatuation with big-name brands, such as hair care and personal care products, the weight of traditional distribution channels is even larger. For example, more than 65 percent of Ajinomoto products, including a particular seasoning used by Thai families and restaurants, are still sold via traditional distribution channels.[24]

TABLE 5.2 Major consumer goods manufacturers in Thailand, as of 2006

	Company name	Sales (million baht)	Main products	Sales ratio of distribution channels (%)
Local Thai	Saha Pathanapibul	15,460	detergent, hair care, personal care, processed-foods (e.g., instant Chinese noodles, artificial flavoring, etc.)	35–50 (MT) 50–65 (TT)
	Osotspa	16,377	medical supplies, drinks (e.g., vitamin drinks), personal care	40 (MT) 60 (TT)
European and American	Unilever Thai Trading	30,390	detergent, hair care, soap, skin care, ice cream	50 (MT) 50 (TT)
	Colgate-Palmolive (Thailand)	9,426	detergent, personal care (e.g., toothpaste, liquid soap, etc.)	n/a
	P&G Trading (Thailand)	7,097	hair care, personal care	n/a
Japanese	Thai Ajinomoto Sales	15,330	processed-foods (e.g., artificial flavoring, instant Chinese noodles, etc.), drinks	33 (MT) 67 (TT)
	Thai Kao Sales	4,618	detergent, hair care, personal care	50 (MT) 50 (TT)

SOURCE: Author interviews; companies' financial statements; Thai-language business magazines.

NOTE: (MT) and (TT) refer to "modern trade" and "traditional trade," respectively. The modern trade percentage of Thai Ajinomoto Sales includes some traditional trade.

Despite these numbers, modern retailing should never be underestimated. Within just twenty years after Makro (cash-and-carry) and 7-Eleven (convenience store) opened their first respective stores in 1989, modern retailing and distribution channels came to occupy nearly 50 percent of all sales of daily necessities and processed foods supplied by major manufacturers. However, as has been repeatedly mentioned, a cloud has been hanging over the growth line of new retail formats since the Thai economy recovered from the serious depression caused by the financial and currency crisis. Moreover, the mosaic structure of Thailand's consumer market, characterized by income and geographic disparity, hinders growth, although it may also offer business opportunities. As a result, the ratio of modern distribution channels is unlikely to rapidly rise in the near future, and traditional distribution channels should continue to occupy a relatively large place in the industry.[25]

It should also be pointed out that, even today, major manufacturers are not only well aware of the importance of traditional distribution channels, but they are also making efforts to reinforce them. Saha Pathanapibul Plc invites wholesalers that sell its products to participate in the company's automatic ordering and inventory control system. This system enables participants to simultaneously achieve inventory reduction and avoid sales opportunity loss. As of November 2006, twenty provincial leading wholesalers agreed to participate in the system (*TNSK*, November 16, 2006). Although Thai Unilever has top-brand products in some daily necessities categories, such as detergent, hair care, and personal care,[26] and positive manufacturer-retailer alliances with hypermarkets and other new retail formats, the company still attaches great importance to traditional distribution channels. For example, the company decided to do joint marketing with both traditional and modern retailers and wholesalers (*PJK-RW*, July 27, 2006). In addition, Thai Unilever had been sending salespersons once every two or three weeks to small-scale grocery stores that sell its products, amounting to more than 200,000 stores throughout the country, and, since 2002, it has increased the frequency of those visits to once a week.[27] This is two to four times as frequent as its competitors, which shows that Thai Unilever also places great importance on traditional distribution channels.

Traditional wholesalers have also been active. One of the typical cases is the Thai Wholesale and Retail Association, consisting of about ninety wholesalers throughout the country.[28] The association has investigated the impact of multinational retailers on the traditional distribution industry, and submitted its results to the government, asking for support. The association has also tried to organize joint sales promotion activities among its members, and asked the major manufacturers to consider the possibility of joint orders. Certain segments of the Thai Chamber of Commerce as well as some major consumer goods manufacturers are actively supporting this movement toward organization among wholesalers (*TNSK*, January 4, 2007). Moreover, leading provincial wholesalers sometimes ask major manufacturers to support their individual managerial reforms,[29] while in other cases provincial wholesalers operate a portion of their distribution centers jointly with manufacturers (*PRCT-TK*, January 8, 2007).

Some traditional wholesalers have rapidly increased sales by actively adopting the operating methods of new retail formats and, in some cases, have grown to become the largest retail store in their locality, exceeding that of hypermarket chains at the local level. Typical examples are Tang Ngee Soon Superstore Co., Ltd. in Udon Thani Province in the northeast and Super Cheap Co., Ltd. in Phuket in the south. Sales of Tang Ngee Soon and Super Cheap in 2006 amounted respectively to more than1.8 billion baht and 3.6 billion baht, each of which was much larger than a hypermarket that earns about 1 to 1.2 billion baht per store (see chap. 4, table 4.1). What is more remarkable is that Tang Ngee Soon, for example, achieved this sales volume by selling mainly processed foods and substantially limiting its goods categories in comparison with hypermarkets. The importance of the company as a retail channel for major manufacturers of processed foods thus becomes even clearer. Similar cases can be seen among many other traditional wholesalers. Even though the total sales volume of traditional wholesalers is smaller than that of hypermarket stores, in some specific goods categories, traditional wholesalers can become manufacturers' most important customers in a given locality.

The reason why major consumer goods manufacturers attach great importance to the role of traditional wholesalers and retailers is twofold. First, manufacturers tend to keep an eye on the increasing buying power of new retail formats and the subsequent abuse that can entail in terms of demanding that manufacturers shoulder the burden of various sales expenses. And, second, traditional wholesalers and retailers remain important marketing channels for manufacturers because they still retain a significant share of the retail market.

Since around 1990, when provincial consumer markets were rapidly expanding, consumer goods manufacturers have made efforts to drastically reorganize their marketing channels. This is common to all manufacturers, however, the way in which the reorganization of marketing channels takes place differs among manufacturers according to the characteristics of their previous marketing channels, the popularity of their product brands, and their market share. Let us look at a few case examples, beginning with Saha Pathanapibul Plc, one of Thailand's largest companies selling daily necessities and processed foods, which began to seek new markets in the provinces and built marketing channels early on.

SAHA PATHANAPIBUL[30]

Saha Pathanapibul Plc (hereafter Saha Pat) is the core sales company of the Saha Group, a major local business group whose main business activity is manufacturing and selling consumer goods. Unlike a sales company in the ordinary sense, Saha Pat has established various manufacturing subsidiaries and has shouldered the responsibility for the sales and marketing of its products.[31] It was the originating company through which the Saha Group eventually developed. This is precisely why the author slightly altered the definition of "sales company" for this book, as mentioned in the introduction, to include any sales company that belongs to a manufacturing business group as well as those that are independent from manufacturing groups.

Saha Pat mainly sells daily necessities such as detergents, hair care, and personal care products, as well as processed foods, such as instant Chinese noodles and seasonings. Selling the products of its subsidiaries (including joint ventures with foreign investors) is its main business. Although the company has recently begun to extend its business into selling other external companies' products (Saha Pathanapibul Plc 2006, 53–55), its characteristics as the core sales company of the group remain essentially unchanged.

Saha Pat established a kind of sales agent (or sales broker) system, *saha rung rueang*, in the 1960s, but found that using outside managerial resources gradually became inappropriate for the rapid changes in the consumer market. The company abolished this system at the end of the 1980s and switched to a new system, in which the company itself basically manages all aspects of its marketing channels. The company closed down most of its warehouses in Thailand's major regional cities and entrusted storage duties for its products to local wholesalers or distribution-related businesspersons. The company called these trustees *So. Ro.*, and as of 2006, had appointed sixty-three businesspersons throughout the country to such positions.[32] At first glance, the word *So. Ro.* may be mistaken as an abbreviation of *saha rung rueang*, but the *So. Ro.* system is entirely different, with a much more limited sales agent role than the former system. *So. Ro.* is responsible for maintaining the daily proceeds that Saha Pat's salespersons collect daily from small-scale grocery stores that sell its products, and remitting the money to Saha Pat's head office every month. Salespersons and drivers travel to small-scale grocery stores in their respective districts using the cash van system to make and collect cash sales, and to conduct inventory control. It would appear that the reason Saha Pat entrusts monthly remittance to *So. Ro.* is that the company believes this will ensure the safety of the daily proceeds and monthly remittance, and will also ensure salespersons devote themselves to their duties on a daily basis. Saha Pat's employees are responsible for the main duties of the cash van system, such as the sales/collection process and inventory management, while *So. Ro.* is only entrusted with minor duties. Figure 5.1 provides a general overview of Saha Pat's new marketing channels.

FIGURE 5.1 Marketing channels of Saha Pat Plc, as of 2006

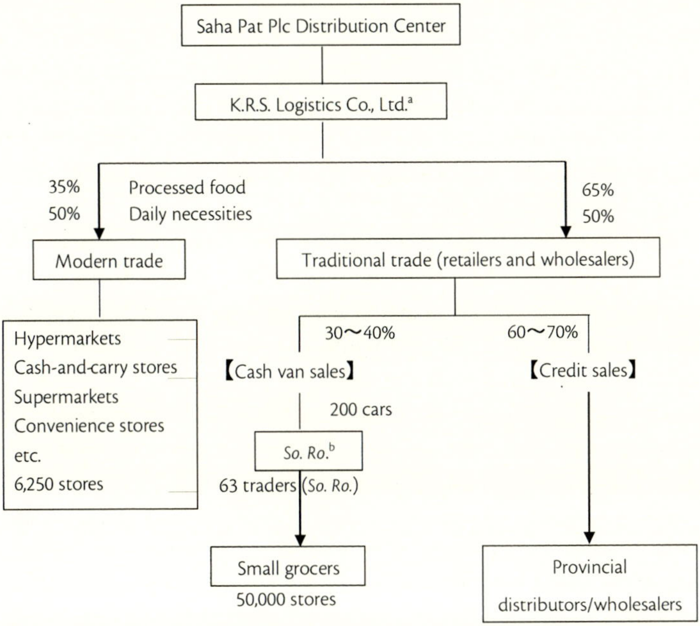

SOURCE: Author interviews; data from company reports.

[a] K.R.S. Logistics is a joint venture between Saha Pat and Q. P. (Japan).

[b] *So. Ro.* is a kind of provincial warehouse whose owners are entrusted by Saha Pat to maintain the daily proceeds that Saha Pat's salespersons collect from small-scale grocery stores.

From figure 5.1, we can see that Saha Pat's traditional distribution division consists of two channels: one for cash van sales using *So. Ro.* and the other for credit sales. While the sum of cash that a small-scale grocery store pays per sales transaction to Saha Pat ranges from about 3,000–5,000 baht, the sum of credit sales of a traditional large-scale distributor (primarily provincial wholesalers) can reach as much as 50 million baht per sales transaction. The cash van sales system covers no less than 50,000 small-scale grocery stores, which accounts for less than 10 percent of the total retailers in Thailand (see table 5.1). Although the credit sales system directly covers only 5,000 distributors, most of them are provincial wholesalers who sell Saha Pat's products to those small-scale grocery stores that are not included in Saha Pat's cash van system. Therefore, the credit sales system actually covers many more stores than the nominal number of distributors. Since large-scale distributors here consist mainly of leading traditional wholesalers (in some cases, running a retailing business simultaneously), the distributors' channels ought to extend to a larger number of small-scale grocery stores. Modern trade channels are, of course, equally as important as the traditional ones for Saha Pat. While in the case of daily necessities the company's sales ratio between modern and traditional trade is fifty-fifty, in the case of processed foods traditional trade makes up 65 percent of Saha Pat's sale of these goods.

As for the physical distribution of its products, Saha Pat entrusts it entirely to K.R.S. Logistics Co., Ltd. (hereafter K.R.S.), a Saha Group subsidiary.[33] With the central distribution center in Si Racha on the eastern seaboard as the starting point of delivery for all Saha Pat's products, K.R.S. usually delivers to modern retailers' distribution centers and directly to each provincial distributor's store or warehouse. In the case of cash van sales, K.R.S. delivers the products to *So. Ro.*, where Saha Pat's cash van teams receive them and then tour small-scale grocery stores in the district to deliver these products.

In this way, Saha Pat entrusts the physical distribution of its products to a group subsidiary, while managing for itself almost all the aspects of making and collecting sales, and inventory management through its salespersons. Compared with its former *saha rung rueang* system, this new system enables the company to spread the head office's sales policies throughout all of its marketing channels more effectively. Yet, the new system, like the former one, depends on leading wholesalers for a considerable part of its traditional trade channels, especially at the provincial level.

THAI UNILEVER

Early in the 1990s, Thai Unilever, Thailand's largest company in the daily necessities market, reorganized its marketing channels, just as Saha Pat did during the same time period. What Thai Unilever did was to convert its former stockist system to a new concessionaire (*sampathan khet*) system.[34] Unlike the stockist system, in which the company depended on external managerial resources for only minor duties such as the establishment and management of warehouses, in the concessionaire system, the company basically entrusts each district's concessionaire with all the duties in its district, including the safekeeping of goods as well as making and collecting cash sales, inventory control, and the arrangements and management of delivery vehicles.[35]

As of early 2006, Thai Unilever had concessionaires in more than sixty provinces throughout the country and built a sales network with them, covering more than 200,000 small-scale grocery stores (*PJK-RW*, February 7, 2006). As for the provinces where the company has not established concessionaires yet or had no successors following the departure of former concessionaires, the company advertised for concessionaires in local Thai-language newspapers. According to one advertisement (December 2006), the qualifications for the position were that the applicant should be a businessperson of the district with funds of at least 5 million baht to invest in establishing and managing his/her own company in cooperation with Thai Unilever, and he/she should be a juridical person with a registered capital of at least 1.5 million baht and at least 1.5 million baht of bank credit. Although not specified in the newspaper advertisements, concessionaires are furthermore expected to solely arrange for such things as warehouses for storing goods, offices, salespersons, delivery trucks, and the like (*TNSK*, December 24, 2006). There are some cases in which Thai Unilever former stockists become concessionaires, but inexperienced persons are preferred because they are easier for Thai Unilever to deal with. As far as the author knows, leading wholesalers in each area never apply for concessionaires in order to avoid the restrictions set by Thai Unilever and other manufacturers using the concessionaire system.

In contrast to Saha Pat's *So. Ro.* system, Thai Unilever's concessionaire system entrusts outside persons with most of the intermediate distribution functions involved in covering small-scale grocery stores. Thai Unilever represents a case of a foreign company, unfamiliar with Thailand's domestic distribution system, entrusting its distribution business to local businesspersons, which is similar to the situation of European trading companies in Thailand that depended on Chinese merchants for domestic sales during the nineteenth century. However, Thai Unilever's present concessionaire system greatly differs from this historical example in two respects. One is that, although concessionaires are entrusted with almost all of the daily duties of a distributor, Thai Unilever still directly supervises them. Specifically, the company sends its own personnel to supervise each concessionaire and to participate in the concessionaire's in-house meetings. In addition, the company has built an online system to track each concessionaire's sales data using personal digital assistants (PDAs), i.e., palm-held computers.

The other difference between the concessionaire system and the practices of the nineteenth century is that the rights and interests of area-exclusive distribution, which Thai Unilever concessionaires enjoy, are much smaller than those of Chinese merchants in former days. The concessionaires' duties entrusted by Thai Unilever consist of covering provincial consumer markets that modern retailing (especially new retail formats) channels cannot cover, or, in other words, covering small-scale and remote retail stores, to which normal routes of delivery are inefficient. As a result, the coverage rate of Thai Unilever products in Thailand's consumer market is extraordinarily high,[36] although it is the concessionaires that must shoulder the burden of the costs of achieving such a high coverage rate.

Even in traditional distribution channels, concessionaires are not always guaranteed exclusive distribution in their appointed area. This is because leading independent wholesalers still play an important role in local areas, which makes it difficult for even Thai Unilever to enforce its concessionaire system and have all the independent wholesalers and small-scale retailers across the country purchase Unilever products from their respective concessionaires.[37] In short, small-scale grocery stores can purchase Thai Unilever products by way of two routes, concessionaires or independent wholesalers.

It is only natural that small-scale grocery stores would prefer to purchase from a cash-and-carry Makro store where prices are comparatively cheaper, provided there is one within relative proximity. Similarly, when hypermarket stores sells goods in bulk at low prices, small-scale grocery stores often use them just as they would use a Makro store. There are usually three or four sources from which small-scale grocery stores purchase their goods.[38] Therefore, it is understandable why leading local wholesalers are unwilling to become concessionaires. Rather, it is generally local businesspersons looking for some stable profit, who accept the role of concessionaire, although such a position does not allow for large profits.[39]

Coupled with this concessionaire system, Thai Unilever is putting a great deal of effort into shelf space management, as a reinforcement measure for traditional trade channels. Shelf space management offers some rewards to leading provincial distributors, according to the shelf space allotted to Unilever products (*KTTK-RW*, July 25, 2005), thereby implementing a more favorable planogram.[40] In addition to this planogram policy, Thai Unilever is also encouraging leading provincial distributors to cooperate in advertising, by hanging banners or setting up shelves dedicated to Unilever products in their stores. Criticism in the industry points to the fact that this method of buying up the goods-display space and advertising space of traditional distributors is an unfair trading practice in contravention of the Trade Competition Act (*TNSK*, July 28, 2005). Whether this is true or not, this method, combined with the concessionaire system, certainly contributes to promoting Thai Unilever products' penetration of the consumer market.

THREE TYPES OF MARKETING CHANNELS

Saha Pat's efforts to internalize intermediate distribution and Thai Unilever's use of external managerial resources contrast with each other in terms of how they each reorganized their traditional distribution and marketing channels. It can be said, however, that Thai Unilever's policy regarding traditional distribution and marketing channels is also, in fact, a very strong integration policy, or a kind of *keiretsu* policy.

Procter & Gamble Trading (Thailand) Co., Ltd. (hereafter Thai P&G) and Colgate-Palmolive (Thailand) Co., Ltd. (hereafter Thai Colgate) have implemented similar systems to Thai Unilever, although their systems are not as thorough. Thai P&G uses a kind of sales district office system,[41] while Thai Colgate uses what could be called a trade partner system. Each of these methods is designed to increase the coverage rate of these companies' products by entrusting traditional trade channels at the provincial level with external managerial resources and requesting these trustees (sales offices and trade partners, respectively)to cover small-scale and remote stores where normal delivery channels are inefficient.

Around 1990, Osotspa Co., Ltd., a major local Thai manufacturer, also made efforts to reorganize its marketing channels, but its method contrasted with the three major Western manufacturing companies.[42] Osotspa established its central distribution center in Bangkok and maintained four regional distribution centers. With the distribution centers as its base of operations, the company had its traveling cash van teams cover the small-scale grocery stores scattered in each region. However, the amount of cash van sales was only 10 percent of the company's total sales, with 50 percent of its sales coming from wholesalers and 40 percent from modern retailers. Special attention should be paid to the high percentage of the company's wholesaler channels. It suggests that the Osotspa attaches greater importance to the role of wholesalers.

In the same way, Thai Ajinomoto Sales also actively began reorganizing its marketing channels at the end of the 1980s, prior to the rise of new retail format chains. The company not only established distribution centers in each region (four centers in total), but also placed a sales office-cum-warehouse in thirty-eight locations throughout the country.[43] Using its sales office-cum-warehouses, the company delivers its products directly to small-scale grocery stores by cash van sales teams (each consisting of one salesperson and one driver). In the case of Thai Ajinomoto Sales, the trade with wholesalers accounts for two-thirds of its entire trade, in other words, significantly more than its trade through cash van sales and with modern retailers.

The marketing channels of Osotspa and Thai Ajinomoto Sales are very similar to each other, and are basically the same as Saha Pat's marketing channels. The difference lies in whether the company chooses to internalize the sales and warehouse bases for small-scale grocery stores in each area (with its own distribution centers and provincial offices) or whether it makes supplementary use of external managerial resources (e.g., *So.Ro.*).

A more thorough internalization of distribution and marketing at the wholesale stage is the direct-sales system introduced by Thai Kao Sales in the early 1990s.[44] Although the company had already started building a direct-sales system in the mid-1970s, it actually entrusted most of its traditional distribution and marketing channels to leading wholesalers in each area. However, many of the leading local wholesalers were simultaneously involved in retail businesses, so that they failed to fulfill the wholesale function that Thai Kao Sales expected from them. In 1992, the company decided to abolish its traditional distribution and marketing channels with wholesalers and to promote a thorough direct-sales system throughout the country. At the same time, the company selected new distributors who had dealings with Thai Kao from among provincial wholesalers who had previously been its customers and re-classified most of them as retailers. As a general rule, the company requested retailers to purchase its products directly from the sales department of the head office or provincial sales offices. This trade practice aims at creating a strong bond with distributors. The company established sales office-cum-warehouses in eighteen regional centers (now reduced to fifteen) throughout the country as part of its direct-sales system. As for physical distribution, the company entrusted this to an external Japanese distribution and warehouse company, while making its employees take full responsibility for product sales, using provincial sales offices as their base. In short, Thai Kao Sales made efforts to build a more thorough

FIGURE 5.2 Classification of marketing channels in Thailand, since the 1990s

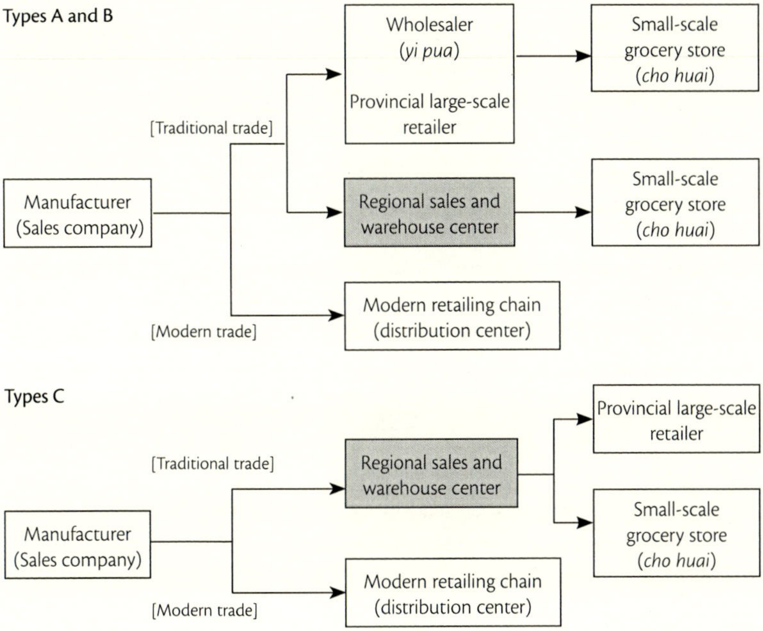

Functions of regional sales and warehouse centers and persons in charge

Type A (Unilever, P&G, Colgate)	Type B (Saha Pat, Osotspa, Ajinomoto)	Type C (Kao)
• full use of external managerial resources • appointment of local businesspersons as regional exclusive distributors, e.g., concessionaires, sales district offices, trade partners	• internalization and partial use of external managerial resources • establishment of sales offices, distribution centers, and warehouses in each region center, e.g., Saha Pat's *So. Ro.*	• internalization • establishment of sales office-cum-warehouses at 18 (later 15) sites through-out the country • in 1992, abolition of cash van system, and thorough separation of physical distribution from commercial activities; • as of 2006, greater importance attached to wholesalers again

SOURCE: Author interviews with major manufacturers and wholesalers.

NOTE: Modern retail formats (e.g., hypermarkets) actually sell goods to small-scale wholesalers and retailers, but such trades are omitted from this figure. Direct delivery from each regional sales and warehouse center to small-scale retailers is done in cash by "cash van sales" tours. Trade with wholesalers is usually done on credit, but sometimes in cash as well.

direct-sales system than its company in Japan. After that, however, the company again came to realize the importance of traditional distribution and marketing channels, while also attaching importance to modern retail distribution channel. Currently, the company is striving to strengthen its business connections with provincial wholesalers, in particular. Figure 5.2 provides a snapshot of the various marketing channels used by Western and local Thai companies, as well as Thai Kao Sales.

As figure 5.2 demonstrates, Western companies (Thai Unilever, Thai P&G, and Thai Colgate) are making positive use of external managerial resources in managing sales offices and warehouses for small-scale grocery stores (*cho huai*) in localities around the country. This pattern is classified as a Type A marketing channel in this study. On the other hand, local Thai companies like Saha Pat and Osotspa, and Thai Ajinomoto Sales, a subsidiary of the Japan-based Ajinomoto, are basically internalizing the functions of sales and warehousing, which is classified as a Type B marketing channel. Although Types A and B differ from each other somewhat, even Thai Unilever, a typical Type A example, depends on leading wholesalers to a certain extent for the sale of its products.[45] Its concessionaires can never cover all of the small-scale grocery stores in their respective districts. This is a phenomenon common to both Type A and Type B marketing channels. Thai Kao Sales meanwhile makes efforts to build a thorough direct-sales system, classified here as a Type C marketing channel, which is different from Types A and B. However, this Type C channel has recently started to fall apart (Hirai 2003, 108–9), and the company is trying to strengthen its relationships with provincial wholesalers. As a result, the difference between Type C and Type B is becoming less clear. In short, although there are some differences among them, all three types of marketing channels attach special importance to modern retailers, but still also greatly depend on traditional provincial wholesalers (*yi pua*) and are striving to strengthen their relationships with them.

THE ROLES OF WHOLESALERS

CASES OF LEADING WHOLESALERS

Intermediate distribution is still playing an important role in Thailand's distribution and marketing channels of daily necessities and processed foods, especially at the provincial level. However, there are all sorts of companies and traders engaged in the intermediate distribution of daily necessities and processed foods, depending on their relationship with manufacturers, the kinds of products for sale, the geographical scope of the business, their position in the distribution channel, and so on. The previous section examined manufacturers' marketing channels and traders directly controlled by manufacturers, that is, exclusive sales companies belonging to the same business groups (e.g., Saha Pat of the Saha Group) and area-exclusive distributors affiliated to the manufacturer (e.g., Thai Unilever's concessionaires). As a result, while these companies made every effort to place intermediate distribution under their direct control, all the major manufacturers still rely on independent wholesalers (*yi pua*) for a considerable part of their traditional trade distribution channels.[46]

The section analyzes the roles and functions of independent wholesalers. Due to data limitations, however, it is impossible to provide an overall view of Thailand's wholesale business. This is why the author can only clarify some aspects of Thailand's wholesale business by considering specific cases of leading wholesalers.

Thai Diethelm. The first case is Diethelm (Thailand) Co., Ltd., a Swiss sales company.[47] Thai Diethelm was established in 1906 and is one of the oldest foreign companies still in operation (Orawan et al. 2004). The company started as an import trader in Thailand, but began to build a domestic distribution network throughout the country both before and after World War II. Under Thailand's import substitution industrialization policy starting about 1960, the company also tried to advance into the manufacturing industry but failed (Somjai 2004, 241–42). After that, it decided to devote its business to selling other companies' products (Suphattara 1993, 265–68), and has continued doing that until the present time. As of 2007, the company had four business divisions: (i) a daily necessities sales division, (ii) a medical supplies and health care goods sales division, (iii) a special goods sales division and (iv) a technology business division. The total sales of the four divisions amounted to about 20.4 billion baht in 2006, which made it one of the largest wholesale companies in Thailand. Among the four divisions, the daily necessities sales division is the largest, accounting for as much as 40 percent of the total sales of the company.

With such an extensive sales network in Thailand's domestic market, Thai Diethelm has been accepting contracts as the sole sales agency (exclusive sales at some stage of distribution) for many manufacturers who have big-name brands but insufficient selling power. Thai Diethelm distributes, for example, foreign brands such as Nivea (personal care products), Cerebos (processed foods, and, at present, an affiliated company of Suntory), and Ovaltine (malt drink), but also local products including the processed foods of So. Khon Kaen Food Industry Co., Ltd., famous for Vietnam-style ham (*mu yo*) and local fermented sausage (*naem*) (*PRCT-TK*, January 18, 2007 et al.). The company's clients consist of approximately ninety foreign and local manufacturing companies, mainly big-name brands of daily necessities and processed foods. Thai Diethelm is also actively involved in the production stage of its manufacturing clients and the sales stage of wholesaler and retailer clients. In this respect, unlike traditional wholesalers in Thailand, this company functions in a similar way as major manufacturers' sales companies like Thai Unilever and Saha Pat.[48]

Thai Diethelm's distribution channels for the products exclusively entrusted to it consist of both modern retailing (mainly new retail formats) distribution channels and traditional distribution channels, representing a ratio of 55 and 45 percent, respectively on a value basis. Because Thai Diethelm trades special goods, including medical supplies, as well as daily necessities and processed foods, the company puts a slightly heavier weight on modern retailing channels, compared with the major consumer goods manufacturers and sales companies mentioned in the previous section. As for traditional distribution channels, Thai Diethelm's customers are mainly wholesalers (including retailer-cum-wholesalers, like cash-and-carry stores) and small-scale retailers (e.g., grocery stores), amounting to approximately 60,000 stores. As for physical distribution, the company has built a direct delivery system with cash vans. This was made possible by establishing two distribution centers in Bangkok and its suburb of Bang Pa-in, Ayutthaya Province, but also by placing depots for cross-docking in three regional centers.[49] In the case of leading wholesalers, however, Thai Diethelm entrusts them with the retail stage as well. In short, according to the classification of marketing channels provided in the previous section, Thai Diethelm belongs to Type B.

Thai Diethelm's marketing channels and distribution system are very useful to manufacturers who lack them. However, the relationship between big-name brand manufacturers and Thai Diethelm is not always a stable one. There have been many cases in which manufacturers were at first unfamiliar with the domestic distribution in Thailand, and so relied on Thai Diethelm, but eventually came to build their own marketing channels after gradually acquiring the necessary market information.[50] Dealings with Thai Diethelm are more important and beneficial for small- and medium-sized manufacturers of weaker brand products than for major manufacturers. Indeed, the dealings with

Thai Diethelm allow small- and medium-sized local manufacturers to drastically expand the markets for their products by using Thai Diethelm's channels. However it is also true that many small- and medium-sized manufacturers have been refused dealings because they did not meet Thai Diethelm's requirements. Moreover, there are only a few independent distributors (sales companies) in Thailand that extend sales networks throughout the country to the same extent as Thai Diethelm.[51]

So, how do small- and medium-sized manufacturers distribute their products when they lack their own marketing channels and cannot trade with sales companies like Thai Diethelm? In such cases, they generally have two options. One is to propose that modern retailers (new retail formats) have direct dealings with them, while the other is to use traditional wholesalers. Since it is difficult for small- and medium-sized manufacturers to trade with modern retailers, the role of traditional wholesalers becomes even more important. Let us now turn our attention to leading local wholesalers, especially at the provincial level.[52]

Tang Ngee Soon Superstore. Tang Ngee Soon Superstore Co., Ltd. in Udon Thani Province is always referred to as a leading local wholesaler, at least by major consumer goods manufacturers operating in Thailand.[53] The forerunner of the company, Ngee Soon Udon Thani Ltd. Partnership, was established in 1960 and was changed to Ngee Soon Superstore in 1988, and later reorganized as a limited company in 2000. It is a typical family business in which five members of the second and third generations of the founding family control ownership and management of the company. At the time of establishment in 1960, it was a small-scale grocery store in Udon Thani City, but later expanded into a leading wholesaler in the northeast. After the vice president (second generation of the founding family) observed cash-and-carry formats during a tour to Western countries around 1990, Tang Ngee Soon decided to imitate this new format in order to further develop its business. The company encouraged three third generation children (two men and one woman) to attend courses related to the family business at famous universities and graduate schools both at home and abroad. At the same time, the company actively implemented information technology systems for efficient inventory management and control.

The first store, located in the central district of Udon Thani City, has two entrances and checkout counters, one in the front facing a main street and one in the back on a back street. The front entrance is for retail goods and the back entrance is for wholesale goods. The store's floor space also has two distinct areas: the front part of the store sells only retail goods, while the back part of the store sells wholesale goods in bulk. Tang Ngee Soon, however, differs from most other wholesalers and general mass merchandisers (especially cash-and-carry) in that it sells goods at the same price per unit, irrespective of the purchase amount, and thus facilitates small-scale retailers' purchases as well. The company does not sell perishable foods whose freshness easily deteriorates, but concentrates mainly on daily necessities and processed foods, always selling them at low prices. Tang Ngee Soon directly purchases goods from about six hundred companies, including major consumer goods manufacturers (and their sales companies) and other manufacturers of various scales. Thai Diethelm is one of them. As a general rule, Tang Ngee Soon purchases goods on non-consignment and is also responsible for inventory management. But in the case of low sales, the company sometimes consults with suppliers to organize a joint sales promotion. Depending on the situation, the company may also return unsold goods to its suppliers.

The reason why Tang Ngee Soon can always sell goods at low prices lies in its low-cost operation. The store is not air-conditioned, and goods for wholesale are left in cardboard boxes piled up to the ceiling. Tang Ngee Soon bears a close resemblance to the cash-and-carry Makro. Customers are divided into retail and wholesale at a fifty-fifty ratio on the basis of sales, and come not only from within the province but also from neighboring provinces and from Vientiane in Laos.[54] Even in the case of wholesale, about 90 percent of the trade is in cash and only 10 percent at most is on credit (30 days). The company does not provide a delivery service for its customers. For these reasons, the format of the company is similar to a cash-and-carry store (however, there is no membership system). The second store, established in November 2007, is a warehouse-style store that is very large and similar to Makro. It is located on a main street in the suburb of Udon Thani City (floor space is 10,000 square meters and a 400-car capacity parking lot). Most of the sales from this second store are wholesale.

Other provincial leading wholesalers. Besides Tang Ngee Soon, there are many leading wholesalers at the provincial level. For example, Super Cheap Co., Ltd. in Phuket Province in the south is in a prominent position at the provincial level in terms of sales, so much so as to attract considerable attention from Thailand's distribution industry. Details of the business are unknown, because the company is reluctant to disclose this information to the mass media. But this company is similar to Tang Ngee Soon in that it has realized low prices by implementing a low-cost operation system and achieving an overwhelming selling power in its locality.[55]

Leng Seng Ltd. Partnership, in Sakon Nakhon in the northeast, is also worth mentioning, as another type of wholesaler.[56] Leng Seng was originally engaged in sales and delivery as an agent (*nuai rot*) for beverages like Boon Rawd Brewery's Singha Beer and Coca Cola. After his succession to the family business in 2001, the first son of the founding family's third generation, Somwang Dechsiriudom (Kasetsart University, MBA), thought that business prospects would be gloomy if the company only depended on the sales agent business for major beverage manufacturers. As a result, the company increased the variety of goods for sale and simultaneously also started running a retail business inside the store. Goods for sale at present are daily necessities (20 percent of total sales) and processed foods, including beverages (80 percent). Compared with Tang Ngee Soon, Leng Seng is a different type of operation in that the percentage of sales from wholesale goods to total sales is overwhelmingly high (80–90 percent), and the company delivers goods to the retail stores that are its customers. The strength of this company resides notably in the physical distribution system that it has built as a sales-delivery agent. Its distribution center was constructed in 2004 in a suburb of Sakon Nakhon City. It is a large-scale facility consisting of two large warehouses and a small one. With this distribution center as its base of operations, the company delivers goods to villages in Sakon Nakhon Province, and at the district level to locales in the neighboring Nakhon Phanom and Mukdahan Provinces. As of August 2008, the company had a fleet of forty delivery trucks, with two or three employees per vehicle responsible for deliveries. Each salesperson when making deliveries to customers carries a notebook computer with a scanner that reads the bar codes of goods. After returning to the distribution center in the evening, the sales data are transferred to the host computer. The company takes care of all the delivery functions itself.

Yongsanguan Group Co., Ltd. in Ubon Ratchathani Province in the same region shares, to some extent, similar characteristics with both Tang Ngee Soon and Leng Seng.[57] Yongsanguan started as a grocery store and later became a sales agent for Bangkok-based major manufacturers. In 1996, the company also began to run a supermarket, Save Land, but soon became exhausted by the competition of a hypermarket (Tesco Lotus at present) from Bangkok. This is why the first son of the founding family's third generation, Prakit Chaisongkhram, was called back from the UK, where he was studying after graduating from the Law Department of Chulalongkorn University. Once he entered the family business, he opened Yongsanguan Wholesale Center in 2002, as a way to set the business apart from new foreign retail formats. This one-storied warehouse-style store has a floor space of 25,600 square meters and mainly sells daily necessities and processed foods (100,000 items, no perishable foods). In the same way as other wholesalers, the store strives to maintain a thorough low-cost operation. The inside of the store is not air-conditioned, and goods are left in cardboard boxes piled up to the ceiling. The ratio of wholesale to retail sales is 65:35, and 90 percent of sales are in cash and 10 percent on credit (15 days). In these respects, Yongsanguan is relatively similar to Tang Ngee Soon. The difference between the two resides in the delivery service they provide to the customers' stores. In this respect, Yongsanguan is similar to Leng Seng. However, Yongsanguan limits its delivery service to customers in Ubon Ratchathani City and only provides delivery service to areas beyond the city in cases of major purchases. The trading area of the company covers an 80-kilometer radius around the store, which is relatively narrow. Yongsanguan actually has another characteristic, which is that the company has expanded its business into the supermarket and minimart formats by establishing separate companies. Yongsanguan Wholesale Center assumes the role of distribution center for these chain stores.

Ekkaphap Super Supply Co., Ltd., in Saraburi Province in the central part of Thailand, is similar to Yongsanguan.[58] As with other leading wholesalers, Ekkaphap started as a grocery store and later expanded its business into a wholesaler. As Ekkaphap came to realize that the traditional wholesaling businesses only achieved very low profits and that its prospects were discouraging, three successors of the thirteen-member, second-generation family each converted their business into a kind of cash-and-carry store in 1999, by adopting certain techniques used by new retail formats. Ekkaphap sells mainly daily necessities and processed foods (no perishable foods) in cash. The sales volume ratio of wholesale to retail is 60:40. In these respects, Ekkaphap is similar to other leading wholesalers. What differentiates Ekkaphap from Makro and Tang Ngee Soon is that the company expanded its business into supermarkets and minimarts. As of August 2008, Ekkaphap was running a regular supermarket chain: two stores in Saraburi, three in Lop Buri, and two in Ayutthaya, all neighboring provinces. In addition, Ekkaphap introduced, also in 2008, a minimart franchise chain system, *ran chumchon Ekkaphap* (Ekkaphap community store). As of August 2008, the company was running four stores in Saraburi and three stores in Lop Buri. The distribution center of the company shoulders delivery for its franchise chain stores as well as its regular stores.

CHARACTERISTICS OF LEADING WHOLESALERS

In provincial cities in Thailand, at present, many traditional wholesalers are trying to convert their operations into new formats by implementing certain aspects of new retail formats' management systems. As provincial entrepreneurs, all of these leading provincial wholesalers exhibit similarly strong business approaches, such as low-cost operations, though their respective formats have different characteristics.

Table 5.3 provides basic information on ten leading provincial wholesalers and their business performances for 2006, based on the companies' financial statements.[59] Each of them is a provincial-city-based, retail-cum-wholesale company. It can be observed that each company's growth rate in sales between 2004 and 2006 is generally very high. Moreover, most of these companies are growing because of an increase in sales at stores opened for at least a year, rather than an increase in the number of stores. In this respect, these wholesalers differ from new retail formats chains.

TABLE 5.3 Leading provincial daily necessities and processed foods wholesalers in Thailand in 2006

			Business performance in 2006				
Rank	Company name	Location (province)	Sales (million baht)	Growth rate 2004/2006 (%)	Gross profit (%)	Ordinary profit (%)	SG&A[a] (%)
1	Super Cheap	Phuket	3,664	36.5	2.6	0.1	2.6
2	Tang Ngee Soon Superstore	Udon Thani	1,836	10.1	1.4	0.8	1.2
3	Yongsanguan Group	Ubon Ratchathani	1,223	21.9	1.9	0.6	3.8
4	Big A Trading	Chanthaburi	987	62.4	2.4	-0.1	2.2
5	Li Wiwat Thawon	Songkhla	813	43.7	3.8	0.5	3.3
6	Leng Seng	Sakon Nakhon	584	62.2	2.0	0.3	2.1
7	Samon Phaibun 2002	Samut Sakhon	511	33.8	2.8	0.4	3.2
8	Ekkaphap Super Supply	Saraburi	506	-0.5	4.4	0.8	5.5
9	K&K Super Kha Song	Songkhla	480	-0.4	6.6	1.0	6.8
10	Thawikit Supercenter	Buri Ram	468	83.7	6.5	1.0	7.7

SOURCE: Financial statements of each company.

NOTE: Gross profit, ordinary profit and loss, and SG&A figures are all represented as sales ratios.

[a] SGA=selling, general, and administrative expenses

However, as table 5.3 shows, each company's gross profit ratio to sales is quite low. This is partly because these companies are mainly running a wholesale business, selling daily necessities and processed foods. The gross profit ratio is indeed remarkably low, even when compared with that of each hypermarket company (9.4 to 20.2 percent in 2006, as shown in chap. 4, table 4.2). For instance, the gross profit ratio is at almost the same level as, or even lower than, the cash-and-carry Makro (5.4 percent in 2006). In short, low prices are realized as a result of a narrower profit margin no less than the combination of a narrow profit margin and a large sales volume, as favored by foreign general mass merchandisers. As a result, the leading wholesalers in table 5.3 show a low ratio of ordinary profit to sales.

Another reason behind the low prices lies in a thorough, low-cost operation. This can be observed in the low ratio of selling, general, and administrative (SGA) expenses to sales, as shown in table 5.3, which is very low even when compared to hypermarkets (17.0 to 21.3 percent in 2006) and the cash-and-carry Makro (6.2 percent in 2006), as shown in chapter 4, table 4.3. How can these provincial wholesalers keep such a low SGA ratio? First, each company makes every effort possible to reduce its operating costs to the lowest level. This is done through various measures, such as not having air-conditioning equipment in their stores, displaying stock goods in cardboard boxes similar to how warehouses maintain their stock, and so on. Second, the costs of opening a new store as well as labor and physical distribution costs are much lower than nationwide chain stores of foreign general mass merchandisers. This is because local wholesalers restrict themselves to local chains in the provinces, where land prices are cheaper and wage levels are lower than in Bangkok. Third, sales associates dispatched by suppliers (manufacturers) are also an important element because this enables wholesalers to reduce labor costs. Sales associates, or promotional salespersons in this context, have a somewhat different role than those in Thailand's department store industry where goods are sold on consignment. Promotional salespersons are extremely common in general mass merchandisers and provincial leading wholesale-cum-retail stores and are generally referred to as product consultants in Thailand.

Product consultants dispatched by daily necessities and processed foods manufacturers generally have the following three duties: (i) to stand by the shelf where their products are displayed and to always keep them clean and displayed properly, (ii) to watch whether their products are sold at the proper prices in the store, and (iii) to send daily sales data back to the head office together with a comparison with other companies' products.[60] In addition, some suppliers have product consultants check their inventories and do sales promotion activities.[61] There are even cases in which suppliers' product consultants and wholesalers' employees cooperate in stocktaking.[62] Suppliers normally cover product consultants' labor costs, and the benefit is generally considered sufficient enough to offset the expense.[63] Product consultants are also helpful to host companies (wholesalers and retailers) since product consultants allow these companies to save on labor costs. Stores with larger sales volume than other stores in the nearby locality are also at a greater advantage in terms of saving on labor costs, because manufacturers determine the number of product consultants and conditions for dispatching according to the sales volume of their products.

Naturally enough, manufacturers dispatch more product consultants to stores that sell larger quantities of their products, than to stores that sell fewer of their products. In the case of stores that sell fewer of their products, manufacturers sometimes adopt a go-around system, in which a product consultant is in charge of several stores. In the case of small- and medium-sized manufacturers, which cannot afford to send a large number of product consultants, the frequency of product consultants' visits between stores is determined according to the sales volume of their products at each individual store. For example, Tang Ngee Soon's first store, the largest daily necessities and processed foods store in the province, has about two hundred employees as well as about two hundred product consultants (probably including a go-around system).[64] These two hundred product consultants are mainly appointed by major manufacturers. Thai Unilever, Osotspa, Thai Kao, Saha Pat, Foremost, and Nestle, in particular, station many product consultants at the store. Foremost, for instance, sends one product consultant per million baht of sales and thus, as of 2007, was dispatching a total of five product consultants to Udon Thani Province. Three of the five product consultants were stationed at Tang Ngee Soon, while the remaining two were in charge of other stores in the province: one to cover a Makro store and a Big C store, and the other to cover a Tesco Lotus store, a Tops supermarket, and other stores.

From this, it is clear that manufacturers attach greater importance to the stores selling the largest quantities of their products in any given locality. Manufacturers are able to encourage leading provincial wholesalers to increase the sales of their products by the assistance provided by product consultants. This is one of the important reasons why leading provincial wholesalers are so eager to increase sales or stick to large sales volume, even though that would reduce their gross profit and ordinary profit ratios.[65]

There is one more thing to add as a characteristic of leading provincial wholesalers.[66] Many of them that have modified their operations are basically selling in cash. Although a large number of provincial wholesalers still sell on credit at customers' request, the percentage of credit to the company's total sales is small. Wholesalers usually purchase goods on credit from suppliers (e.g., 14, 30, 45 days, and so on, according to the suppliers' policies), though sometimes in cash. When buying goods on credit, wholesalers can make money from the difference in the turnover rate, i.e., the time lag between purchasing on credit and selling in cash.[67] Due to data limitations, it is difficult to know exactly how much money each company can gain from the turnover rate differential and in what ways each company uses this additional revenue, but it certainly provides wholesalers with ample cash flow.

THE ROLES OF WHOLESALERS AND THE PROBLEMS THEY FACE[68]

Wholesalers, especially leading provincial wholesalers, still play important roles in the marketing channels of manufacturers. One of their most important roles is selling manufacturers' products, both at the retail level for consumers and at the wholesale level for small-scale stores and service businesses. Even major manufacturers rely heavily on the selling powers and sales networks of wholesalers, which is why their role is such a significant one. In addition to their sales functions, leading provincial wholesalers also play an important role in the delivery and finance (credit sales) of goods for small-scale retailers,[69] although some wholesalers have abandoned these functions following their conversion into a kind of cash-and-carry format.

Compared with Japanese wholesalers, however, Thai wholesalers tend to lack some of the functions of their Asian counterparts, or haven't sufficiently developed these functions.[70] For example, Thai wholesalers, in general, prefer fast-moving items, and tend to take a passive attitude toward new items, because they can't predict how well they will sell. Thai wholesalers are also reluctant to offer sales promotions to their existing small-scale store customers, and do not always actively seek new customers. In addition, they are unwilling to supply sufficient sales data to manufacturers, in spite of the fact that this is expected of them, even under sales agency contracts. Thai wholesalers usually enter into sales agency contracts with several manufacturers in order to avoid becoming an exclusive distributor for a specific manufacturer. As a result, there is often little difference between independent wholesalers and sales agents.[71] Consequently, manufacturers find themselves unable to sufficiently enforce their marketing policies even to the wholesalers who are under agency contract, not to mention independent wholesalers. Nevertheless, manufacturers have no other choice but to rely on the wholesalers' selling powers and sales networks, notably in provincial consumer markets. Thus, manufacturers attach greater importance to the wholesale functions, even though they are not always totally satisfied with them. It would seem that manufacturers send product consultants to wholesalers in order to provide wholesalers with product assistance and also to complement those functions of wholesalers that manufacturers deem insufficient.[72]

Wholesalers cannot simply continue doing business in traditional ways only, despite the fact that they are regarded as indispensable to major manufacturers' marketing channel policies. Wholesalers need to engage in some type of self-reform. Tang Ngee Soon and other provincial leading wholesalers have begun this process by modifying their store formats and adopting certain aspects of new retail formats' management systems. Thong Thai Chan Khlang Sinkha (Nakhon Sawan) Co., Ltd.,, one of the three largest wholesalers in Nakhon Sawan Province, is making efforts to improve its logistics system. For example, upon receiving a phone order from a retail store, the company immediately sends out a truck to deliver the ordered goods to the store. By maintaining this kind of customer service, the company seeks to differentiate itself from foreign general mass merchandisers. Its efforts have paid off. Thai Diethelm granted the company a contract for delivery of its goods at the provincial level (*TNSK*, August 13, 2006).

Mr. Boonchai Chokwatana, president of Saha Pat and chairperson of the Committee of Wholesale and Retail Businesses of Thailand's Board of Trade, pointed out that strengthening traditional wholesalers (*yi pua*) is necessary for local small-scale retail stores (*cho huai*) to continue to exist. He identified four actions necessary to implement such a strengthening strategy: (i) organize industrial networks among wholesalers within a province or neighboring districts; (ii) reduce sales prices through the control of a sales cost structure; (iii) improve store convenience for customers, by providing a parking area, for example; and (iv) introduce and develop logistics and information technology (*TNSK*, November 16, 2006). Tang Ngee Soon and Thong Thai Chan Khlang Sinkha have each already implemented points two through four. As for the first point, which is to organize a wholesaler network by district or province, it is not clear how practical and effective this measure would be for provincial family businesses, particularly those with a strong independent streak. In any case, it is certain that wholesalers should implement some new functions in order to respond to the structural changes in the distribution industry. Whether they can break out of the mold of tradition or not will likely determine their future success.

6

WHERE IS THE THAI GOVERNMENT'S DISTRIBUTION POLICY HEADING?

THE DISTRIBUTION INDUSTRY'S RESPONSE TO THE ADVANCE OF FOREIGN RETAILERS

We have seen that the rise of new retail formats has not always brought difficulties to the Thai distribution industry. Nevertheless, a significant number of distributors, both retailers and wholesalers, now face a crisis of vital importance, even if it is only partially or locally. In response to this, the Thai government has taken a series of measures to address the distribution problem, which in the last several years has become a significant political issue in Thailand. However, the government has been confronted with strident opposition to these measures from various players in the retail and distribution industries. Table 6.1 outlines the responses of Thailand's domestic distribution industry to the advance of foreign retailers, which were made around 2002, when individuals in the industry actively expressed their opinions on government policy, as Thai officials were presenting a series of laws and regulations in rapid succession.[1]

TABLE 6.1 Responses of local industries to the advance of foreign retailers, circa 2002

	Thai Retailers Association (led by large retailers)	Thai Wholesale and Retail Association (led by wholesalers)	Thai Salvation and Solidarity Club (led by manufacturers)
Organizational background	• consists mainly of major local retailers • about 140 members (in 2001) • President PhitthayaJi-arawisitthakun (vice president-director, C. P. Seven Eleven Co., Ltd.)	• consists mainly of local wholesalers (*yi pua*) • established on August 4, 2002 • mission is to achieve buying and selling powers as large as hypermarkets by organizing small-scale grocery stores, and organizing joint marketing among its members • President Somchai Phonrattanajaroen (Bangkok-based wholesaler)	• formed by family members of local consumer goods manufacturing business groups • established in mid-2001
Position towards the advance of foreign retailers and new retail formats	• basically against regulation towards large-scale retailers and foreign investors (positive evaluation of the influences of new foreign retail formats and technology) • recognizes some support for small- and medium-sized enterprises is needed	• expresses concern about the harm to small-scale suppliers caused by the expansion of foreign hypermarkets (e.g., forced to reduce wholesale prices and pay various fees, confronted with severe competition with the private label goods of foreign hypermarkets)	• criticizes the regulations against foreign hypermarkets for making little progress, though the Thaksin government does make a positive statement about the regulations at the time of its establishment
Measures to be taken	• participating in the Draft Working Committee for the Retail and Wholesale Business Act • stresses that the commercial practices of hypermarkets are ordinary trade practices, so the government should be careful in judging whether they are unfair	• planning to cooperate with suppliers (manufacturers) in order to compete with foreign hypermarkets (i.e., wholesalers and small-scale grocery stores plan to cooperate to build a new marketing channel for manufacturers)	• cooperating with consumer organizations and business associations, as well as small- and medium-scale retailers in asking for the dismissal of Deputy Commerce Minister Suwan • cooperating with local retailers in the east and northeast who oppose the opening of foreign hypermarkets

Other organizations, business groups, and companies			
Organizational background and activities	Retailers Organization • consists of small- and medium-sized retailers, and is a separate organization from the Thai Retailers Association • on December 19, 2000, holds a symposium on the future prospects of the retail business Provincial Chambers of Commerce and Municipalities • complain to the government (via the Thai Chamber of Commerce) that the commercial practices of foreign hypermarkets fall under unfair trade practices • survey the influences of new retail formats on local small- and medium-sized retailers • enact a municipal ordinance in Chanthaburi to regulate the expansion of large-scale retailers	Various large-scale foreign retailers • On May 10 and 29, 2002, the chairperson of the board of directors of UK-based Tesco and the managing director of the Thai local company of France-based Carrefour speak with Prime Minister Thaksin to express their cooperation with Thailand's government • Foreign hypermarket companies point out the demerits of regulation to the government both directly and through diplomatic channels as well The Central Group • again concentrates managerial resources into its traditional core business—department stores • establishes a cross-docking and distribution center	C. P. Seven Eleven Co., Ltd. • complains that the regulation on operating hours and trade fees would make it impossible to operate convenience stores WinStore Co., Ltd. • established in August 1999 • Thailand's first Third Party Logistics (3PL) provider • devotes its activities by making full use of IT (outsources physical distribution) Major consumer goods manufacturers • took the lead in reorganizing small-scale retailers in order to build new marketing channels, which represented a kind of distribution integration at an individual maker level (e.g., Saha Group, Unilever) • the Saha Group organized small-scale retailers to develop its "108 Shop" chain, where the group's products are sold at below market prices

SOURCES: Author interviews with representatives of the industries and persons concerned; Thai-language newspapers.

The Thai Retailers Association, a representative association in the industry led by major local retailers, had about 140 members in 2001 (Thai Retailers Association, n.d.). According to the then president of the association, who was executive vice president-director of C.P. Seven Eleven, this association was fundamentally opposed to regulation against large-scale retailers and foreign investment (Kanjana and Sanlaya 2001). One reason for this was that members of the association believed new retail formats and the innovations introduced by foreign retailers had brought positive influences to Thailand's retail industry. The association also argued that requiring manufacturers/suppliers to pay rebates and charging them special fees were common commercial practices among foreign general mass merchandisers, and that the government should be careful in intervening to determine whether it constituted an unfair trade practice. The association also expressed its opinion that the government needed to support small- and medium-sized retailers who were on the verge of a crisis. The Thai Retailers Association has never been particularly critical of the rise of new retail formats, at least not officially. This stems, in part, from the fact that the association's president ran 7-Eleven, a convenience store chain that is one of the most promising of the new retail formats, without direct competition from other new retail formats. 7-Eleven is the largest company in the convenience store format.

Meanwhile, the Thai Wholesale and Retail Association was against the advance of foreign retailers, which is natural enough given its mandate. The purpose of this association is to gain sufficient bargaining power to compete with general mass merchandisers. It was established in August 2002 and consists mainly of local wholesalers (*yi pua*). One of the association's main concerns is that the expansion of foreign general mass merchandisers in Thailand had caused fierce competition, resulting in ever-increasing price reductions. Another concern is that the new commercial practices and private label goods' marketing strategies, which were introduced by foreign investment, drove small-scale manufacturers into a disadvantageous situation. The association's president, Somchai Pornrattanacharoen, believed that the government should regulate such unfair practices by applying the Trade Competition Act, B.E. 2542 (1999), and was unsatisfied by the little progress made in terms of administrative measures. As of 2002, the association was working on a countermeasure against foreign general mass merchandisers by constructing a new distribution channel for manufacturers based on cooperation between its wholesalers members and small-scale grocery stores (*cho huai*), including joint marketing.

There was also another opposition movement active during the same period led by the Thai Salvation and Solidarity Club and local manufacturers. This club was formed in mid-2001 by businesspersons from local manufacturing *zaibatsu* (large business group) families who were concerned with the rise of foreign retailers. Just as the Thai Wholesale and Retail Association blamed the Thaksin government for inaction, so, too, did the Thai Salvation and Solidarity Club. Prime Minister Thaksin Sinawatra took no specific political action to address the distribution problem in Thailand, although he did state, at the time of his inauguration, that the government would take some regulatory measures against foreign general mass merchandisers. In response, the Thai Salvation and Solidarity Club, on the base of its political power, started a joint movement with consumer organizations and business organizations as well as small- and medium-sized retailers, to put pressure on the government to dismiss Suwan Walaisatien, the then deputy commerce minister in charge of the distribution policy.[2] By November 2002, in cooperation with small- and medium-sized retailers, the club organized a movement against new store openings of large-scale foreign retailers in northeastern and eastern Thailand.

Other organizations were also actively involved in responding to the distribution problem between 2001 and 2002. For example, each province's chamber of commerce investigated the actual situation of small- and medium-sized distributors, which were its members, and alleged that the advance of foreign general mass merchandisers into provincial cities was harming their businesses. They also demanded that the government, via the Thai Chamber of Commerce in Bangkok, take measures against foreign investment. In addition, some municipalities strove to enact municipal ordinances to protect small- and medium-sized local distributors. As this movement for government regulation became more active, foreign investors attempted to prevent the Thai government from adopting regulatory policies by organizing talks between Prime Minister Thaksin and the top management of foreign companies already operating in Thailand or overseas affiliated companies. Foreign investors also made use of diplomatic channels.

Local companies had varied responses. For example, following the financial and currency crisis, the Central Group concentrated its managerial resources again into the department store format, which was the group's traditional core business, in order to avoid dispersion of its managerial resources through corporate restructuring. In addition, the group also established a cross-docking and distribution center, following the example of foreign new retail formats, in order to build an efficient logistics system. Another example is WinStore Co., Ltd., which established itself as a kind of third-party logistics (3PL) provider by foreseeing the future importance of logistics. WinStore foresaw that logistics would be critically important in the future as new retail formats expanded their chains. Consumer goods manufacturers, expressing concerns about the rise of foreign investment, also took the lead in reorganizing small-scale retailers in order to build new marketing channels, which represented a kind of distribution integration strategy.[3] Although these companies each held different positions toward foreign retailers, they have in common that they individually strove to achieve more efficient logistics by following strategies used by foreign retailers, including the use of information technology to some extent. On the other hand, however, it is true that a number of small- and medium-sized distributors failed to cope with such a rapid fundamental change. That is why Thailand's government had no choice but to attach greater importance to the country's distribution policy.

DISTRIBUTION POLICIES UNDER THE THAKSIN ADMINISTRATION

BACKGROUND

Prior to Thaksin, no Thai government had ever adopted policies directly regarding the retail and distribution industries, whereas the Thaksin government formulated and applied various regulatory measures concerned with the recent distribution issue, whether they were right or wrong. The contents and implications of the Thaksin government's policies for the distribution industry from February 2001 until September 2006 are considered in this section. Table 6.2 shows a general overview of the changes in the distribution policy in the period between the post-currency crisis and the end of the Thaksin government.

The distribution policy of the Thaksin government can be divided into five periods of time. The first period begins in 2001 around the time of his inauguration. Prime Minister Thaksin, paying attention to the difficulties of domestic distributors caused by the rise of foreign retailers, expressed his opinion that the government should adopt certain regulations to protect domestic distributors. Commerce Minister Adisai and Deputy Commerce Minister Suwan, in charge of the distribution policy, also clearly expressed similar stances. Accordingly, the domestic distribution industry expected the new government to succeed in drafting and enacting the Retail and Wholesale Business Act, a piece of legislation that had begun to be developed in late 2000 towards the end of the Chuan government's term in office.

TABLE 6.2 Changes in the Thai government's distribution policy, 1997–2006

	Timeline of government actions regarding a national distribution policy
1997	Chawarit government/ Chuan government
Nov	establishment of second Chuan government
1998	Chuan government
Dec 25	BOI designates retail and distribution industries as eligible for industry investment promotion (until December 31,1999)
1999	Chuan government
Mar 22	promulgation of Trade Competition Act B.E. 2542 (1999)
Nov 24	promulgation of Foreign Business Act B.E. 2542 (1999)
2000	Chuan government
Dec	establishment of Draft Working Committee for the Retail and Wholesale Business Act
2001	Chuan government / Thaksin government
Feb	establishment of Thaksin government
	at a national meeting in Phuket, the Thai Chamber of Commerce decides to ask the government for early enactment of the new law and an amendment to the existing Foreign Business Act in order to strengthen industry regulations; Commerce Minister Adisai and Deputy Minister Suwan emphasize the need for regulations against large-scale retailers
Aug 6	the government announces it is considering the enforcement of zoning regulations and operation hours regulations using the existing Urban Planning Act B.E. 2518 (1975), and the Building Control Act B.E. 2522 (1979) (the enactment of the Retail and Wholesale Business Act is shelved)
Oct 22	the cabinet discusses measures for retail and wholesale businesses and decides not to adopt regulations against foreign investment
2002	Thaksin government
Mar 6	following a cabinet reshuffle, Newin is appointed deputy commerce minister
Mar 28	Newin invites delegates of small-scale retailers and suppliers, as well as three hypermarkets and one cash-and-carry store to discuss matters, declaring that he will apply the Trade Competition Act B.E. 2542 (1999) if he finds that the hypermarkets and cash-and-carry stores have applied unfair trade practices; Newin simultaneously stresses the need to establish a joint-purchase organization to support small-scale retailers
Apr	the Examining Working Committee on Unfair Trade Competition Practices is established

	Timeline of government actions regarding a national distribution policy
2002	Thaksin government (con't)
May 7	the Commerce Ministry's Internal Trade Department sponsors a seminar to discuss unfair trade practices by large-scale retailers, and consider applying the Trade Competition Act against them
Apr–Jun	arrangements are made by the Commerce Ministry's Internal Trade Department for the establishment of ART (Allied Retail Trade) Co., Ltd. to support small and medium-sized retailers, and the resumption of a procedure for the enactment of the Retail and Wholesale Act
May 7	at a cabinet meeting, the budget for relief to local small- and medium-sized retailers (395 million baht) is approved
May 31	the Examining Subcommittee on Unfair Trade Competition Practices, on the basis of its working committee's report, decides to conduct an inquiry by asking delegates of three hypermarkets and one cash-and-carry store to meet with Deputy Commerce Minister Newin on June 19
Jun	the adviser to the commerce division of the UK embassy and the French ambassador to Thailand ask to speak with Newin
Jun 19	an inquiry into unfair trade practices by three hypermarkets and one cash-and-carry store begins
Jun 25	the establishment of ART (Allied Retail Trade) Co., Ltd. is approved at acabinet meeting
Jul 8	members of ART's board of directors are made public
Aug 6	ART Co., Ltd. is established by the government with capital investment and is to begin operations on September 1, 2002
	the Commerce Council sponsors a seminar on Thailand's retail issues
	75 provincial Chambers of Commerce throughout the country request the government to suspend the expansion of hypermarket and cash-and-carry chains and to provide the chambers with a chance to speak to the prime minister
Sep 1	ART begins operations
Sep 11	the Internal Trade Department sponsors a seminar to discuss the draft of the Retail and Wholesale Business Act
Sep 23	the Examining Subcommittee on Unfair Trade Competition Practices completes its review of a two-pointed complaint about large-scale retailers made by suppliers, and concludes that: (1) by virtually forcing its suppliers to use its distribution center the Central Group engaged in an unfair trade practice; and (2) by insisting that suppliers obey their demands, foreign hypermarkets and cash-and-carry stores engaged in an unfair trade practice
Oct 2	the Examining Subcommittee on Unfair Trade submits a draft of criteria for unfair trade to the Examining Committee on Unfair Trade
Oct3	following a cabinet reshuffle, Wattana is appointed deputy commerce minister (Newin is transferred to deputy agriculture and cooperative minister)
Nov 4	for fear of sending a wrong signal to foreign investors, Wattana states that the Retail and Wholesale Business Act is unnecessary

	Timeline of government actions regarding a national distribution policy
Nov16	Prime Minister Thaksin states that the government will withdraw the Retail and Wholesale Business Act bill and, instead, promises to take measures based on the existing Urban Planning Act within four months
Dec 15	ART officially begins its bulk-purchasing system
2003	Thaksin government
May 19	notification of the Mandate of the Public Works and Town & Country Planning Department, based on the Urban Planning Act, announcing that 72 provinces had no comprehensive urban planning (i.e., urban planning was in place in only certain areas of each province) and, therefore, land use regulations should be enforced for those areas without urban planning, is published in the Official Gazette (enforced May 20)
Sep 10	notification of the Notice of the Public Works and Town & Country Planning Department, based on the Urban Planning Act, is published in the Official Gazette (valid until May 19, 2006)
Sep 12	notification of the Notice of the Ministry of Interior, based on the Building Control Act B.E. 2522 (1979), announcing that 72 provinces had no comprehensive urban planning (i.e., urban planning was in place in only certain areas of each province) and that land use regulations should be enforced for those areas with urban planning already in place, is published in the Official Gazette (enforced Sep 13, and valid for 1 year)
2004	Thaksin government
Mar 3	the Public Works and Town & Country Planning Department jointly sponsors a seminar with the Ministry of Commerce and the Board of Trade of Thailand on deregulation of retail business
Mar 17	the Thai Chamber of Commerce, Thai Retailers Association, Thai Wholesale and Retail Association, and consumer organizations jointly establish a working committee to reconsider the content of the Interior Ministry Notice, dated September 12, 2003
Mar 22	promulgation of the Notice of Ministry of Interior regarding site plan regulations of large-scale retailers in Bangkok
Apr 30	notification of the Notice of the Ministry of Interior regarding site plan regulations of large-scale retailers in Bangkok is published in the Official Gazette (enforced May 1)
Aug 4	ART signs an agreement to enter into a business partnership with the Phranakhon Cooperative
Sep 3	notification of the Ordinance of the Ministry of Interior, based on the Building Control Act, is published in the Official Gazette (enforced the same day)
2005	Thaksin government
Apr 27	notification of the Bangkok Municipal Ordinance, based on the Building Control Act, announcing that the Bangkok Metropolitan Administration should enforce site plan regulations for its jurisdiction, is published in the Official Gazette (enforced Apr 28)
2006	Thaksin government / Surayud government
May 16	the New Bangkok Comprehensive Plan (revised second edition) is published in the Official Gazette (enforced May 17, and valid for 5 years)
May 19	the 2003 Notice of the Public Works and Town & Country Planning Department expires

	Timeline of government actions regarding a national distribution policy
2006	Thaksin government (con't)
Aug	the Internal Trade Department, Ministry of Commerce, makes efforts to reenact the Retail and Wholesale Business Act, also issuing guidelines on trade between distributors and manufacturers
Aug 29	notification of the Notice of the Public Works and Town & Country Planning Department, based on the Urban Planning Act, announcing that 72 provinces have no comprehensive urban planning and urging enactment of such planning, is published in the Official Gazette (enforced Aug 30, and valid for 3 years)
Sep	Business Development Department, Ministry of Commerce, begins planning the Nework project for local stores
	The guidelines for retail businesses, based on the Trade Competition Act, are developed by the Ministry of Commerce
Sep 13	Deputy Commerce Minister Pricha calls on15 large-scale retailers to discuss their impact on small-scale grocery stores and asks them to sign the Ministry of Commerce's MOU, but none do
Sep 20	collapse of the Thaksin government due to a coup d'état

SOURCES: Author interviews with government authorities; Thai-language newspapers.

Prime Minister Thaksin, however, gradually came to express his disapproval of regulations against foreign investment about six months after coming into office. This marks the second period of distribution policy under Thaksin. Given that Thailand's economy relied heavily on foreign investment and that economic globalization was increasingly intensifying, the government could not really take explicit regulatory measures against foreign investment. So, instead of referring directly to the source of retail investment, the regulations were simply aimed at "large-scale retail stores." It was, nevertheless, obvious that the government was actually targeting foreign general mass merchandisers. Yet, there was a chance this would send an unfavorable signal that the government was leaning towards adopting regulations against foreign industrial investment and not just retail businesses. Based on this realistic assessment, in August 2001, Thaksin announced he was considering enforcing zoning regulations and business hours regulations based on the Urban Planning Act B.E. 2518 (1975) and the Building Control Act B.E. 2522 (1979) already in force, to express his belief that the government could cope with the distribution issue by using existing legislation. Around the same time, the prime minister began to consider postponing the enactment of the Retail and Wholesale Business Act, and was determined to shelve the introduction of foreign investment regulations at the cabinet meeting in October 2001.

The conversion of the Thaksin government's distribution policy, from supporting foreign investment regulations at the beginning of his term to then postponing it half a year later, caused strong dissatisfaction and criticism among the retail and distribution industries. As a result of this, during a cabinet reshuffle in March 2002, Thaksin replaced Deputy Commerce Minister Suwan, who was the one most severely criticized by the general public, and appointed Newin Chidchob as the new deputy commerce minister in charge of the government's distribution policy. The third period begins at this point and lasts until the next cabinet reshuffle that took place in early October 2002, when the deputy commerce minister was replaced once again. Immediately after becoming minister in March 2002, Deputy Commerce Minister Newin had invited representatives of small-scale retailers, suppliers (manufacturers and sales companies), and general mass merchandisers for talks. He asserted that the government would strictly apply the Trade Competition Act B.E. 2542 (1999) if general mass merchandisers abused their advantageous position by conducting unfair trade practices, which were disadvantageous to their business connections and/or competitors.[4] Newin simultaneously insisted that the government should establish a joint purchasing organization to support small-scale retailers. After that, for a short period of time under Newin's leadership, the government successively adopted various policies to support local distributors. Among these measures were (i) the establishment of the Examining Subcommittee on Unfair Trade Competition Practices and its working committee (April 2002), for which Deputy Commerce Minister Newin served as chairperson for both committees, (ii) a seminar sponsored by the Commerce Ministry's Internal Trade Department to discuss unfair trade practices by large-scale retailers and to consider applying the Trade Competition Act against them, (iii) arrangements for the establishment of ART (Allied Retail Trade) Co., Ltd., a joint purchasing organization, to support small- and medium-sized retailers, and (iv) the resumption of a procedure for the enactment of the Retail and Wholesale Act.

Actually, in August 2002, ART Co., Ltd. was established by the government with capital investment and was to begin operations on September 1, 2002. The working draft of the Retail and Wholesale Act was also making steady progress. In addition, the Examining Subcommittee on Unfair Trade Competition Practices, led by Deputy Commerce Minister Newin, reached the conclusion in the last ten days of September that large-scale retailers' trade practices, such as requests for entrance and planogram fees, were unfair (*KTTK-RW*, September 24, 2002). In short, the government was about to investigate and expose the unfair trade practices of foreign general mass merchandisers. It is actually surprising that it only took seven months for such a broad array of distribution policies to be put into action in Thailand, where no direct laws regarding the retail industry had ever been in force.

However, with the cabinet reshuffle on October 3, 2002, Thailand's distribution policy went through various changes yet again. The fourth period marking distribution policies under Thaksin begins with this cabinet reshuffle and lasts until mid-November of the same year. Deputy Commerce Minister Newin, who had actively led the government's distribution policy, was transferred to the post of deputy minister of agriculture and cooperatives, and Wattana Muangsuk took Newin's place as the deputy commerce minister in charge of the country's distribution policy. Many people in the domestic retail and distribution industries were concerned that the government's distribution policy might swing back and withdraw support for regulations against large-scale and foreign retailers with the appointment of Wattana.[5] This concern came from the fact that the distribution policy powerfully led by his predecessor could clash with the business expansion of C.P. Seven Eleven (currently, CP All), a subsidiary of the CP Group, with whose founding family Wattana was related by marriage.[6] Although the first targets were foreign general mass merchandisers, the Examining Committee on Unfair Trade was about to extend the target to major local retailers, such as Central Department Store and 7-Eleven, which could use their advantageous positions against suppliers and small- and medium-sized businesses in the same way as foreign retailers (*PJK-RW*, October 3, 2002). It is unknown, however, whether or not Wattana attempted to convert existing government policy by placing his personal interests as a top priority. Since Thaksin intended to control the unexpectedly rapid progression of foreign investment regulations, he replaced Newin, his point person in charge of the distribution policy, with Wattana. In any case, it soon became obvious that the regulations against large-scale and foreign retailers were being weakened all at once following Wattana's appointment. By mid-November 2002, Prime Minister Thaksin declared that the government was going to withdraw the Retail and Wholesale Business Act bill, just prior to the completion of the draft. While the government suggested the possibility that it would eventually enact ministerial guidelines, notices, and ordinances based on existing laws if fair competition was hindered, it also clearly expressed its concern that the Retail and Wholesale Business Act, which was virtually aimed at foreign retailers, could send a wrong signal to the market. On the other hand, however, the government began to support the operations of the ART project, as planned, whose purpose was to protect and support small-scale retailers.

It is likely that Prime Minister Thaksin did not intend for the government to adopt a laissez-faire policy towards the business expansion of general mass merchandisers. For instance, at the end of November 2002, soon after withdrawing the draft of the Retail and Wholesale Business Act, the prime minister declared that the government would take legal measures within four months to realize a fair competitive environment for retail business in accordance with the Urban Planning Act. Eventually, in the latter half of 2003, the government issued the Notice of the Public Works and Town & Country Planning Department, based on the Urban Planning Act, B.E. 2518 (1975), announcing that seventy-two provinces had no comprehensive urban planning (i.e., urban planning was in place in only certain areas of each province) and, therefore, land use regulations should be enforced for those areas *without* urban planning. The government also issued the Notice of the Ministry of Interior, based on the Building Control Act, B.E. 2522 (1979), announcing that among the seventy-two provinces with no comprehensive urban planning, land use regulations should also be enforced for those areas *with* urban planning already in place. It was determined to choose a method to regulate the store openings of large-scale retailers, especially general mass merchandisers. In other words, while the government shelved the enactment of the Retail and Wholesale Business Act to which foreign retailers and others were vehemently objecting, it considered the situation of local small- and medium-sized retailers, wholesalers, and consumer goods manufacturers and took some political measures within the framework of existing laws. This marks the fifth period, extending from the end of November 2002 to Thaskin's downfall in September 2006. While it may seem, at a glance, that the Thaksin government once again shifted its distribution policy back to a reinforcement of regulations during this period, the author thinks otherwise. This is because, even though the content of the Public Works and Interior Ministry notices was very strict, its actual application was not effective, as will be later discussed. Another reason is that the government was actually planning to reexamine its regulatory measures. In this sense, the fifth period can be regarded as a continuation of the fourth.

The Thaksin government's distribution policy thus began supporting various regulations against foreign retailers, and then entered a period of deregulation. This period was followed by a fundamental review of its policy as a result of the severity of criticism that had emerged from domestic industries. It stimulated a move to reinforce the application of regulations again, with Newin at the helm. After Newin's transfer and the appointment of Wattana to lead the government's response to the country's distribution problem, the Thaksin government actually began to get the reinforcement of regulations under control, making efforts to prevent extreme regulation while simultaneously addressing the interests among local companies, which continued up until the collapse of the government as a result of the September 2006 coup d'état. To fully understand the implications of the Thaksin government's distribution policy, it is necessary to go back in time to look at the process involved in the drafting of the controversial Retail and Wholesale Business Act.

DRAFTING OF THE RETAIL AND WHOLESALE BUSINESS ACT

Just prior to completing the working draft of the Retail and Wholesale Business Act (the "Act") and submitting it to the cabinet, the government discarded its proposal to enact the Retail and Wholesale Business Act (the "bill"), which had been long awaited among the domestic retail and distribution industries as a measure that would help protect their businesses. Examining the content of the Act will help not only to better understand distribution policies under Thaksin but will also provide a clearer picture of the distribution issues that Thailand is presently facing.

The working draft of the Act was actually started in 1999, during the Chuan government.[7] In the midst of the post–currency-crisis period, small- and medium-sized local retailers in each area were in distress, in contrast with foreign retailers that were on the rise. As a consequence, local retailers petitioned the provincial chambers of commerce in their respective provinces for help. The Thai Chamber of Commerce in Bangkok gathered the petitions to submit them to the Ministry of Commerce. Upon receiving them, the Ministry of Commerce had the Department of Internal Trade discuss countermeasures against foreign retailers and reached a conclusion that the government should draft a bill to protect small- and medium-sized local retailers and wholesalers. The then deputy commerce minister, Newin, accelerated work on the drafting of the Act that had been delayed since the change of governments. The key points of the Act, which consists of five chapters and fifty-five articles, are summarized in table 6.3, while table 6.4 provides the names of the committee members that would be in charge of implementing the Act.[8]

TABLE 6.3 Main features of Thailand's Retail and Wholesale Business Act

	Key Points
Purpose	To provide a framework for coexistence of all retailers and wholesalers, irrespective of business size and format
	• to support the capacity of small- and medium-sized distributors without impeding fair competition • to remove disadvantages between distributors • to prevent negative influences on the community and the environment
Chapter I	Establishment of the Retail and Wholesale Supervision Committee and its authority
	Central Supervision Committee (chaired by the Commerce Minister) • to prescribe the format and size of retail businesses subject to regulation, while developing a policy and plan that enables small-scale retailers to coexist with large-scale ones • to prescribe measures to control retail and wholesale businesses, e.g., to prescribe criteria for the establishment of new companies and new stores, application procedures, and other requirements • to request an impact analysis for the opening of large-scale retail stores and to order suspension and revision of business projects, as well as to request an explanation of circumstances • to prescribe penal codes for violations of the law Provincial Supervision Committee (chaired by the provincial governor in each province) • to transfer implementation authority to local self-governing bodies • to prescribe detailed criteria and measures according to the specific circumstances of each locality, within a framework fixed by the Central Supervision Committee • to examine the applications for new store openings and grant permission • to regulate unfair trade practices and unfair sales to consumers
Chapter II	Establishment of the Office of Retail and Wholesale Supervision Committee and its authority
	• to make the Internal Trade Department of the Ministry of Commerce the secretariat of the Central Retail and Wholesale Supervision Committee responsible for overseeing retail and wholesale businesses and supervising the Appeal Hearing Committee and the Subcommittee for Cooperation between the Central Supervision and Provincial Supervision Committees • to have the authority to call the parties concerned and request them to explain a situation and present necessary data including financial statements

	Key Points
Chapter III	Maintenance of order in the retail and wholesale businesses
	• to maintain order in the retail and wholesale businesses, e.g., by preventing disadvantages and unfair bargaining practices between traders • to implement zoning regulations of retail business (based on the locality's population, the number of retail stores, the distance between large-scale stores, and so on) • to prescribe the number of operating days and operating hours • to prohibit an excessively heavy burden on suppliers and the imposition of disadvantageous conditions on suppliers • to require permission from the chief of the Internal Trade Department or the provincial governor for new store openings, and to determine the influence on the business, people, and environment in the locality and to develop an improvement plan • to prescribe measures to support small-scale retailers (e.g., low cost purchasing, preparation of sales locations and a distribution system for goods, construction of a network between retailers and wholesalers, implementation of joint-marketing activities)
Chapter IV	Examination of appeal
	• anyone denied an application for a store opening by an order issued by the Central Supervision or Provincial Supervision Committees is given a right to appeal to the Appeal Hearing Committee • the chief of the Internal Trade Department appoints members to the Appeal Hearing Committee, consisting of two groups: individuals from among the staff of the department, including a secretary and an assistant secretary, and up to six individuals from outside of the department
Chapter V	Penal regulations
	• administrative penal codes are prescribed clearly and in detail • for a single offense, the penalty can reach up to 200,000 baht and the announcement of the offender's name • in the case of a refusal to pay the penalty, up to 3 months imprisonment or up to a 5,000 baht penalty per day, or both

source: Based on the draft of the Retail and Wholesale Business Act (Judicial Affairs Section of Internal Trade Department, Ministry of Commerce); author interviews at the Judicial Affairs Section, Internal Trade Department; Thai-language newspapers.

TABLE 6.4 Members of Supervision Committees, based on the Retail and Wholesale Business Act

	Central Retail and Wholesale Supervision Committee	Provincial Retail and Wholesale Supervision Committee
Chairperson	Commerce Minister	Provincial Governor
Secretary	• Chief of the Internal Trade Department	• Chief of the provincial office of the Ministry of Commerce
Assistant secretary		• Chief of the provincial office of the Internal Trade Department
Committee members	• Permanent Secretary of Commerce • Permanent Secretary of the Interior • Permanent Secretary of Industry • Permanent Secretary of Public Health • Secretary General of NESDB • Governor of the Metropolis of Bangkok • Representative of Thai Chamber of Commerce • Representative of Federation of Thai Industries • Representatives of consumer organizations • Persons of learning and experience (4–6 persons, more than half from the private sector)	• Chief of the provincial office of the Department of Public Works and Town & Country Planning • Representative of the provincial Chamber of Commerce • Representative of provincial Association of Thai Industries • Representative of provincial Federation of Thai Industries • Staff of local self-governing bodies • Representatives of commercial organizations • Representatives of consumer organizations • Persons of learning and experience (4–6 persons, more than half from the private sector)

SOURCE: *KTTK-RW*, August 9, 2002.

First of all, let us consider the purpose of the Act. As noted in table 6.3, the Act never stated, at least nominally, that the government would regulate large-scale retailers and completely protect small- and medium-sized distributors. The government persistently aimed at securing a fair competitive environment in order to prevent extreme advantages and disadvantages from arising, according to business size and the differences in format. The government also directly avoided referring to foreign retailers as the target of the Act. In addition, the government paid attention to the benefit of local residents and consumers and to the competing interests among the related industries. In short, compared to Japan, the Act was more similar to Japan's Large-Scale Retail Store Location Law than Japan's Large-Scale Retail Store Law, the latter of which is characterized by strict regulations.

Let us observe the responsibilities of the organizations in charge of implementing Thailand's Retail and Wholesale Business Act, as outlined in table 6.3. The organizations in charge were roughly divided into two governmental levels: the Retail and Wholesale Supervision Committee, with the commerce minister as its chairperson and its bureau at the central level, and the Provincial Retail and Wholesale Supervision Committee, with each provincial governor as its chairperson and its bureau at the provincial level (as for the names of the committees' members, see table 6.4). The committee at the central level was authorized to do the following: (a) prescribe criteria for the format and size of retail business and to draw up policies and projects that would enable small-scale retailers to co-exist with larger ones; (b) prescribe regulatory measures, such as principles of permission and approval, "how-to" procedures, and requirements for new store openings; (c) assess the impact of large-scale store openings and to order the restraint and amendment of business plans, as necessary, as well as ask for explanations regarding certain facts; and (d) prescribe penal regulations in cases of violation of the law. On the other hand, the provincial committee, which was established in each province outside of Bangkok, was authorized not only to prescribe criteria and measures in more detail within the framework provided by the central committee, according to the actual circumstances of each province, but also to permit and approve the opening of new stores. In short, the central government attempted to transfer much of the executive authority to each provincial committee, which was consistent with the promotion of decentralization incorporated into the Constitution of Thailand, B.E. 2540 (1997).

It is in the third chapter that the content of the regulations is defined, that is, to maintain a competitive environment for both retail and wholesale businesses by preventing unfair bargaining practices between traders. If we look at the Act more closely, we can see that it not only included commercial zoning regulations, rules regarding days and hours of business operation, the prohibition of unfair trade practices, and so on, but it also adopted a license system regarding the opening of new stores. The Act suggests that, in addition to foreign general mass merchandisers, convenience stores could also be a target of these regulations. It is very natural that the senior management of both general mass merchandisers and convenience stores would criticize the potential new law, given that they were continually expanding their businesses. In the third chapter of the Act, there is an article about providing support to small-scale retailers, but this article had no direct relation to the establishment of ART Co., Ltd., which was a joint purchasing organization.[9]

Under the fourth chapter of the Act, applicants that are denied approval for opening a new store have a right to appeal. The same appeals process applies to persons accused of engaging in unfair trade practices. The Appeal Hearing Committee is responsible for reviewing the content of appeals, in which representatives of the Internal Trade Department and persons of learning and experience are to be appointed as committee members. In the fifth chapter of the Act, penal regulations are prescribed in detail.

The Commerce Ministry's Internal Trade Department sponsored a seminar on September 11, 2002, to discuss the Retail and Wholesale Business Act, where all the parties that would be affected met to exchange their views on the Act.[10] Large-scale retailers, who would be most impacted by the Act, proposed the following five revisions: (a) define more clearly terms such as "retail business," "wholesale business," and "selling;" (b) increase the ratio of private sector representatives in the Retail and Wholesale Supervision Committee and its provincial committee; (c) clarify the criteria for regulating retail and wholesale businesses, but do not discriminate by business size or store floor space; (d) clarify the conditions and methods of supervision and support by the provincial committee (e.g., business hours, store floor space, and division of retail formats), and unify those throughout the country; and (e) delete the article regarding the prohibition of unfair trade practices, given that it overlaps with the existing Trade Competition Act. Large-scale retailers were against the article on unfair trade practices because it specifically targeted a certain type of business, and would restrict the freedom of business activities. They also argued that regulating large-scale retail stores would reduce the choices of shopping venues for general consumers and increase prices.

As large-scale retailers argued, while it might be true that the Act was actually targeted at a specific business type, which would be disadvantageous for the business, it was not, however, clear whether it would actually be disadvantageous for general consumers. There was, indeed, a risk that those companies, which were putting a great deal of effort into selling goods at low prices for the short term due to severe competition, would become oligopolistic. A further risk was that these companies would change their business strategy and raise their prices in the medium and long term. Another possibility was that, after driving out older local distributors, such companies would close their stores due to a lack of profitability, and consumers would lose places to shop. In addition, the low-price sales strategy of general mass merchandisers would reduce the profits of their competitors and suppliers, thus bringing about a negative effect on the entire local economy. Nevertheless, large-scale retailers were against the Retail and Wholesale Business Act and were pressuring policy makers to at least minimize the extent of the regulations if the government was determined to enact the bill. It seems that the pressures from foreign retailers and local large-scale retailers, who had strong political influence, had a role in Prime Minister Thaksin's decision to discard the bill.

Although the Retail and Wholesale Business Act, which was aiming direct regulation against foreign retailers and large-scale retailers, was finally withdrawn, ART Co. Ltd., a joint purchasing organization whose purpose was to support local small-scale retailers, made progress even after Newin's resignation.

ESTABLISHMENT AND DEVELOPMENT OF ART

One of the most important reasons why small-scale local retailers have been hurt by the rise of foreign new retail formats lies in the fact that small-scale retailers were at a disadvantage in terms of trade with suppliers because they purchased much smaller quantities of products than new foreign retail formats and, as a result, did not have the bargaining power to negotiate lower prices. It was believed that if small-scale retailers were organized and a head office purchased goods in bulk, the amount of orders to suppliers would then drastically increase to such an extent that small-scale retailers would be able to compete with large-scale retailers. It was this belief that led to the launch of ART, as a joint purchasing organization. At first, however, the government had no intention to establish ART as a company. It was only after the appointment of Newin as deputy commerce minister that ART became a limited company.[11]

On June 25, 2002, it was decided at a cabinet meeting to establish ART (Allied Retail Trade) Co., Ltd., and on August 6 of the same year, the company was founded with the use of public funds. The registered capital was 395 million baht, of which the Small Industry Finance Corporation (SIFC) under the jurisdiction of the Ministry of Industry contributed 49 percent, while the Office of Small- and Medium-Sized Enterprises Promotion (Office of SMEs Promotion) under the jurisdiction of the Ministry of Finance contributed the remaining 51 percent. The main function of the company was to organize small-scale retailers by adopting a membership system. Under the company's first business plan, two kinds of stores would be able to participate in ART: franchise chain stores and independent stores. ART expected a total of one hundred thousand stores to become members by 2004 (as of February 2004, approximately forty thousand stores had applied for membership). The head office not only taught members how to modernize the management of their businesses but also conducted joint marketing and advertising activities. Moreover, SIFC, one of the company's investors, set out to finance the remodeling and business expansion of members' stores at lower than open market rates. The state-owned Krung Thai Bank and later, Siam City Bank, as well, were supposed to offer loans to ART members.

Immediately following its establishment, ART's president-director, Pennapha Dhanasarnsilp, was interviewed by a Thai-language newspaper and said:

> The revenue of the company comes from collecting only one percent of the total sum of orders from the joint purchasing organization users, and collecting one percent of sales from the franchise chain stores. The goods ART jointly purchases are daily necessities items and limited to two to three hundred items. Compared with general wholesalers (*yi pua*) who sell more than two thousand items, ART sells a much smaller variety of items. Therefore, wholesalers should not be influenced negatively by the activity of ART. Similarly, the cash-and-carry Makro should not be affected either, because the number of items that ART sells is only one percent of that of Makro, while small-scale grocery stores (*cho huai*) sell around one thousand items. Since the sales increase of small retailers would cause an increase in the sum of purchases from wholesalers and Makro, the support of ART to small-scale retailers seems to have a positive influence on wholesalers and Makro as well. (*PRCT-TK*, August 26, 2002)

In short, the president argued that ART's aim was not to compete directly with large-scale retailers, such as foreign general mass merchandisers, but mainly to provide the infrastructure necessary to improve the competitiveness of small-scale retailers.

Figure 6.1 shows the order, payment, data, and delivery flow of ART's distribution system at the time of its establishment. The head office gathered order data from each member store and then sent a collective order to manufacturers/suppliers. In Bangkok, online orders from members were sent directly to the head office, while in the provinces, members' orders were first collected by the designated department in each provincial chamber of commerce and then sent to Bangkok. Accordingly, the mode of payment for purchases differed to some extent between Bangkok and the provinces. In Bangkok the head office paid suppliers by way of the financial institutions with which ART had dealings, while in the provinces each provincial chamber of commerce was in charge of payments. As for the physical distribution of goods, ART basically organized joint delivery to reduce costs. In Bangkok, where the number of members and the amount of orders were significantly larger, goods were first delivered to the distribution center in bulk and then divided before being sent to each store. In the provinces, too, a similar system was to be implemented as members increased in number. ART chose to entrust the operation of the distribution center and the delivery to outside companies.[12]

FIGURE 6.1 Distribution System of ART Co., Ltd., at time of establishment

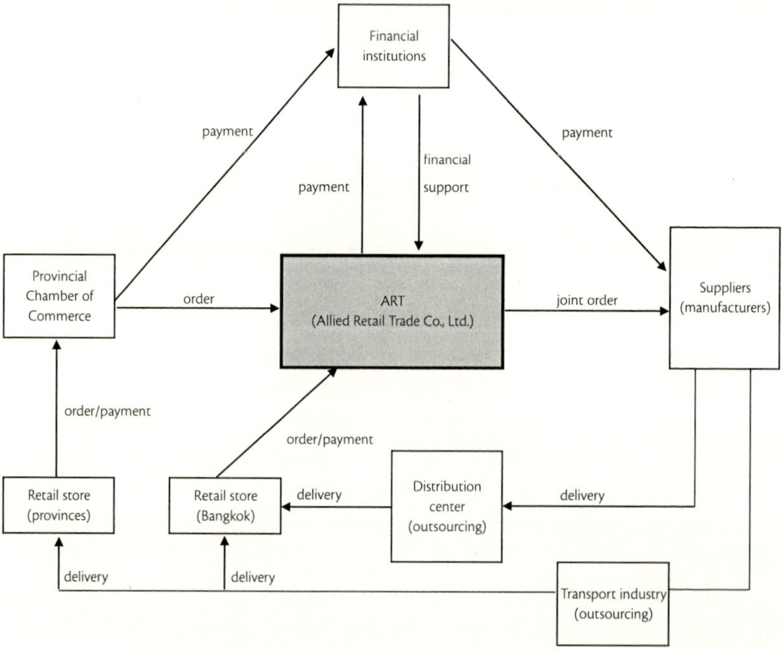

SOURCE: Author interview with the Office of Business Support, Internal Trade Department, Ministry of Commerce (Bangkok, October 22, 2002).

Considering the great number of members expected in the future and the complexity of the system, advanced special knowledge was needed to manage ART. This is why ART invited the very best professional managers from among the industry as directors of the company. Table 6.5 shows the top management of the company at the time of establishment. Ms. Pennapha was installed as president of ART. She was one of the founding family members of the Saha Group and a member of its administration. Mr. Anuchai, a former executive officer of a foreign-led general mass merchandiser in Thailand, was installed as managing director. The other five directors, from the private sector, were also managers of Thailand's leading companies. It can be said that the management consisted of an extraordinary cast. In addition to these seven private sector delegates, the following four representatives from the government sector participated in the management of ART: the permanent secretary to the Ministry of Commerce, the chief of the Bureau of Fiscal Policy in the Fiscal Policy Office of the Ministry of Finance, the secretary general of Office of SMEs Promotion, and the director of SIFC.

TABLE 6.5 Senior management of ART, at the time of establishment

Position	Name	Brief career history
7 representatives from the private sector		
President	Ms. Pennapha Dhanasarnsilp	• Director, Saha Pathanapibul Plc • Former President, Marketing Association of Thailand
Managing director	Mr. Anuchai Wiraphatthanakun	• Former Executive Officer, Siam Makro Plc (in charge of foods) • Former Vice President and Executive Officer, Big C Supercenter Plc (in charge of foods)
Director	Mr. Somphop Amatayakun	• Vice President, Thai Chamber of Commerce
	Mr. Montri Khongtrakunthian	• Chief, Agriculture Division, CP Group
	Ms. Lakkhana Lilayut-yothin	• Managing Director, Cerebos Thailand Co., Ltd. • President, Marketing Association of Thailand
	Mr. Phaibun Damrongchaitham	• Chairperson, Board of Directors, GMM Grammy Plc
	Mr. Chaiyut Pilan-owat	• Vice Chairperson, Board of Directors, Surathip Group • Vice Chairperson, Board of Directors, Berli Jucker Plc
4 representatives from the public sector		
Director	• Permanent Secretary of Commerce • Chief of the Bureau of Fiscal Policy, Fiscal Policy Office, Ministry of Finance • Secretary General, Office of SMEs Promotion • Director, Small Industry Finance Corporation (SIFC)	

SOURCE: *TNSK*, July 14, 2002; annual report of each company; almanacs of various companies.

Since its establishment, however, various concerns about the feasibility of ART had been expressed both inside and outside of the industry. One common concern was that it would be extremely difficult to compete with foreign general mass merchandisers, who had superior data tracking and physical distribution systems as well as advanced managerial know-how. There was also the concern that the sum total of the capital investment was far too small to run such a big project, and that decision-making would be complicated because the management consisted only of very influential figures (*PRCT-TK*, July 4, 2002; *TNSK*, July 14, 2002).[13]

Given both the high expectations for ART as well as concerns about its shortcomings, would ART be able to achieve its stated goals? Examining the management structure of the company as of August 2003, one year after its establishment, may provide some answers.[14] ART was located on the 29th floor of the Italthai Tower, rising high along New Phetburi Road, one of the main streets in Bangkok. The company was equipped with a host computer that collected order data from member stores as well as a call center that accepted orders by phone and fax from members who had not yet been provided with an online system. ART had dealings with more than thirty manufacturers and sales companies, including major local business groups like the Saha Group and major foreign companies such as P&G, Colgate, Nestle, and Diethelm. According to the *Ordering Guidebook* (as of August 2003), the goods that ART distributed to its members consisted of five categories: (a) personal care (e.g., soap, shampoo, and toothpaste), (b) processed foods (e.g., instant coffee, sugar, instant noodles, *nam pla*, and cooking oil), (c) confectionary, (d) beverages (e.g., milk, juice, etc.), and (e) other daily necessities, all of which amounted to a total of around five hundred items. Most of these items were cheaper than the over-the-counter prices of foreign general mass merchandisers.[15] Furthermore, prices of ART's goods did not differ between members regardless of how large or small the size of their order.

According to Mr. Niphon Nakhasuriyawong, operation director of the company, ART's purchasing and physical distribution systems had to be altered in some respects from original plans (see fig. 6.1). The most important change was the shift in the relationship between member stores and financial institutions. The head office of ART in Bangkok (and each provincial chamber of commerce in the provinces) initially was expecting to pay manufacturers/suppliers via its own bank, but this ended up not working, so instead each member store individually remitted payment for the goods they bought to a bank that ART had designated and from these funds ART then paid suppliers.

Unlike purchases on credit, which was the traditional way of trading with wholesalers in Thailand, ART's system was based on non-interest trade for forty-five days (if customers missed the payment deadline, though, they were charged interest). In order to institute the non-interest trading system, each member store first had to undergo a credit check by one of ART's designated banks and receive approval to open a current account. Relationships with manufacturers/suppliers changed also as the company came to depend more heavily on outside (or third-party) logistics service providers (3PLs).[16] As a result, ART came to play a role in selecting the most appropriate financial institutions, suppliers, and 3PLs in order to build a supply chain connecting these three parties with member stores and acting as the coordinator when adjustments needed to be made.

As of August 2003, forty three thousand stores throughout the country applied for ART membership. Nevertheless, according to Mr. Niphon, only about a thousand stores actually participated in the project at that time. A year later in 2004, this situation, which did not represent anything near full operation, remained unchanged. The reason behind this was that the designated banks, Krung Thai Bank and Nakhon Luang Thai Bank, were conducting such strict background checks of the applicant stores that only a very limited number of them were allowed to open accounts (*PJK-RW*, February 19, 2004).[17] Yet, these financial institutions had little choice but to check applicants thoroughly because each loan to an ART member store was about 15,000 baht, which was too small a sum of money to make the transactions profitable for the banks. As a result, many member stores were unable to borrow money or make sufficiently large amounts of orders. Since the collective orders placed by ART were rather small, suppliers could not offer wholesale prices as low as originally planned. Shipping companies also suffered financial losses because of the lack of efficiency of low loading conditions and the high cost structure. Moreover, they were required under the contract to pay one percent of the total sum of the cost of goods delivered to ART.[18]

Given this situation, ART expressed its intent to personally provide member stores with the financial support they needed. Under this new system, the company set out to use a portion of the money allocated by the government that remained uninvested, about 100 million baht, as funds for loans. When ART became short of funds, SIFC, one of the two major stockholders of the company, would step in and provide support from 2005 onwards (*PJK-RW*, February 19, 2004). ART also decided to affiliate with cooperatives.[19] Since the rise of foreign general mass merchandisers, some cooperative stores had experienced a dramatic drop in sales, while others had to even close down. It was thought, therefore, that cooperatives decided to affiliate with ART as a survival measure. ART put a great deal of effort into jointly developing private label goods with cooperatives. In addition, it announced that it would start a mobile store business with cooperatives, consisting of remodeled pick-up trucks loaded with goods for sale that traveled to residential districts.

Such a new direction meant that ART would continue to play a coordinating role, while also taking on an executive role as well. However, as its duties, including financial support for member stores, sharply increased, ART found itself stuck in a situation where the actual practices of its operations were vastly different from had been originally conceived. In October 2007, at a cabinet meeting, ART decided to finally close down (*PRCT-TK*, October 18, 2007). Although the ART project ended in failure, the government began to develop site plan regulations that continue to affect large-scale stores in certain respects.

SITE PLAN REGULATIONS FOR LARGE-SCALE STORES

FEATURES OF THE REGULATIONS

In November 2002, after discarding the draft bill of the Retail and Wholesale Business Act, which was almost completed, Prime Minister Thaksin announced that the government would promptly enforce some protective measures for small- and medium-sized retail and wholesale businesses in conformity with the existing Urban Planning Act B.E. 2518 (1975). Site plan regulations based on the Urban Planning Act were already being discussed under the leadership of Deputy Commerce Minister Suwan, Newin's predecessor (*PJK-RS*, August 13, 2001). Such discussions did not spring from a casual idea that just popped out of Prime Minister Thaksin's head to evade industry criticism of the withdrawal of the new Act. The idea that the government would protect small- and medium-sized retail and wholesale businesses with zoning controls based on the Urban Planning Act had already been discussed at the Ministry of Commerce during the last stages of the Chuan government (*PRCT-TK*, January 25, 2001).

In the latter half of 2003, site plan regulations based on existing laws were actually put into practice.[20] On September 10, 2003, the Notice of the Public Works and Town & Country Planning Department, B.E. 2546 (2003), based on the 1975 Urban Planning Act, was published in the Official Gazette and was to be enforced the next day. The notice was valid for about three years from September 11, 2003 until May 19, 2006.[21] It applied to all the areas of the seventy-two provinces where urban planning was not yet in place. Two days later, on September 12, 2003, the Notice of the Ministry of Interior, B.E. 2546 (2003), based on the 1979 Building Control Act was published in the Official Gazette and was to be enforced the next day. It applied to all the areas of the seventy-two provinces where urban planning was already in place. The Building Control Act prescribed that this particular official notice would lose validity unless a ministerial or municipal ordinance was enacted within one year. Consequently, on September 3, 2004, the Interior Ministry Ordinance on Commercial Buildings, B.E. 2547 (2004), based on the Building Control Act was published in the Official Gazette and enforced on the same day. It applied to all the areas of the seventy-two provinces where urban planning was already in place.

Tables 6.6 and 6.7 outline the main features of the Public Works notice and the Ministry of Interior ordinance, as applied in Chiang Mai Province. In the Public Works notice, which was targeting areas without urban planning (table 6.6), the store floor space to be controlled was 300 square meters and over, and the content of the regulation differs between stores up to 1,000 square meters and stores over 1,000 square meters in size. The 300-square-meter criterion seems to be based on the fact that the store floor space of small- and medium-sized stores in Thailand was generally less than 300 square meters (*PRCT-TK*, January 25, 2001). In the case of stores between 300 and 1,000 square meters, the legal building coverage ratio (floor area-to-plottage ratio) was prescribed to be up to 30 percent. For example, when constructing a one-storey building on a 1,000-square-meter building area,[22] 3,334 square meters would be required for the premises. In such a case, a 467-square-meter park or green area would also be required within the premises. Similarly, in the case of a two-storey building with a total floor space of 50,000 square meters (each floor having 25,000 square meters), 125,000 and 20,000 square meters would be required respectively for the premises and a park. The legal building coverage ratio was very strictly prescribed as being up to 20 percent. Other strict provisions were also included, such as setbacks from the front road. These provisions would lead to a sharp increase in the costs of opening a large-scale retail store chain. Moreover, some provinces required that stores with a store floor space of over 1,000 square meters should be located more than 15 kilometers away from the central urban (municipal) area. Compared with existing stores, new stores undeniably had to face disadvantageous conditions. In addition, the Ministry of

Interior ordinance targeting areas that already had urban planning (see table 6.7) established strict construction requirements for commercial buildings in each area. Construction of commercial buildings with a store floor space over 1,000 square meters was prohibited, and this provision applied to existing buildings as well, in the case of modification or change of use. The content of the regulations set forth in the Ministry of Interior ordinance were actually stricter than those of the Public Works notice.

TABLE 6.6 Main features of the 2003 Notice of the Public Works and Town & Country Planning Department, Chiang Mai Province

Clause 1	Definition of commercial building (retail and wholesale) Buildings with a store floor space of 300 sq m or more are subject to regulation, except wet markets
Clause 2	This notice does not apply to areas where urban planning has already occurred
Clause 3	(omitted)
Clause 4	Construction requirements for commercial buildings with a store floor space of between 300 and 1,000 sq m: • Should face a public road with at least four lanes or over 20 m wide • Vehicle entrances should be at least 100 m from crossings • Legal building coverage ratio should be 30 percent or less • Floor area ratio (FAR) should be 80 percent or less • More than 20 percent of the premises should be covered by a park, woods, or recreation facilities • Front road setback should be at least 50 m • Side and back setbacks should be at least 15 m from public roads and other people's properties • Buildings 10m or higher should be at least 200 m from government offices, religious facilities, historical buildings, and educational facilities • Parking lots should have a capacity of one car per 20 sq m of store floor space • Garbage collection areas should be at least 10 m from public roads and other people's properties
Clause 5	Construction requirements for commercial buildings with a store floor space over 1,000 sq m: • Should face a public road 40 m or more wide • Vehicle entrances should be at least 500 m from crossings • Legal building coverage ratio should be 20 percent or less • Floor area ratio (FAR) should be 80 percent or less • More than 20 percent of the premises should be covered by a park, woods, or recreation facilities • Front road setback should be at least 75 m • Side and back setbacks should be at least 20 m from other people's properties • Buildings 10 m or higher should be at least 200 m from government offices, religious facilities, historical buildings, and educational facilities • Parking lots should have a capacity of one car per 40 sq m of store floor space • Garbage collection areas should be at least 10 m from public roads and other people's properties
Clause 8	This notice comes into force on the day following notification in the official gazette

SOURCE: English translation by the author of the 2003 Notice of the Public Works and Town & Country Planning Department.

NOTE: This notice was intended for areas outside the urban planning areas in 72 provinces, except the Bangkok Metropolis and the provinces of Nonthaburi, Samut Prakan, and Phuket. While other provinces have the requirement that commercial buildings should be located at least 15 km away from municipal areas, Chiang Mai Province does not have this provision.

TABLE 6.7 Main features of the 2004 Ministry of Interior Ordinance on Commercial Buildings, Chiang Mai Province

Clause 1	Definition of commercial buildings (retail and wholesale) Classification of areas
Clause 2	Construction requirements for commercial buildings by classified areas (First area): Construction of commercial buildings with a store floor space of 300 sq m or more is prohibited. (Second area): Construction of commercial buildings with a store floor space over 1,000 sq m is prohibited. Construction of commercial buildings with a store floor space between 300 sq m and 1,000 sq m should meet the following requirements: • Should face a public road with at least four lanes or over 20 m wide • Vehicle entrances should be at least 100 m from crossings • Legal building coverage ratio should be 30 percent or less • Floor area ratio (FAR) should be 80 percent or less • More than 20 percent of the premises should be covered by a park, woods, or recreation facilities • Front road setback should be at least 50 m • Side and back setbacks should be at least 15 m from public roads and other people's properties • Buildings that are 10m or higher should be at least 200 m from government offices, religious facilities, historical buildings, and educational facilities • Parking lots should have a capacity of one car per 40 sq m of store floor space • Garbage collection areas should be at least 10 m from public roads and other people's properties
Clause 3	Changes or modified uses of buildings within the area concerned pertaining to provisions in Clause 2 are prohibited.
Clause 4	Existing buildings constructed on or before the day of enforcement are exempt from the regulations in this ordinance. However, changes or modified uses of the buildings pertaining to the provisions in Clause 2 are prohibited.
Clause 5	Buildings under construction that have obtained permission for construction, changes, and/or modified uses before the day of enforcement are exempt from the regulations in this ordinance. However, any change in the content of the permission pertaining to the provisions of this ordinance is prohibited.

SOURCE: English translation by the author of 2004 Ministry of Interior Ordinance on Commercial Buildings.

NOTE: This ordinance was intended for those areas within the seventy-two provinces with urban planning already in place, but excludes the Bangkok Metropolis and the provinces of Nonthaburi, Samut Prakan, and Phuket. Some provinces allow for, under specific requirements, the construction of buildings with a store floor space over 1,000 sq m, but Chiang Mai Province does not.

The government also issued another Ministry of Interior notice, which included many provisions that strictly regulated the store openings of large-scale retailers and wholesalers in the Bangkok metropolis and the three provinces of Nonthaburi, Samut Prakan, and Phuket, where comprehensive urban planning was already in force. In the Bangkok metropolis, for example, the original mandate stipulated that the requirements for constructing commercial buildings would be based on three classified areas: (i) store floor space between 2,000 and 6,000 square meters, (ii) over 6,000 square meters and below 30,000 square meters, and (iii) over 30,000 square meters. However, certain amendments were implemented to make the Ministry of Interior's mandate and notice consistent with the Public Works notice that had already been published (*PRCT-TK*, November 24, 2003). On March 22, 2004, the Notice of the Ministry of Interior on Regulations of Construction, Reconstruction, and Change of Use of Retail and Wholesale Buildings in the Bangkok Metropolis was promulgated and published in the Official Gazette on April 30 to be enforced the next day on May 1, 2004. Enforcement in the Bangkok metropolis would be substantially later. Finally, after several amendments were made, on April 27, 2005, the Bangkok Municipal Ordinance was published in the Official Gazette to be enforced the next day, in order to ensure the validity of the Interior Ministry notice. Table 6.8 shows the main features of the municipal ordinance.

The "first area" noted in clause 4 of the municipal ordinance represents sparsely populated areas in Bangkok in which the construction of stores with a store floor space of 300 square meters and over is, in principle, prohibited.[23] In the "third area," which represents Bangkok's central districts, there is a large concentration of small- and medium-sized retail and wholesale stores and many large-scale retailers were already established there as well, so that site plan regulations for this area were the second strictest, after the first area. Site plan regulations were the least strict in the "fourth area," which represents sub-centers located in the suburbs, while the strictness of the regulations for the "second area" was at a level between the third and fourth areas. The municipal ordinance also contained provisions such as requiring businesses to conduct environmental impact assessments reports, as needed, including obtaining necessary ministerial approval from the Office of Natural Resources and Environmental Policy and Planning, the Ministry of Natural Resources and Environment. In the case of stores with a 100-car capacity or more parking lot, to prepare plans to mitigate the negative influences on traffic and obtain approval from the metropolitan government.

TABLE 6.8 The Bangkok Municipal Ordinance on the Regulation of Construction, Reconstruction, and Changes of Use of Retail and Wholesale Buildings in the Bangkok Metropolis

Clause 1	This municipal ordinance is named the Bangkok Municipal Ordinance on the Regulations of Construction, Reconstruction, and Changes of Use of Retail and Wholesale Buildings in the Bangkok Metropolis B.E. 2548 (2005)				
Clause 2	This municipal ordinance comes into force on the day following notification in the government's Official Gazette.				
Clause 3	Definition of commercial buildings (retail and wholesale) Buildings with a store floor space of 300 sq m or more are subject to regulations, except wet markets				
Clause 4	Classification of areas and provisions of each area				
		First area	Second area	Third area	Fourth area
	Area	all the areas of Bangkok, except the second, third, and fourth areas (sparsely populated areas)	the fringe area in the north and east of the third area and the outskirts of the fourth area (e.g., the sub-center of the suburbs)	the central district of Bangkok, including Old Bangkok (i.e., the northern end of Chatuchak, the eastern end of Bang Kapi, the southern end Bang Na, the western end Phasi Charoen and Phetkasem Road)	the sub-center of the suburbs (i.e., Saphan Mai, Ram Inthra Road, Min Buri, Nong Chok, Lat Krabang, Bang Khun Thian)
	Store floor space, subject to regulations	300 sq m or more is prohibited	between 300 and 2,000 sq m (stores over 2,000 sq m are prohibited)	between 300 and 1,000 sq m (stores over 1,000 sq m are prohibited)	stores over 4,000 sq m
	Width of public roads fronting the store		20 m or more	30 m or more	20 m or more
	Distance between vehicle entrances and crossings		100 m or more	200 m or more	100 m or more

Clause 4	Classification of areas and provisions of each area				
(con't)		First area	Second area	Third area	Fourth area
	Setback from the front road		30 m or more	50 m or more	30 m or more
	Side and back setback from other people's properties		6 m or more	6 m or more	6 m or more
	Legal building coverage ratio		70 percent or less	70 percent or less	70 percent or less
	Requirement for use of vacant land		more than 50 percent should be a park or woods	more than 50 percent should be a park or woods	more than 50 percent should be a park or woods
	Distance from temples, remains, educational facilities, and hospitals		500 m or more	500 m or more	500 m or more
	In the second, third, and fourth areas, developers, depending on the situation, must submit environment assesment reports and obtain approval from the Office of Natural Resources and Environmental Policy and Planning, Ministry of Natural Resources and Environment. In the case of a parking lot with a capacity exceeding 100 cars, the store must draw up plans to prevent negative influences on traffic and obtain approval from the Bangkok Metropolitan Administration.				
Clause 7	Existing buildings constructed on or before the day of enforcement are exempt from the regulations of this ordinance. However, changes or modified uses of buildings pertaining to the provisions in Clause 4 are prohibited.				
Clause 8	Buildings under construction that have obtained permission for construction, changes, and modified uses before the day of enforcement are exempt from the regulations of this ordinance. However, any change in the content of the permission pertaining to the provisions of this ordinance is prohibited.				

SOURCES: English translation by the author of the Bangkok Municipal Ordinance on the Regulations of Construction, Reconstruction, and Changes of Use of Retail and Wholesale Buildings in the Bangkok Metropolis.

NOTE: Clauses 5, 6, and 9 are omitted.

THE HYPERMARKETS' RESPONSE TO GOVERNMENT NOTICES AND ORDINANCES

While some differences exist in the content of the site plan regulations between the provinces and Bangkok, a common point was that restrictions came to be imposed primarily on the establishment of new stores by large-scale retailers. As a result, it presumably became difficult for general mass merchandisers to open large new stores (around 10,000 sq m of store floor space) like they had in the past.

The enforcement of site plan regulations did not immediately affect the opening of such stores, however. Since none of the Interior Ministry's ordinances or Public Works notices or Bangkok municipal ordinances had retroactive clauses, stores already in operation were not subject to the regulations, nor were stores in the planning, if they had obtained their construction permits prior to the enforcement date of the notices and ordinances. In fact, prior to the issuance of the Public Works notice, general mass merchandisers in various districts rushed in to apply for permission from municipal or provincial offices to build new stores (*KTTK-RW*, August 25, 2003; *PRCT-TK*, March 8, 2004).

It is worth noting here that, except of Carrefour, the three other largest foreign general mass merchandisers had already started to develop new downsized-format stores before the site plan regulations were being drafted (see chap. 4). For example, in addition to the existing large-scale hypermarket format of an approximately 10,000-square-meter store floor space, Tesco Lotus had started to develop a medium-sized hypermarket format, Lotus Value (Khum Kha) (4,000 sq m), a supermarket format, Talad Lotus (800 sq m), and a new format combining a supermarket and a convenience store, Tesco Lotus Express (300 sq m). Makro regarded its existing stores of 10,000-square-meter floor space as "large-scale stores" and its 6,000-square-meter floor space stores as "medium-sized stores," and began in 2001 to open downsized stores (*PJK-RS*, January 1, 2001). Beginning in 2002, Big C opened Leader Price, a small-sized discount store (with a store floor space of 800–1,000 sq m), which mainly sold its private label goods. Behind the development of these downsized formats was over-competition among large-scale stores, a saturation of the consumer market, and rising opposition movements in the districts where store openings were planned.

The enforcement of site plan regulations only accelerated the development of such new businesses. From 2004 onwards, general mass merchandising companies declared that they would mainly open downsized stores rather than their existing standard-sized stores (*TNSK*, January 22, 2004).[24] Ek-Chai

Distribution System Company, running Tesco Lotus, was particularly active. Tesco Lotus Express, which had only eleven stores at the end of December 2003, expanded to 135 stores as of June 2006, including several stores in Chiang Mai, where large-scale retail chains had surprisingly been present from early on for a provincial city and where competition in the opening of stores was fairly fierce (*PRCT-TK*, July 6, 2006).

Simultaneously with the development of downsized stores, Tesco Lotus adopted another way to avoid regulations. It began to affiliate itself with local stores in provincial cities, where it had become difficult to establish new stores. Specifically, this consisted mainly of renting part of an existing store or shopping center and opening a Talad Lotus supermarket. Many provincial companies including provincial representative retail companies, such as Fairy Plaza (Khon Kaen Province), Fairy Land (Nakhon Sawan Province), and Topland Plaza (Phitsanulok Province), invited Tesco Lotus's downsized stores as tenants (*TNSK*, April 16, 2006). Laemthong Group, in Chonburi Province, had been at the core of a movement against the opening of large-scale retailers' new stores in eastern Thailand, but, in the end, also allowed Tesco Lotus to rent a part of its store, since it was unable to withstand the burden of increased cost caused by intensifying competition (*TNSK*, April 13, 2006). Besides Tesco Lotus, Central Group's supermarket chain Tops also adopted a similar strategy to advance into provincial cities. Tops not only opened its downsized format, Tops Daily, on the first floor of Edison Department Store in Chiang Rai Province, but also came to an agreement about a lease with Aphi Plaza Department Store, in the same province (*TNSK*, June 25, 2006).

THE PROBLEMS OF SITE PLAN REGULATIONS

Although some points remain unclear regarding the effects of site plan regulations, it is true that foreign general mass merchandisers, who were the main targets of these regulations, have been taking some countermeasures against them. Foreign general mass merchandisers are, indeed, facing a certain amount of restrictions due to these regulations. However, site plan regulations are not always a sufficient policy to protect small- and medium-sized retailers and wholesalers. This is due to several problems with the regulations.

One of the first problems lies in the fact that the regulations do not fully consider the specific conditions of each area. For example, in Chiang Mai, the largest city in northern Thailand, all four of the largest general mass merchandisers, Makro, Tesco Lotus (two stores), Big C, and Carrefour, had already opened stores along the city's major thoroughfares and streets, and, as a result, local industries took a critical stance on the regulations, saying that it was too late for the government to attempt to control the situation.[25] The Chiang Mai Chamber of Commerce asked the Chiang Mai Province Joint Public and Private Sector Consultative Committees (JPPCCs) to postpone the application of site plan regulations, saying to the press:

> Even if the government regulated the opening of large stores, foreign chains would continue opening their downsized stores. Rather, the government should make efforts to correct unfair trade practices. The biggest problem is that large-scale retailers force suppliers to sell their goods at very low prices. (*KTTK-RW*, August 25, 2003)

Although the circumstances are different from Chiang Mai, strong opposition to the regulations was also heard in Krabi Province in the south. There, many people were actually hoping for the opening of large stores because they believed that the advance of general mass merchandisers would stimulate competition among retail stores in the locality and reduce prices. The provincial chamber of commerce also asked for the application of site plan regulations to be postponed (ibid.).

Another problem with the site plan regulations in the official notices and ministerial ordinances is that the definition of the formats subject to regulation is unclear. The official notices state that their target is retail and wholesale businesses selling foods and non-food daily necessities. Foreign general mass merchandisers expanding their chains in Thailand belong to these very target categories. However, it is difficult to judge whether supermarkets, which sell primarily food, and department stores, which sell primarily non-food shopping goods such as clothing, fall into this category. For example, in 2004, Central Department Store, which had planned to open a new store in Pattaya in eastern Thailand, argued that department stores selling only non-foods should not be included in the scope of the regulations. According to one newspaper, the Public Works and Town & Country Planning Department, after deliberation, announced its decision to approve the construction on the condition that the store would not sell goods at lower prices than local retail stores (*KTTK-RW*, February 27, 2004). According to another newspaper, lawyers for the Public Works and Town & Country Planning Department presented the view that stores selling only foods or only non-food goods would be considered outside of the scope of the regulation, and would, therefore, receive approval for construction (*PRCT-TK*, March 8, 2004).

A third problem of the site plan regulations is that the size of stores subject to regulation is problematic. The regulations provide that the minimum store floor space to be regulated is 300 square meters both in Bangkok and in the provinces. This means that convenience stores, which are the real competitors to small-scale grocery stores (*cho huai*), are not within the scope of the regulations. Foreign general mass merchandiser companies have been developing downsized stores for some time, as we have seen, and these downsized stores fall out of the regulation's scope. As a result, foreign mass merchandisers have been putting great efforts into opening these types of stores. In addition, by making the new entry of large-scale stores more difficult, the regulations are actually protecting existing foreign mass merchandisers' stores. Moreover, the regulations do not only bring more direct competition to local distributors but also restrict the opening of their medium-sized stores of more than 300 square meters. Thus, it can be said that these regulatory measures are actually cause small- and medium-sized local retailers and wholesalers more harm than good.

Taking this into consideration, the local industry, with small- and medium-sized retailers as its leaders, requested the government to institute more effective regulatory measures. For example, the Chiang Mai Chamber of Commerce argued that the government should control the unfair trade practices of large-scale retailers rather than site plan regulations per se. Mr. Somchai, president of the Thai Wholesale and Retail Association, however, complained that the biggest problem was the manufacturers/suppliers who reduced their wholesale prices to unreasonably low levels due to the pressure of general mass merchandisers' low prices. He also had very little hope that the government would eventually enact the necessary regulatory measures, and expressed the opinion that the government had never seriously tried to apply the Trade Competition Act.[26] Conversely, large-scale retailers, irrespective of whether they were local or foreign, requested the government to enact deregulation for the industry. In March 2004, a movement began demanding that the government reexamine its regulatory measures before the official notices were upgraded to ministerial ordinances (*KTTK-RW*, March 19, 2004). For example, an assistant managing director of CRC, one of the core companies of the Central Group, emphasized that the criterion the government used to determine which formats would be subject to regulation should be based on whether the formats were directly competing with small-scale grocery stores (*cho huai*). In addition, he requested that deregulation be implemented such that the construction of stores with a store floor space of 3,000 square meters or below in municipal areas would be approved and the construction of stores with a store floor space over 3,000 square meters would also be approved if they were located at least three kilometers away from municipal areas (*PRCT-TK*, March 8, 2004). Since disputes over the government's site plan regulations cannot be simply characterized as large-scale stores vs. small-scale stores or foreign capital-led vs. domestic capital-led, it becomes ever more difficult to address the interests among the various parties concerned.

THE DISTRIBUTION POLICY BEFORE AND AFTER THE 2006 COUP D'ÉTAT

RECURRING OPPOSITION BY SMALL-SCALE RETAILERS

Site plan regulations stimulated large-scale retailers to develop downsized stores and affiliate with provincial stores that were locally-owned, which caused an increasing threat to traditional grocery stores (*cho huai*). In the past, grocery stores could somehow differentiate themselves from larger competitors by targeting particular classes of customers and their purchasing patterns. They could also use the larger stores as a source for purchasing goods for resale. The downsizing of large-scale retailers' stores forced them to compete directly with these downsized stores.

Even Tesco Lotus Express, which is considered to be the greatest threat in the domestic retail industry, never had many stores in comparison with Thailand's largest convenience store chain 7-Eleven, for example. However, considering the enormous amount of sales of Tesco Lotus' hypermarket business and the ample funds provided by the head office in the UK, there is an undeniable possibility that the group's small-scale store business will grow drastically in the near future.[27] The fact that local self-governing bodies, such as municipalities, were entitled to authorize new store openings made things even more complicated, because the application of policy varied between areas.[28] Some local self-governing bodies applied the Public Works notice rigidly, answering the demands from local industries, and only allowed new store openings after careful consideration. Others loosened the regulations and easily authorized store openings, disregarding the wishes of local industries.

Local retailers came to feel a growing sense of crisis and dissatisfaction with the administration and since the latter half of 2006 have thus often opposed the expansion of large-scale retailing chains in various places. For example, local retailers in the district of Pak Chong in Nakhon Ratchasima Province formed the Acting Committee for Expelling Tesco Lotus and requested the municipality not to permit the opening of a new store (*TNSK*, September 3, 2006).[29] A group of local retailers from various provinces have also organized a network called the Federation of Thais Opposing Foreign Retailers. On September 5, 2006, the federation made a direct appeal to the king of Thailand, in which it stated that the business expansion of large-scale foreign retailers had caused local distributors great difficulties. The federation also sent parliament and the Ministry of Commerce a document requesting that measures be taken to resolve the retail problems facing the country (*TNSK*, September 7, 2006). On September 20, 2006, immediately following the coup d'état, the federation further announced that it expected the new government to promptly take measures to restrict the business expansion of major multinational retailers (*The Nation*, September 21, 2006).

Small-scale retailers were not the only ones to take the lead in opposing the advance of large foreign new retail formats. The Thai Wholesale and Retail Association criticized the trade practices of foreign large-scale retailers in August 2006, claiming that they impeded fair competition in the industry and requesting the government to enact a law to strengthen existing regulations (*PRCT-TK*, August 21, 2006). Some of the major national-level industrial associations, such as the Board of Trade of Thailand (BOT) and the Federation of Thai Industries (FTI), also expressed their concern with the country's ongoing retail problems. In September 2006, the chairperson of the Wholesale and Retail Businesses Committee at the BOT, Boonchai Chokwatana (also president of shopping giant, the Saha Group), was particularly critical of how little effect site plan regulations, based on the Urban Planning Act, actually had. He demanded that government authorities go back to drafting and then enacting the Retail and Wholesale Business Act, and reinforce regulations on foreign large-scale retailers (*TNSK*, September 3, 2006; *PRCT-TK*, September 11, 2006).

Thailand's government could no longer disregard all these opposition voices in the local retail and distribution industries and by the latter half of 2006, it had developed three new distribution policies.

REDRAFTING OF THE RETAIL AND WHOLESALE BUSINESS ACT

Although the draft bill of the Retail and Wholesale Business Act was withdrawn in November 2002, the Ministry of Commerce came to the conclusion that it would be indispensable to apply the laws related to it and also to enact a new law aimed at retail and wholesale businesses in an attempt to resolve the retail problem. It set out to draft the Act again, under the lead of the Internal Trade Department.

The new bill, based on the previous one, consists of fifty-five articles, but as of November 2012 had still not been enacted. According to one newspaper, however, the new bill, which is still supervised by the central and provincial committees, includes permission requirements regarding new store openings and floor space expansions, as well as specific provisions regarding store floor space, business size in terms of sales, number of stores, and the distance between stores (*PJK-RW*, August 17, 2006). Other provisions relate to the population density in target areas and the prohibition to run various formats with only one authorization, according to Siriphon Yordmuangjaroen, former head of the Internal Trade Department at the Ministry of Commerce (*PRCT-TK*, September 18, 2006). The latter provision seems to be targeting cases such as Tesco Lotus. It means, for example, that a company running hypermarkets, which decides to develop a downsized format, has to apply for a new business permit from the authorities in order to open a new type of store.

Just prior to the coup d'état, the Internal Trade Department was planning on holding a public hearing in October 2006 to make an amendment to the draft bill of the Retail and Wholesale Business Act and then submit the draft bill to a cabinet meeting. With the collapse of the Thaksin government, the enactment of the bill became more uncertain. Yet the Ministry of Commerce remained determined to continue the distribution policy under the new government (*PRCT-TK*, October 2, 2006). The Retail and Wholesale Business Act, which the small- and medium-sized local distributors had been longing for, was expected to come into existence in the near future, though to what degree its regulations would be effective was unclear. The steps needed to enact a new bill can take a considerable amount of time, which is why the new government attached particular importance to taking two temporary political measures.

TEMPORARY MEASURES UNTIL ENACTMENT

One measure was the guidelines for retail businesses based on Section 29 of the Trade Competition Act, B.E. 2542 (1999) developed by the Ministry of Commerce in the form of regulation B.E. 2549 (2006) (the "Guidelines"). The Guidelines are derived from work that has been done on defining standards for unfair trade practices, which were actively discussed in 2002. The Guidelines specified the following eight items as "unfair trade practices," with provisions that violators would be subject to up to three years imprisonment, or up to 6 million baht in fines, or both:

1. Unfair price fixing (e.g., selling below cost)
2. Unfair fees collection (e.g., raising entrance fees without advance notice, collecting fee for every minor change in goods, etc.)
3. Unfair return of goods (e.g., return of goods not prescribed in trade contract)
4. Unfair consignment contracts
5. Unfair compulsory sales and service fees collection (e.g., advertising costs)
6. Unfair use of product consultants
7. Unfair refusal of pre-ordered products (e.g., returning private label goods despite having ordered the manufacturing of such goods)
8. Other unfair trade practices (e.g., unreasonable delays in ordering or selling, removing goods from display without reason, etc.)

(*TNSK*, September 10, 2006; *PRCT-TK*, October 5, 2006).

The Thai Retailers Association, which consisted of large-scale retailers, expressed strong concern over the establishment of the Guidelines. The president of the association, Thanaphon Tangkhananan, who belongs to the Central Group, the largest local retail business group, complained that private sector members of the sub-committee under the Trade Competition Committee, which established the guidelines, were led by representatives of consumer goods manufacturers and suppliers, such as the Federation of Thai Industries (FTI) and the Board of Trade of Thailand (BOT). He also pointed out that these Guidelines only targeted large-scale retailers, unlike the former guidelines established in 2002, which also included regulations targeting manufacturers, such as the prohibition against tying and bundled discounting (*PRCT-TK*, September 11, 2006).[30] Large-scale retailing companies also suspected that these guidelines would only benefit the manufacturers (*PRCT-TK*, September 18, 2006). However, Boonchai, the chairperson of BOT's Wholesale and Retail Business Committee, pointed out that, because the guidelines were based on self-assessment by the parties concerned, manufacturers/suppliers might worry about losing business dealings with large scale retailers if they complained about unfair trade practices, and ended up accepting unfair trade practices. Boonchai thus expressed some doubts about the guidelines' effectiveness (*PRCT-TK*, October 9, 2006). In spite of these doubts and opposition from various sides, the first meeting of the Trade Competition Committee was held on October 3, 2006, and the guidelines regarding trade practices between manufacturers, wholesalers, and retailers were approved (*PRCT-TK*, October 5, 2006).

In addition to the guidelines, another urgent measure was put forth. On September 7, 2006, Deputy Commerce Minister Pricha invited fifteen large-scale retailers to come to his office to discuss the impact their businesses were having on local grocery stores (*cho huai*). Representatives of the Thai Chamber of Commerce, the Public Works and Town & Country Planning Department, the Ministry of Interior's Local and Provincial Administration Departments, the National Economic and Social Development Board (NESDB), the Business Development Department of the Ministry of Commerce, and the Office of Natural Resources and Environmental Policy and Planning in the Ministry of Natural Resources and Environment were also present (*TNSK*, September 10, 2006). This meeting was held to request that large-scale retailers sign a Memorandum of Understanding (MOU) to be presented by the Ministry of Commerce stating that they would refrain from opening new stores until the enactment of the Retail and Wholesale Business Act. The fifteen companies that were targeted included seven foreign and eight local companies, of which five were department stores, four were general mass merchandisers (cash-and-carry stores and hypermarkets), one was a supermarket, two were convenience stores, one was a category killer, and two were specialty stores. All of them were major chain stores (see chap. 3, table 3.10). Among them, Tesco Lotus, 7-Eleven, Tops, and Big C, the most active in new store openings, would likely be the most severely affected by this measure. For this reason, Tesco Lotus maintained a negative position toward the MOU, in contrast with the other fourteen companies that showed some willingness to comply (*PRCT-TK*, October 2, 2006).

The MOU was scheduled to be presented for signature on September 13, 2006, but, in the end, each company refused to sign it, notably because the period of time during which they would have to stop opening new stores was not clearly defined (*PRCT-TK*, September 18, 2006). In response, the Deputy

Commerce Minister Pricha warned that he would publish a Commerce Ministry's ordinance more rigid and with stronger legal force, if they did not sign the MOU by the September 22 deadline (*TNSK*, September 17, 2006). As it turns out, the deadline was postponed due to the coup d'état, so no retailer signed it. Later, however, with the exception of Tesco Lotus, all fourteen of the other retail companies agreed to temporarily freeze new store openings and sign the MOU (*PRCT-TK*, October 2, 2006), and then in November, Tesco Lotus also agreed to freeze the opening of new Tesco Lotus Express stores for three months (*The Nation*, November 12, 2006). In order to find a point of compromise among the parties concerned about store opening regulations, the Ministry of Commerce established the Joint Public and Private Sector Working Committee for the Resolution of Large-Scale Retail Business Issues. This committee included representatives of small-scale retailers, the BOT (consumer goods manufacturers representatives), and professionals as well as large-scale retailers, who had been stridently complaining about being excluded from the policy-making processes (*PRCT-TK*, October 2 and 5, 2006).

WHERE IS THE GOVERNMENT'S POLICY HEADING?

As opposition against the business expansion of new retail formats, especially hypermarkets, arose again within the local retail and distribution industries in the latter half of 2006, the Thai government continued to move forward with its distribution policy, despite the political discontinuity brought about by the fall of Thaksin and the rise of the Surayud government as a result of the coup. In addition to the continuation of site plan regulations for commercial buildings, efforts regarding a national distribution policy consisted of redrafting the Retail and Wholesale Business Act and implementing temporary measures until the enactment of the law.

Although the fifteen large-scale retailers signed the Ministry of Commerce's MOU and promised to temporarily freeze the opening of new stores, they actually continued to construct new stores in certain areas. One reason for this, some of them explained, was that it was impossible to simply stop construction of a project once a contract had been signed with contractors. Another reason was that nothing prevented them from opening stores with a floor space under 300 square meters (*PRCT-TK*, February 1, 2007). The government's Guidelines have not been very effective either. Despite complaints from consumer goods manufacturers about the pressure from large-scale retailers to produce low-priced goods (*The Nation*, January 29, 2007; February 3, 2007), these complaints have not led to any concrete measures, since administrative measures require many steps to be put into practice and often end up not being executed at all. Moreover, site plan regulations have not been sufficiently effective in protecting traditional small- and medium-sized distributors, and, in fact, have even intensified competition with new retail formats. Site plan regulations stimulated hypermarket chain companies, in particular, to put more effort into developing downsized-format stores. Since the Public Works notice (2003) lost validity in May 2006, areas without urban planning within seventy-two provinces, which had been subject to site plan regulations, no longer have any site plan regulations.

For these reasons, the Thai Wholesale and Retail Association and the Federation of Thais Opposing Foreign Retailers as well as traditional distributors, whose survival is threatened by the growth of new retail formats, strongly urged the government to enact a more effective Retail and Wholesale Business Act as soon as possible (*KTTK-RW*, August 23, 2007). However, partly because of large-scale retailers' pressure, the bill was sent back many times before being submitted at a cabinet meeting and the enactment procedure was substantially delayed (*TNSK*, May 3, 2007; September 27, 2007).[31] As of November 2012, the situation still remains unchanged.[32]

Although no one can predict how the content of the regulation will change in the future, it can at least be said that openly strengthening the regulations against large-scale retailers (foreign companies, in particular) is a difficult task. This is particularly the case since the reinforcement of distribution regulations would basically be incompatible with Thailand's present economic growth policy, which is based on international trade and foreign investment. Moreover, reinforcement of site plan regulations does not always bring the expected results. Even if store floor space subject to regulation were fixed below the 300 square meters presently in force, foreign retailers with ample funds and managerial know-how would develop yet another new format to avoid such regulation, which could once again intensify the competition with local retailers and wholesalers. Reinforcement of other provisions could also hamper local retailers and wholesalers' opportunities for new businesses. The author believes another reason why it is doubtful that regulations will be dramatically strengthened is due to the powerful political voices of major local and foreign retailers that the government simply cannot ignore.

In any case, even though small- and medium-sized local retailers and wholesalers are on the verge of a crisis, it is practically impossible to protect them exclusively. And, in reality, some small- and medium-sized retailers and wholesalers have actually continued growing, despite the severe business environment.

There is still plenty of room for opening new businesses in areas that the new retail formats have thus far been unable to include in their trading networks. This can be seen by the increase in the number of small-scale retail and wholesale stores. Behind the coexistence of new retail format chains and local distributors lies the mosaic structure of Thailand's consumer market. Yet for local distributors this type of consumer market could ultimately work against them if they do not engage in some form of self-reform. Should Thailand continue to move forward into a mass consumption market as economic development continues, a further geographical expansion of new retail formats chains would very likely make the competition with the traditional distribution industry even more severe. The Thai government should, therefore, not devote itself to simply protecting local industry based on a short-term vision, but rather, it should embrace a medium- and long-term vision, and encourage local distributors to transform themselves so as to increase their competitiveness, by using as models the cases of those local distributors who have successfully adapted to changing market conditions. Ultimately, what the government should do is to implement a system devoted to this specific purpose and, to ensure its effectiveness in maintaining a sufficiently competitive environment, notably using regulations against unfair trade practices.[33]

7

DIVERSIFYING RETAIL AND DISTRIBUTION INDUSTRIES IN A MOSAIC-STRUCTURED CONSUMER MARKET

OVERVIEW

New retail formats, especially hypermarkets, have been on the rise in Thailand since the late 1990s. The most remarkable characteristic of these new formats is their use of a chain store operation in which logistics are efficiently managed using information technology. The expansion of chain stores has allowed new retail formats to increase their bargaining power against manufacturers and to conduct direct dealings with manufacturers, thereby bypassing wholesalers. New retail formats have also simultaneously introduced new commercial practices that require suppliers (i.e., manufacturers) to pay various fees and offset various costs, such as advertising, sales promotions, distribution center warehousing, etc.; this is particularly true in the case of hypermarkets. As a result, new retail formats have succeeded in realizing low prices as well as improved the convenience of consumers' shopping in many instances.

Based on the research presented in this study, the growth rates of new retail formats and their impact on Thailand's distribution system seem, however, to have been overestimated. It is true that the sales of new retail formats, especially that of hypermarkets, have rapidly increased, but, not to the extent that local newspapers and current analyses by Thai and foreign scholars have emphasized, primarily because they do not always consider the whole consumer market. While foreign capital-led new retail formats in Thailand rose rapidly before and after the financial and currency crisis and have, indeed, increased their sales in absolute value, their share of the entire country's retail sales has decreased or at least has stagnated since recovery from the crisis.

In reality, new retail formats are facing various problems and their potential growth is somewhat limited. As for hypermarkets and cash-and-carry stores, suitable places to open new stores are decreasing in Bangkok and its vicinity. Site plan regulations imposed by the government have made it more difficult for them to seek new locations. Companies are making efforts to overcome these problems by expanding their businesses into the provinces and developing new downsized formats. Yet this change in company strategy also causes new problems, such as the rise of physical distribution costs. From the very beginning, new retail formats were unable to cover Thailand's entire consumer market, which is characterized by a mosaic structure that sees large disparities in household income levels between and within urban and rural areas. In this kind of consumer market, new retail formats, whose break-even point is relatively high, find it difficult to expand their chain operation into provincial areas. This suggests that there is still enough room for traditional wholesalers and retailers to play a role in Thailand's distribution system.

Supermarkets, which mainly sell daily foods, have shown less growth than other new retail formats. Central Group's Tops Supermarket, the only national supermarket chain in Thailand, is suffering from low profitability and high operating costs, as well as other managerial problems. Some local chains are doing relatively well, but they have adopted niche market strategies that target a limited customer base, e.g., the upper class and foreign residents. They, therefore, can only expand their chain stores at a slow pace. Moreover, supermarkets must compete with wet markets (*talat*) in the sales of perishable foods, as well as with hypermarkets in the sales of processed foods and daily necessities. Because of this, they have not yet managed to establish a competitive advantage within the retail industry.

Convenience stores are similarly confronted with some limits to further growth. Although as a distinct format they present a remarkable growth rate as a whole, the largest chain, 7-Eleven, is considerably larger both in sales and in number of stores than the other convenience stores operating in Thailand. Despite this, 7-Eleven still has various problems to address. For example, the proportion of its corporate stores, as opposed to franchise stores, is so high that the head office is saddled with huge management costs. The older type of franchise chain stores (designated as Type A) have not increased as expected. At the present time, the head office is making efforts to promote a new franchise chain system by introducing a new type of store (Types B and C). Types B and C stores, however, are inferior to Type A stores because they increase the managerial resources of the head office and do not provide enough incentives to franchisees. In addition, since the proportion of strategic goods, like ready-to-eat foods, is much lower than in Japan, for example, the convenience store system in Thailand has not yet reached the stage where convenience stores construct close business connections with suppliers, as is the case in Japan. In other words, convenience stores in Thailand have not impacted the domestic distribution system as they have in Japan.

Under these circumstances, what marketing strategies have manufacturers taken? Needless to say, new retail formats are indispensable to manufacturers, given their huge sales volume. Major manufacturers and new retail format companies have attempted to engage in various kinds of producer-retailer alliances, such as private label goods development and category management (planogram proposals). However, manufacturers are concerned that large-scale retailers are controlling channel leadership, as they increase their sales volume. Leading consumer goods manufacturers have, once again, come to attach greater importance to the functions of traditional wholesalers and retailers, who can more easily distribute goods into provincial areas than some large-scale retailers.

Based on a series of case studies conducted by the author, major manufacturers' marketing channels can be classified into three types, according to their involvement in intermediate distribution processes. Western manufacturing and sales companies, like Thai Unilever, are making positive use of external managerial resources by outsourcing the management of its sales offices and warehouses to sell their products to small-scale grocery stores in each provincial area. Meanwhile, local companies, like Saha Pat, and some Japanese companies, like Thai-Ajinomoto Sales, are internalizing their sales and warehouse functions in the provinces, while Thai Kao Sales has been attempting to build a thorough direct-sale system. All three marketing channels, nevertheless, rely heavily on leading provincial wholesalers for the distribution of their products and strive to strengthen their relationships with wholesalers. Yet, these manufacturers are not always satisfied with the roles wholesalers play in the provincial markets, but they have little choice but to rely on wholesalers' selling abilities and sales networks.

With this ongoing situation, what distribution policies have the Thai government put into place? Under the Thaksin administration, several political measures were attempted to address the country's distribution problems, especially in 2002. Most of these measures failed, with the exception of certain site plan regulations involving new store openings that were implemented based on already existing city-planning regulations. These regulations, however, were not necessarily effective in protecting small- and medium-sized local retailers and wholesalers. On the contrary, these regulations likely have had a detrimental effect, because they stimulated general mass merchandisers to devise strategies for store-miniaturization, which, in turn, intensified the direct competition between new retail formats and local traditional retailers and wholesalers.

The Thai government, therefore, should pay attention to the growing hybrid format of wholesale-cum-retail stores that are developing in the provinces. Such stores could be used as model cases to promote institutionalization that would stimulate traditional distributors' self-reform.

CONCLUSIONS

New retail formats have recently been on the rise in Thailand. They are driving Thailand's traditional distribution system towards a fundamental change. Yet, it does not appear as though any structural change has actually occurred in the distribution of daily necessities and processed foods in Thailand.[1] At the stage of intermediate distribution, in particular, leading traditional wholesalers still play an important role. In this respect, Thailand's traditional distribution system remains unchanged. While expanding direct dealings with new retail formats, consumer goods manufacturers have come to attach importance to traditional distributors, especially wholesalers, once again. As happened in Japan during its period of high economic growth, large-scale retailers are becoming major players in Thailand's retail and distribution industries, but this has not directly led to a declining role for traditional wholesalers.

The changes occurring in Thailand's distribution system at present differ greatly from Japan's experience in one respect, in particular. In Japan, supermarkets, including general merchandise stores, emerged in the 1950s, while convenience stores did not become prominent until the 1970s. Because of the time lag between the emergence of these two formats, distribution innovations, such as a central purchasing system and information technology, were introduced at different times. In Thailand, new retail formats, such as general mass merchandisers, supermarkets, convenience stores, and so on, emerged one after another beginning around 1990, and distribution innovations were thus introduced simultaneously with the emergence of all these new retail formats. As a result, new retail formats that were developed with foreign capital and know-how engaged in direct dealings with manufacturers from a very early stage in Thailand, and did not need to rely on traditional wholesalers. Even as new retail format chains expanded at the national level, provincial wholesalers in Thailand, unlike in Japan, have never been motivated to extend their scale or functions through mergers and acquisitions to become nationwide wholesalers. The structure of the consumer market in Japan and Thailand also contributes to differing distribution practices between the two countries. In Thailand, there is still ample room for the traditional distribution sector to continue to exist due to the country's mosaic consumer market. Leading provincial wholesalers, in particular, armed with considerable selling abilities and sales networks, are playing an important role.

In Japan, many wholesalers succeeded in maintaining an important position in the country's distribution system by not only expanding their business scale but also by strengthening their logistics functions. In contrast, the present advantageous position of Thai wholesalers is based on the premise that new retail formats cannot cover the entire mosaic consumer market; however, there is no guarantee that this will be the case in the future. In fact, site plan regulations regarding new store openings enacted by the Thai government have motivated new retail format companies to further develop smaller, compact stores. While previously these companies concentrated their efforts on opening new stores in Bangkok and its vicinity as well as other major regional centers, they are now also extending their chain operations deeper into other less prominent areas. Meanwhile, certain leading provincial wholesalers have adopted aspects of the new retail formats' operation systems and have succeeded in rapidly increasing their sales volume. This marks, as it were, their conversion into a hybrid format, which combines the strengths of traditional wholesale businesses with the strengths of new retail formats.[2] However, the strategy of these hybrid formats is to maintain extremely narrow profit margins and large sales volumes, as seen in provincial cities. Hybrid formats also rely, in part, on dealer assistance, including product consultants sent by suppliers. Whether these hybrid wholesalers can maintain a competitive advantage in the long run remains uncertain. To subsist in the increasingly competitive business world, Thai wholesalers will need constant self-reform. Instead of simply protecting traditional distributors, Thailand's government should probably encourage traditional distributors to increase their competitiveness by using the cases of these new hybrid wholesalers as models.

RECENT RETAIL AND DISTRIBUTION TRENDS IN THAILAND

Certain trends in Thailand's retail and distribution industries can be observed by looking at the ranking of the country's top thirty retailers across time. Tables 7.1 and 7.2 compare the 2006 and 2010 ranking of the country's top thirty retail companies based on sales. If we compare tables 7.1 and 7.2 to tables 3.5, 3.6, and 3.10 in chapter 3, which show the same rankings for the years 1999 to 2006, we can see that while there have been no major changes in the rankings of the Thailand's top retailers between 1999 and 2010, some noteworthy differences can nevertheless be observed.

First, the sales concentration ratio of high-ranking companies increased between 2006 and 2010. While the weight of the top five companies to the whole country's retail sales barely increased between 1999 and 2006 (12.3 to 12.5 percent), it increased by two percentage points, to 14.5 percent, in 2010 (see table 7.2).[3] Nevertheless, the concentration ratio is still not as high as generally expected. This is an important point to emphasize. Since the weight of these companies may well continue to increase, we should keep an eye on the development of foreign-affiliated general mass merchandisers, in particular.[4]

Second, 7-Eleven, at the top of Thailand's convenience store industry, has made remarkable growth. It is, of course, caused by the increase in the number of stores, which totaled 3,784 as of the end of 2006 and 5,790 as of the end of 2010.[5] The increasing number of stores by 2010 includes some provincial city-based, sub-area licensees, namely, Choice Mini Store in Chiang Mai (ranked 22nd among Thailand's top 30 retailers), Yingyong Minimart in Ubon Ratchathani (ranked 27th), and Ngan Noeng in Phuket (ranked 28th), among others. The Japan-based Siam FamilyMart is also gradually expanding its chain. The reasons for its high growth rate are that (i) small-scale stores, like FamilyMart and 7-Eleven convenience stores, fall out of the area of the government's site plan regulations compared to large-scale stores; (ii) ample space still exists to open new convenience stores; and (iii) there are increasing numbers of convenience-oriented consumers. Hypermarket and supermarket companies have also developed a small-scale store format with a floor space under 300 square meters, and are putting a great deal of effort into opening such stores, including Tesco Lotus' "Tesco Lotus Express," Big C's "Mini Big C," Tops's "Tops Daily," and AEON's "Max Vale Than Jai," among others (*PRCT-TK*, June 28, 2010,December 9, 2010, February 15, 2012). This means that hypermarkets and supermarkets are in direct competition with traditional small-scale grocery stores (*cho huai*)—a point that should attract considerable attention in the future.

TABLE 7.1 Thailand's top thirty retailers in sales, 2006 vs. 2010

Ranking[a]		Company/ chain store name[b]	Year of establishment	Group name (nationality)	Format[c]	2010 sales (million baht)	2006/2010 sales (% change)
2006	2010						
1	1	Ek-Chai Distribution/ Tesco Lotus	1993	Tesco (UK)	HM	137,350	46.2
2	2	C.P. Seven Eleven (CP All) (Plc)	1988	CP	CVS	131,656	99.3
4	3	Siam Makro (Plc)	1988	Makro (Holland)	C&C	86,459	55.7
3	4	Big C Supercenter (Plc)	1994	Casino (France)	HM	70,236	21.0
6	5	CenCar/Carrefour	1994	Carrefour (France)	HM	32,041	42.4
5	6	Central Dept. Store	1974	Central	Dept.S	29,311	29.4
7	7	Central Food Retail/ Tops	1996	Central	SM	23,097	14.9
8	8	The Mall Group(+)/ The Mall	1980	The Mall	Dept.S	21,145	15.2
9	9	Robinson Dept. (Plc)	1983	Central	Dept.S	14,794	36.8
10	10	Power Buy	1996	Central	CK	13,930	39.9
11	11	Siam FamilyMart	1992	FamilyMart (Japan)	CVS	9,050	49.1
12	12	Siam Paragon Retail/ Siam Paragon	2001	The Mall et al.	Dept.S	7,484	26.7
13	13	Central Watson/ Watson	1996	Central et al.	SS	5,753	21.2
15	14	Super Cheap	1995	Anantajarun-wong family	W/SM	5,457	48.9
14	15	City Mall Group/ The Emporium	1997	The Mall et al.	Dept.S	4,268	1.6
16	16	Foodland Supermarket	1972	Foodland	SM	4,173	15.6
17	17	CRC Sports/ Super Sports	1996	Central	CK	3,998	24.1
19	18	Boots	1996	Boots (UK)	SS	3,652	39.2
22	19	Tang Ngee Soon Superstore	2000	Wirarattanarot family	W/SM	3,529	92.2
25	20	CRC Power Retail/ Home Works	2001	Central	HC	3,248	97.9

Ranking[a]							
2006	2010	Company/ chain store name[b]	Year of establishment	Group name (nationality)	Format[c]	2010 sales (million baht)	2006/2010 sales (% change)
23	21	Villa Market JP	1988	Phusanakhom family	SM	3,149	73.3
26	22	Choice Mini Store/ 7-Eleven	1988	Tantraphan	CVS	3,128	101.7
18	23	B2S	1995	Central	SS	2,971	7.7
21	24	AEON [Thailand]/ (Siam-Jusco)	1984	AEON (Japan)	SM	2,891	55.1
28	25	Yongsanguan Group	1994	Yongsanguan	W/SM	1,872	53.0
20	26	Tang Hua Seng Dept. Store	1976	Tang Hua Seng	Dept.S	1,861	-3.4
NL	27	Yingyong Minimart /7-Eleven	1993	Yingyong	CVS	1,836	163.1
NL	28	Ngan Noeng/ 7-Eleven	1992	Ngan Thawi	CVS	1,560	77.9
30	29	Chiang Mai Siam TV	1981	Ploemphithak-kun family	CK	1,445	55.3
NL	30	Liwiwat Thawon	1983	Arunoprayot family	W/SM	1,427	75.5

SOURCE: Annual reports of listed companies; financial statements of unlisted companies.

NOTE: Retail-cum-wholesalers are included in the list of companies/chain stores, while automobile and motorcycle dealers are excluded. "Sales" refers to sales income only (it does not include other income, such as rental income). The sales for all formats were calculated by the author as follows: in the case of a public limited company, consolidated figures were used; among non-listed companies with chain stores that have the same store name, which are designated by (+), the sales figures of each store were added together for a single total. As for C.P. Seven Eleven Plc, the figures are based on company data (not consolidate figures) from their annual reports, because the company operates subsidiary hypermarkets in China, representing approx. 30 percent of consolidated sales. The sales figures for The Mall Department Store, Nakhon Ratchasima Branch (The Mall Ratchasima), founded in 1997, were added to the sales figures of The Mall Group Company.

[a] "NL" in the "ranking" column indicates that the company was not listed as one of the top thirty companies for 2006.

[b] The code "(+)" in the "company/chain store" column indicates a non-listed company with chain stores that have the same store name.

[c] Codes used in the "format" column represent the following: C&C=cash-and-carry store; CK=category killer; CVS=convenience store; Dept. S=department store; HC=home center; HM=hypermarket; SM=supermarket; SS=specialty store; W/SM=wholesaler-cum-supermarket.

TABLE 7.2 Thailand's top thirty retailers as a percentage of total retail sales, 2006 vs. 2010

	2006		2010	
	million baht	Percentage of total retail sales (%)	million baht	Percentage of total retail sales (%)
Cumulative sales				
Top 5 companies	296,186	12.5	457,742	14.5
Top 10 companies	377,916	16.0	560,019	17.7
Top 20 companies	416,652	17.6	610,631	19.3
Total of top 30 companies	431,428	18.2	632,770	20.0
By business group				
Central Group	75,889	3.2	97,102	3.1
CP Group	66,055	2.8	131,656	4.2
The Mall Group	28,471	1.2	32,897	1.0
By nationality				
Thai	187,960	7.9	291,091	9.2
Foreign	243,468	10.3	341,679	10.8
By format				
Department stores	66,782	2.8	78,863	2.5
General mass merchandisers	229,982	9.7	326,086	10.3
Supermarkets	27,395	1.2	33,309	1.1
Convenience stores	73,677	3.1	147,230	4.7
Other	25,882	1.1	34,997	1.1
Provincial wholesaler- cum-supermarkets	7,710	0.3	12,284	0.4
Total for the entire country	2,364,814	100.0	3,157,05	100.0

SOURCE: Annual reports of listed companies and financial statements of unlisted companies for individual company data; author's estimate for total sales of Thailand's entire retail industry (for calculation method see Appendix).

NOTE: "Sales" refers to sales income only; it does not include other income, such as rental income. Business group and nationality are determined based on the major stockholders and who controls the management of the company. "Other" includes category killers, specialty stores, and home centers.

Third, some provincial city-based, retail-cum-wholesalers have risen in the ranks since 2006. They are as follows: Super Cheap in Phuket (ranked 14th), Tang Ngee Soon Superstore in Udon Thani (ranked 19th), Yongsanguan Group in Ubon Ratchathani (ranked 25th), and Liwiwat Thawon in Songkhla (ranked 30th). All of them are companies that have successfully converted into a hybrid format, combining the strengths of traditional wholesale businesses with the strengths of new retail formats. This does not necessarily mean, however, that all provincial wholesalers are thriving. There is the possibility that many other wholesalers have been forced into decline as a result of the rise of Thailand's leading wholesalers. A further study on this kind of intermediate distribution is, therefore, needed.

LOOKING AHEAD

In Japan, during the period of its high economic growth, the changes to its distribution system remained partial. The recent changes in the Thai distribution system also remain partial. Thus, we cannot regard these changes to Thailand's distribution system as a "revolution" in the strict sense of the word, just like the case in Japan. One of the reasons for this lies in the mosaic structure of Thailand's consumer market, which features very large disparities in income strata between and within geographical areas. Another reason is that new foreign retail formats have been an *addition to* rather than a *replacement of* traditional distributors. New retail formats have also provided traditional distributors with additional sources from which to purchase their goods. Moreover, some leading provincial wholesalers have successfully converted into a hybrid format by adopting some of the features of new retail formats. In other words, Thailand's retail and distribution industries are, for the time being, heading towards diversification rather than uniformity.

What significance does this case study of Thailand have for studies on retail and distribution industries in other emerging markets, into which multinational retail companies have dramatically advanced in recent years?

Many emerging markets, like Thailand, have mosaic structured consumer markets. However, the extent and depth of multinational retail companies' impact should be expected to differ among countries according to the importance of their traditional distributors, especially wholesalers. Differences in historical backgrounds also influence the structure of the traditional distribution industry and the degree of its development. In Thailand, Chinese (or Thai-Chinese) wholesalers have consistently occupied a dominant position in the domestic distribution industry. In other countries, this is necessarily different. In the case of Thailand, the government's distribution policies have never been very effective, while its site plan regulations regarding new store openings have even been detrimental. Yet other countries, where more effective regulations are enacted, may have better success in protecting their traditional distribution industries. Keeping in mind the issues discussed throughout this book, scholars will need to develop area studies and business history studies that center on Asian countries and emerging markets in order to determine to what degree the experience of Thailand has generality in other emerging markets, and what kinds of experience can be observed. Other points at issue will also need to be considered. For instance, how diversified are the distribution systems in emerging markets? And, to what degree has the rise of multinational retail companies caused uniformization? Such further studies will undoubtedly make a significant contribution to the field of comparative business history as well as to studies on retail internationalization processes.

APPENDIX

Method used for calculating Thailand's retail sales, 1995–2006

	Retail sales at current market prices, according to Bank of Thailand internal documents (million baht)	Retail sales index at 2002 prices	Consumer price index at 2002 prices	Estimated retail sales at 2002 prices (million baht)	Estimated retail sales at current market prices (million baht)
1995	796,625	0.702	0.794	982,489	780,096
1996	983,931	0.770	0.841	1,077,659	906,311
1997	958,029	0.772	0.888	1,080,458	959,446
1998	660,793	0.493	0.960	689,981	662,382
1999	863,332	0.642	0.962	898,515	864,372
2000	1,066,269	0.779	0.978	1,090,255	1,066,269
2001	–	0.872	0.994	1,220,413	1,213,091
2002	–	1.000	1.000	1,399,557	1,399,557
2003	–	1.157	1.018	1,619,287	1,648,434
2004	–	1.373	1.046	1,921,591	2,009,984
2005	–	1.470	1.093	2,057,348	2,248,682
2006	–	1.477	1.144	2,067,145	2,364,814

The method used to calculate estimated sales figures for Thailand's retail industry was as follows: I compared official data (1995–2000), provided by internal documents from the Bank of Thailand, with my estimated figures (1995–2000) by using the same method in which I estimated industry sales for 2001–2006, in order to confirm the accuracy of the method.

The method entailed the following steps:

1. Retail sales for all of Thailand, as of 2000, based on Bank of Thailand's internal documents, were divided by the consumer price index at 2002 prices, as of 2000.
2. The quotient was, then, divided by the retail sales index for Thailand at 2002 prices, as of 2000.
3. This estimated figure was multiplied by the retail sales index at 2002 prices, as of each year, representing the estimated retail sales for the entire country at 2002 prices, as of each year.
4. The estimated figures, arrived at in step 3, were, then, multiplied by the consumer price index at 2002 prices, representing the estimated retail sales for the whole country at current market prices, as of each year.

SOURCES: Bank of Thailand internal documents for retail industry sales at current market prices (1995–2000); Bank of Thailand (www.bot.or.th) for the country's retail sales and consumer price indices at 2002 prices.

NOTES

INTRODUCTION

1. This retail format is generally known as a "hypermarket" in France and a "supercenter" in the US, but they are, in fact, so similar that it is very difficult to strictly distinguish between them. In Thailand, the appellation differs according to the company, but the two are almost the same format. Given this, only the term "hypermarket" will be used in this study.

2. See, e.g., Kawabata (1999, 2000, 2005, 2011); Davis and Yahagi (2000); Yahagi (2003); Yahagi (2007); Dawson et al. (2003); Dawson and Lee (2004).

3. Studies on the retail internationalization process are popular among economic geographers as well. The conceptualization of "territorial embeddedness," highlighting the circumstances of host countries, in particular, is very interesting. See, e.g., Dicken and Malmberg (2001); Coe (2004); Hess (2004); Wrigley et al. (2005); Coe and Lee (2006); Coe and Wrigley (2007); Dawson (2007); Reardon et al. (2007). As these studies indicate, however, further case studies on the topic are needed.

4. As for the case of Thailand, see Endo (1998a).

5. See, e.g., Athiwat (2002); TDRI (1999); Rewadi and Sunantha (2000); Sombun (2002); Waraphon (2000); Warunrat (2001).

6. See, e.g., Khunathip (2001); Worawan (2001).

7. As for the viewpoints of horizontal and vertical relationships in the distribution system, see Takaoka (1997, 1999a, 1999b).

8. An interesting study by Wirayut (2006) examined the Thai distribution system from a neo-institutional economics point of view. However, this study, too, is insufficient as a positive analysis of the vertical relationships in the distribution system, since it also tends to overestimate informal business connections between actors.

9. There are two main reasons for widening income differentials in an emerging market country. First, the structural change in employment comes behind the structural change in production, resulting in differentials of per capita labor productivity between industrial sectors. Second, while the high-income class has greater advantages in assets formation, allowing for acquisition of higher income, the government's income redistribution policy to equalize the gap is ineffective.

10. Private research companies like AC Nielsen sometimes make public a portion of their original research findings, but they fail to discuss their research methodology. The reliability of the data is, therefore, unknown to outsiders. Niphon et al. (2002, 14) also pointed out this issue.

11. There have been very few studies on retail and distribution in emerging markets in Asia from the viewpoint of area studies. The author, therefore, made full use of earlier studies on the distribution industry in Japan as a point of comparative reference.

12. An exception is Saha Pathanapibul Plc, a long-established Thai company that publishes a report of its company history at various intervals of time. Kao Industrial (Thailand) Co., Ltd. has also published a report in Thai on its twenty-year history. In addition, the public relations department of Osotspa, another long-established Thai company, provided the author with a DVD on the history of the company.

13. Business Online Plc, a Thailand-based private research company, provides general customers with fee-based online services for copies of the financial statements of all companies registered at the Department of Business Development, under a concession contract with the department. As will be noted in chapter 3, the author made use of this service and also collected data directly from the department. An affiliated company of Business Online Plc also publishes a company yearbook covering the top 2,000 companies in terms of total revenues in which some corporate data, including financial statements, is provided (Advanced Research Group Co., Ltd.). However, since the listing is limited to the top 2,000 companies, in which only a partial number of domestic wholesalers and retailers are included, one cannot obtain sufficient data from this yearbook.

14. According to a research paper by Thailand's central bank, no governmental organization, except the National Taxation Bureau within the Ministry of Finance, gathers sales data for the entire retail industry (Rewadi and Sunantha 2000, 55). As will be shown in chapter 3, however, the bureau's data has its own peculiar limitations and, moreover, is closed to the public. Although the National Statistical Office has recently begun to publish *Retail Survey*, which includes the sales volume of individual companies, these statistics lack credibility, as there is an unnaturally sharp fluctuation in the data between consecutive years. Meanwhile, the industrial associations are fairly inactive as regards public information. The Thai Retailers Association consisting of leading retailers in Thailand has tried to gather some business performance data, such as sales figures, but has failed due to insufficient cooperation among its members (author interview with Ms. Varaporn Namatra, executive director, Thai Retailers Association, Bangkok, November 1, 2001).

CHAPTER 1

1. For the socioeconomic impact the development of railways had on the provinces, see Phunphon (1987); Plaio (1987); Suphaphan (1991); Kakizaki (2005, 2012).

2. European trading companies not only traded with Chinese merchants but also employed Chinese personnel with abilities in business and foreign languages as compradors (Skinner 1957, 102–3; Khomsan 2006, 363).

3. Chinese paddy middlemen probably played a leading role in rural areas. They were engaged not only in the purchase of paddy from farmers, but also in the sale of Bangkok-manufactured goods to farmers in rural areas (Ingram 1971, 70–72; Phanni 2002, 164–86). In addition, Chinese merchants settled down in provincial cities, purchasing manufactured goods for resale in big lots from Bangkok-based wholesalers (Endo 1996, 56–61; Endo 2001, 29–31). As for the relationship prior to World War II between these two kinds of province-based merchants, it is believed that their businesses were divided, to some extent, by the scale of capital and the type of customers, although complete details are unknown.

4. A similar explanation was heard from local, large-scale consumer goods manufacturers (e.g., Saha Pathanapibul Plc) and leading provincial companies (author interviews).

5. Hiap Seng Chiang was reorganized in 1952 as Saha Pathanapibul Co., Ltd.

6. Thiam Chokwatthana (1991, 57); author interview with Mr. Samrerng Manoonpol, previously employed with Saha Pat (joined in 1952) and, as of 2006, current director, Saha Pathana Inter-Holding Plc of the Saha Group (Bangkok, December 14, 2006).

7. Author interview with Mr. Samrerng.

8. Ibid.

9. The physical base that enabled many more consumption goods to be distributed was the construction of road networks. For further details, see Kakizaki (2009).

10. Author interviews with Mr. Udomsak Lerthanapoke, director, Sutthiphan (1991) Co., Ltd., one of the largest wholesalers in northern Thailand (Chiang Mai, January 3, 2007); Mr. Milin Veraratanaroj, managing director, Tang Ngee Soon Superstore Co., Ltd., one of the largest wholesalers and retailers in northeastern Thailand (Udon Thani, August 23, 2007).

11. Saha Pat increased its own warehouses in each area in accordance with increases in provincial sales.

12. These new marketing channels were created during different periods, depending on the type of goods sold. In the case of household electric batteries, for example, every brand was sold via the Sampheng-based wholesalers until the 1970s. It was at the beginning of the 1980s that Panasonic Siew Sales Co., Ltd., which had about a 75-percent share of the household battery market as of 2006, started to build its own marketing channels. Author interview with Mr. Tanimoto Takuya, deputy director, Battery Sales Division, Panasonic Siew Sales [Thailand] Co., Ltd. (Bangkok, September 13, 2006).

13. In an author interview, Mr. Samrerng said that the Chiang Mai-based Tantraphan Group doing retail-cum-wholesale business had such a great influence in Chiang Mai,

that even Saha Pat couldn't sell its products without the sales network of the Tantraphan Group. Further details on the Tantraphan Group are discussed in chapter 2.

14. The author confirmed this point during his interviews with many persons connected with the industry, such as Mr. Somchai Phonrattanajaroen, president, Thai Wholesale and Retail Association (Bangkok, September 1, 2004); Mr. Samrerng, director, Saha Pathana Inter-Holding Plc (Bangkok, December 14, 2006); Mr. Somboon Rujikhajorn, co-editor of *Brand Age* (Bangkok, December 22, 2006), and so forth.

15. In this section, data on the Central Department Store is based primarily on the funeral book (*nangsue chaek ngan sop*) commemorating Mr. Samrit Jirathiwat, a second-generation leader of the Central Group (Samrit 1992).

16. Central Trading was a rare store in the sense that it took risks by directly importing foreign goods.

17. Such well-known brands include, for example, Manhattan and Esquire for shirts, Crepe de Chine for pomade, Helena Rubinstein for cosmetics, and so on.

18. After Tiang died on July 12, 1968, the Silom branch opened and Tiang's eldest son Samrit succeeded him as the leader of the Jirathiwat family business.

19. The site for the store was on land that Tiang had bought in the early days of his company at a relatively low price (7,000 baht per *tarang wa*, the equivalent of approx. 4 sq m). The land was bought with the intention of building on it for future business (Wirat, Pandop, and Somsak 2003, 45). Given that the land price had increased to more than ten times its value at the time of the construction of the Chidlom store, it is obvious that Tiang had foresight. As to the construction expenses, Central Department Store borrowed 60 million baht from Bangkok Bank.

20. Similarly, this study does not distinguish between native Thai and ethnic Chinese when referring to the Thai people, unless it is necessary.

21. The discussion on Central Plaza here is primarily based on the company's prospectus (Central Pattana Plc 2000) and the report by Wirat et al. (Wirat, Pandop, and Somsak 2003, 50–56). The view that the project took the initiative into the suburbs ahead of large-scale commercial institutions has already been pointed out in Suehiro (1989, b: 60); Suehiro and Nanbara (1991, 169–70).

22. Central Plaza Co., Ltd. was financially backed at the time of its establishment by the Tetchaphaibun family and the Saha Union Group. After that, the company changed its name to Central Pattana, and in 1995 listed its stocks with the Stock Exchange of Thailand (SET).

23. Author interview with Mr. Matsumura Kazuyuki, managing director, and Mr. Kuribayashi Yoshio, director, Thai Daimaru Department Store (Bangkok, May 29, 1997).

CHAPTER 2

1. US dollar figures are based on the yearly average currency exchange rate.

2. For the characteristics and some of the weak points of NSO's *Household Socio-Economic Survey*, see Shigetomi (1998, 153–66). For a comparison between NSO's statistics and GDP statistics by NESDB (National Economic and Social Development Board of Thailand), see Suehiro (1995); Ikemoto (1997).

3. If we use GRP (Gross Regional Product) and GPP (Gross Provincial Product) as an index for comparison, the differentials between geographic areas are larger.

4. The population figures in this paragraph are based on Thailand's official census, which is taken every ten years. The latest census, for 2010, was still being prepared for publication as of September 2012 when this book was in press, which is why these population figures are based on the year 2000.

5. A similar view appeared in the Japanese newspaper *Nihon Keizai Shimbun* (November 25, 2007).

6. The six provincial Robinson affiliate department stores had a total net loss of 241 million baht in 1996, and Robinson Department Store Plc, the parent company, had a consolidated net profit of 372 million baht in the same year, while six of Robinson's seven provincial department stores experienced a total net loss of 302 million baht in 1997, and Robinson Department Store Plc had a consolidated net loss of 7,628 million baht, which was primarily due to the currency crisis that Thailand was undergoing at the time. See Robinson Department Store Plc (1999).

7. Robinson Department Store was founded in 1979 by a group of apparel manufacturers who owned the company. They poached Mr. Preecha Vejsupaporn (then manager of Thai Daimaru Department Store) and his subordinates from Thai Daimaru and entrusted the management of Robinson to them. Author interview with Mr. Kanda Masao, former employee, Thai Daimaru and director and store manager, Isetan [Thailand] Co., Ltd. (Bangkok, November 1, 2001).

8. Author interview with Mr. Sutthiphan Jirathiwat, a member of Central Group's founding family (Bangkok, August 7, 2000).

9. The leading provincial department stores that were PDS Club members included, for example, Tantraphan Department Store in Chiang Mai, Topland Arcade in Phitsanulok, Fairy Land Department Store in Nakhon Sawan, Charoensi Plaza in Udon Thani, Fairy Plaza in Khon Kaen, Yingyong Department Store in Ubon Ratchathani, Ocean Department Store in the southern provinces, Saha Thai Department Store in Surat Thani and Nakhon Si Thammarat, and Diana Department Store in Songkhla (Hat Yai city), all of which were typical department stores in each region.

10. Unless mentioned otherwise, information on the Tantraphan Group is based on author interviews with the following central figures of the group: Mr. Thawat Tantranon, leader of the group (Chiang Mai, June 7, 1997); Mr. Worawat Tantranon, president, Tantraphan Department Store Co., Ltd. (Chiang Mai, August 13, 1996); Mr. Phairot Phatsoraphin-Yosakun, president, Tantraphan Supermarket (1994) Co., Ltd. (Chiang Mai,

August 19, 1997 and August 3, 2000). For details on the development and managerial organization of the Tantraphan Group, see Endo (2001).

11. This is why in the 1970s Thawat not only expanded the store's floor space on Thaphae Road to 4,000 square meters and established a private wet market, but also diversified into transportation, construction contracting, mining, and other businesses that had little relation to his department store business. This business development strategy was probably motivated by the difficulty Thawat faced in trying to deepen his retail business by concentrating on one format or one particular category of goods due to the geographical limitations of consumer markets in provincial cities.

12. Kad Suan Kaew shopping center was developed by the Hin Suan Nam Sai Group, a provincial property developer that had no relationship capital with the Central Group.

13. In April 1993, Tantraphan Department Store Co. Ltd. increased its registered capital from 100 million to 150 million baht through the allocation of new stocks to S&P Syndicate Co., Ltd., a major foodservice company in Thailand. At the time, S&P, which was expanding its branches into provincial cities as well as the Bangkok metropolitan area, found that the affiliation with provincial department stores would benefit the company (*PJK-RS*, April 26, 1993).

14. CR Chiang Mai Co., Ltd. was established with joint investment from the Tantraphan Department Store and CR Company. Tantraphan put in 10 percent, while CR contributed 90 percent towards the joint venture. The store name was also changed to Robinson Tantraphan Department Store and four of the five directors were from Robinson Department Store, while only a single director, Worawat (the second son of Thawat), was from Tantraphan. Robinson, therefore, held decision-making authority over important matters.

15. Information on the PDS Club is based mainly on author interviews with three leading members of the club: Mr. Worawat Tantranon, the first president (Chiang Mai, August 13, 1996), Mr. Surachai Luangchairat (Chiang Mai, August 15, 1996), and Mr. Santi Kunawong (Nakhon Sawan, August 29, 1996), who served two terms, third and fifth, as president. For further details on the PDS Club, see Endo (1998c).

16. Initially, only five big manufacturers (Unilever, Nestle, P&G, Colgate, and Saha Pat) agreed to deliver goods to PDS Club's members at the TDC distribution center, though later on approximately four hundred small- and medium-sized manufacturers followed suit (*TNSK*, August 19, 1993).

17. Author interview with Mr. Somchai Sirivichayakul, managing director, Davids Distribution (Thailand) Limited (Nonthaburi, May 30, 1997)..

CHAPTER 3

1. Author interview with the Bank of Thailand (Bangkok, August 20, 2001).

2. Here, the term "unemployed people" includes seasonal unemployed persons. Meanwhile, the unemployment figures for each year correspond to the mean value of NSO's *Labor Force Survey*, which is conducted four times a year in February, May, August, and November.

3. The "oligopoly of the retail industry" is characterized by a small group of companies that sell similar or identical products within the same geographical area and collude to raise prices on those products because of excess demand. Oligopolies tend to have little incentive to lower costs, which usually results in fewer innovations and improvements in their sector.

4. Table 3.2 shows that the total sales of Carrefour Group in 2000 roughly US$60 billion (approx. 2.4 trillion baht), whereas table 3.1 shows the total retail sales for all Thailand in 2000 were roughly US$27 billion (approx. 1.1 trillion baht).

5. The exception was US firms that were allowed full ownership as a result of America's special relationship with Thailand during the Cold War (Pasuk and Baker 2008, 20).

6. Author interview with the Business Development Department, Ministry of Commerce (Nonthaburi, August, 16, 2000).

7. Prior to the enactment of the new law, the Board of Investment decided to offer retail and wholesale industries investment promotion measures for the first time in December 1998 and permit 100-percent foreign capital stockholding (BOI, 1998). However, this was for a limited time only, until December 31, 1999, and only two companies actually received the investment promotion (Yutthasak, 2001c, 43). It can, therefore, be concluded that deregulation of foreign investment implemented by the BOI had a very limited effect on Thailand's retail and wholesale industries.

8. The total sales of department stores may be overestimated. According to the author's calculations based on data collected from the Business Development Department, Ministry of Commerce (for further details see note 12 in this chapter), the total sales of major department stores throughout the country were, as of 2000, less than 56 billion baht, which is substantially lower than the figure of approximately 106 billion baht noted in the internal documents from the Central Bank of Thailand (the original data came from the Revenue Department, Ministry of Finance). The reason for this discrepancy may be that many companies were actually engaged in other businesses even though they were nominally listed as "department stores" in the commercial registry. Therefore, general mass merchandisers may have exceeded department stores in sales at an earlier time.

9. The reason for this will be examined in the next chapter.

10. As a side note, the author calculated the total sales of hypermarkets and cash-and-carry stores (i.e., general mass merchandisers) as a percentage of private consumption expenditures and found that it rapidly increased during the post-crisis recession but did not show as much growth as expected during the recovery period (see table 3.4).

11. For example, the Thailand Development Research Institute [TDRI] (1999) argued that the sales ratio of traditional trade to modern trade drastically changed from 75:25 in 1990 to 30:70 in 1997, but it unquestionably overestimated the percentage of modern trade.

12. Business Online Plc, a Thailand-based private research company, provides general customers with an online, fee-based service for copies of financial statements of all companies registered at the Business Development Department, Ministry of Commerce under a concession contract with the department. Using this service, the author selected all the retail companies with total revenues exceeding 100 million baht or total assets exceeding 100 million baht to create an original database. Data not available from Business Online Plc was then gathered directly from the Business Development Department and added to the database. Tables 3.3 and 3.5 as well as several other tables are based on the contents of this database. It should be noted that unlisted companies do not make public their consolidated financial statements. For this reason, in those cases where several companies from the same business group run chain stores using the same store name, the sales figures of each company were added together to reach a total sum. If among those companies, commodity trading took place, the total sales of those companies, needless to say, would be overestimated. However, the author believes that the data represent a sufficiently accurate enough estimation to observe a rough trend in retail sales in Thailand. Using Robinson Department Store as a test case, the author compared that company's consolidated sales with the total of sales of individual stores that were simply added together, and found that the difference between the two figures proved to retain the essence of this argument.

13. The Central Group sold the stock of these companies with an optional right to repurchase within five years, according to the author's interview with Mr. Sutthiphan Jirathiwat, a founding family member of the Central Group (Bangkok, August 7, 2000).

14. HCDS's balance sheet showed a sharp decrease in its inventory, as of the end of 1995, compared with the previous year. From that point on, the inventory gradually decreased and finally reached "0," as of the end of 1998, according to the company's financial statements.

15. This can be seen from the list of CRC's stockholders maintained at the Business Development Department, Ministry of Commerce. As of the end of 1999, the company's board of directors consisted of fifteen persons, thirteen of whom were from the Central Group's founding family, and two persons were from the Robinson Group's founding families.

16. In contrast with the disposal of Lotus, the CP Group expressly stated that it would maintain ownership and management of 7-Eleven, even during the post-crisis, business-restructuring period (Phujatkan 2000, 65). As for the positioning of 7-Eleven in the CP Group, see Athiwat (2001).

17. As of the year 2000, the Central Group consisted of various businesses, including retail, real estate development, hotel and resort development, and fast food, as well as consumer goods manufacturing and wholesale. The core business of the group was retail.

The group's revenues in 1999 were approximately 70 billion baht, of which 74 percent was earned from its retail businesses (Pandop 2000, 71, 89).

18. For example, the amount of foreign-currency corporate bonds Robinson Department Store issued in 1994 was 1,879 million baht (equivalent to 18.4 percent of total capital for the same year), 3,107 million baht in 1995 (representing 17.1 percent of total capital), 5,583 million baht in 1996 (25.8 percent of total capital), and 13,090 million baht in 1997 (71.6 percent of total capital). As can be seen, the amount of foreign-currency bonds increased every year. The figure for 1997, despite its significant amount, includes a currency exchange loss following the weak baht. By contrast, basing its experience with a significant currency exchange loss due to the devaluation of baht in 1981 and 1984, the Central Group was more careful, comparatively speaking, in borrowing foreign currency even during the financial liberalization of the 1990s (Pandop 2000, 83).

19. As a result of this extraordinary currency exchange loss, CRC, Robinson's main stockholder, and the Effective Planners Company, as the representative of the creditors, established Robinson Planner Ltd., an equally joint capital investment venture to carry out the reorganization plan for Robinson (Robinson Planner Ltd. 2000).

20. During the post-crisis period, the Central Group, in particular, carried out a drastic restructuring—mainly of its core business—in order to concentrate managerial resources into the core business again.

21. Calculated based on the company's financial statements.

22. Ibid.

23. On February 6, 2006, Robinson Department Store requested the Central Bankruptcy Court to revoke the Company Resuscitation Law application. The court accepted the request (Robinson Department Store Plc 2007, 8).

24. The nine companies that were forced to close down or sharply reduce their business following the financial and currency crisis were Asia, Banglumpoo, Edison, Imperial, Merry Kings, New World, Pata, Piriyapul, and Welco, all of which were Bangkok-based medium-sized department stores.

25. According to Mr. Viroj Chunprathipthong, president of the only surviving Bangkok-based medium-sized department store, Tang Hua Seng, the success of Central and The Mall was attributed to the appropriate selection of location and customers (author interview, Bangkok, August 6, 2008).

26. Author interview with Mr. Phairoj Phatsorpinyosakul, president, Tantraphan Supermarket (1994) Co., Ltd. (Chiang Mai, August 22, 2002).

27. Although sales of the group's supermarket business consistently decreased from 1996 to 2001 (451 million baht in 1996, 310 million baht in 1999, and 194 million baht in 2001), the group rebuilt its business with a clear differentiation strategy against competitors and recovered its losses by expanding to 365 million baht in 2005 and 527 million baht in 2006, according to the company's financial statements.

28. Author interview with Mr. Adachi Akihiko, sales department manager, Thai Glico Co., Ltd., for which Super Cheap is its agent (Bangkok, January 26, 2007).

29. Author interview with Mr. Milin Veerarattanaroj, managing director, Tang Ngee Soon Super Store Co., Ltd. (Udon Thani, August 23, 2007).

30. Examples are Leng Seng Limited Partnership in Sakon Nakhon (*TNSK*, April 20 and 23, 2006); Ekkaphap Super Supply Co., Ltd. in Saraburi (*PRCT-TK*, July 13, 2006; *PRCT-TK*, January 8, 2007); Samon Phaibun 2002 Co., Ltd. in Samut Sakhon (*TNSK*, October 7, 2007); Ruam Sinthai Co., Ltd. in Ubon Ratchathani (*TNSK*, December 27, 2007).

31. The next chapter approaches this point by dividing general mass merchandisers by format and by company.

32. To compete with The Mall Group, the Central Group expanded Central World, located very near to Siam Paragon, renovating it as a similar type of high-class shopping center. For further information on the competition between the two groups in Bangkok's commercial district, see Sutjanya and Saran-ya (2006).

CHAPTER 4

1. The consignment sales system and the sales representative system were first introduced and diffused throughout the Thai retail industry by Thai Daimaru Department Store. As of 2001, the percentage of consignment sales to total sales in Thailand's department store industry was estimated between 60 and 70 percent on average. Author interview with Mr. Kanda Masao, store manager, Isetan Department Store (Thailand) (Bangkok, November 1, 2001).

2. However, the buying price, or cost of sales, then becomes more expensive and the gross profit ratio declines.

3. Percentages of bulk delivery to the distribution center differ among chains. For Tesco Lotus, the percentage, at present, reaches almost 100 percent. As for other chains, the percentages for some goods are relatively low since they purchase those goods from selling agents in nearby localities.

4. Author interviews with Mr. Justin H. Barnett, senior vice president, Ek-Chai Distribution System Co., Ltd., which operates Tesco Lotus (Bangkok, August 21 2003); Ms. Titima Bantrapiwat, Vice CEO, Ek-Chai Distribution System Co., Ltd. (Bangkok, December 26, 2003).

5. In the case of Tesco Lotus, the central distribution center's rate of use as of 2003 had already reached 80 percent for perishable foods and 90 percent for other goods (Arun 2004, 100–103).

6. Author interview with Mr. Barnett.

7. Author interview with the store manager of Carrefour's Chiang Mai branch (Chiang Mai, August 23, 2002).

8. Big C has entrusted its physical distribution to Excel Distribution (Thailand) Co., Ltd. Based on the registry book at the Business Development Department, Ministry of Commerce, the forerunner of Excel Distribution was DDT (Davids Distribution [Thailand]

Co., Ltd.), a joint venture between the Central Group and Australia-based Davids Holding Group. The company name was changed in 2005 after Big C allocated new stock to a third party, the UK-based Tibbett & Britten Group, representing up to 40 percent of the company's total capital.

9. Author interview with Ms. Suchada Ithijarukul, president, Siam Makro Plc (Bangkok, December 24, 2003). Siam Makro Plc has entrusted its cross-docking activities to the local-based Blue & White Logistics Co., Ltd. In June 2008, a new distribution center for fresh and frozen products was opened with a focus on distribution efficiency and food safety standards (Siam Makro Plc annual report).

10. According to author interviews, the percentage of virtual wholesaling to total sales of a hypermarket is unknown, but some provincial leading wholesalers estimate it at approximately 10 to 20 percent.

11. The clever usage of data on members' purchases enabled Makro to realize its primary customers' needs and then to buy goods accordingly, thus reducing stock loss of less popular items and brands, which, in turn, helped to avoid direct competition with hypermarkets.

12. The number of SKU in hypermarkets greatly differs between companies. Big C offered about 100,000 SKUs, as of 2006 (Big C Supercenter Plc 2007, 42).

13. Author interview with Ms. Suchada.

14. Due to limited data, the differences of the opening day and floor space between stores are not considered. Since all general mass merchandisers had established similarly standard stores (floor space approx. 10,000 sq m), this does not really matter when roughly estimating sales efficiency.

15. Hypermarkets' gross profit ratios and SG&A cost ratios are much lower than department stores. For example, Thailand's top department store Central (CDS) showed a gross profit ratio of 27.1 and a SG&A cost ratio of 25.1 percent in 2006 (author calculations based on the company's financial statements).

16. Ordinary profit = operating profit + non-operating revenue (mainly "other revenue") – non-operating expenses. In the cases of these four companies, non-operating revenue is much larger than non-operating expenses. Actually, the operating profit of each company is almost 0, or in the red.

17. One of the possible causes for the decreasing sales per store is that Makro began to put emphasis on medium-sized stores when opening new stores. Another possible cause, based on the company's financial statements, is that since 2000 Makro has shifted some part of its sales to non-operating revenue (especially "other revenue").

18. Mr. Milin Verarataanaroj, managing director, Tang Ngee Soon Super Store Co., argued that the start-up and management costs (i.e., selling, general, and administrative expenses) of establishing one of their new stores was much lower than that of the three hypermarkets operating in Thailand, which enabled the company to have a competitive advantage (author interview, Udon Thani, August 23, 2007). For further details, see chapter 5.

19. A new type of pick-up truck has been recently developed, in which the loading platform is reduced, while the seat space is enlarged. Pick-up trucks are generally utilized for business, but Thais also purchase a pick-up truck as an automobile substitute, although they are not always satisfied with it because the seat space is small. That is why automobile companies have developed the new type of pick-up truck for general customers who utilize a pick-up truck as an automobile substitute. These customers do not need a large loading platform because they purchase consumer goods at a hypermarket store just for their family use.

20. It should also be pointed out that while it is true that the number of motorcycles is quite high throughout Thailand, including in rural areas, these types of vehicles (which are not factored into motorization rates) do not allow for the transport of large quantities of household goods as one might purchase from a hypermarket or cash-and-carry store.

21. The forerunner of Foodland was a supermarket that Foodland's founder Somsak Tiraphatthanakun had initially established as a joint venture with a Hong Kong businessman. Since his partner later returned to Hong Kong, Somsak developed the chain by himself (Arun 2002a, 44–45).

22. The Delhaize Group purchased a supermarket business (Sunny's) from the CP Group.

23. Author interviews with Mr. Hiramatsu Kenji, assistant division manager, Personnel and Management, Siam-Jusco Co., Ltd. (Bangkok, May 29, 1997); Mr. Takani Takashi, president, Siam-Jusco Co., Ltd. (Bangkok, August 14, 2002).

24. Author interview with Ms. Chiranun Poopat, senior vice president (buying and marketing), Central Food Retail Co., Ltd., which runs Tops supermarket (Bangkok, February 20, 2007).

25. Author interview with Mr. Shibata Eiji, managing director, Siam-Jusco Co., Ltd. (Bangkok, January 26, 2007).

26. Although wet markets are, in reality, divided into wholesale and retail markets, there is no legal distinction. Data here on wet markets is mainly based on author interviews with Ms. Udomluck Pongsuphan, promotion and public relations manager, Thai Agro Exchange Co., Ltd., which runs Talat Thai (Pathumthani, August 15, 2008); Mr. Parinya Tumwattana, managing director, Suwapee Holding Co., Ltd., which runs Talat Yingcharoen (Bangkok, August 15, 2008); Ms. Pradap Komut, president, But Lae Luk Co., Ltd., which runs Talat Sot Bang Khun Si (Bangkok, August 16, 2008).

27. Information on Tops' logistics system is primarily based on the author's interview with Ms. Penchan Jongthavornvitaya, assistant vice president, Logistics and Distribution, Central Food Retail Co., Ltd. (Bangkok, February 20, 2007).

28. Tops further established a "quality-guaranteed team" division within the head office to implement quality control and inspection.

29. MASCI stands for Management System Certification Institute (Thailand) and was established by the Ministry of Industry. HACCP (Hazard Analysis and Critical Control Points) handles food safety and hygiene control and conducts hazard analysis. TQCSI (Total Quality Certification Service International) Co., Ltd. is a certification organization

for quality management, including internationally recognized ISO management system standards.

30. In 1995, Jusco established a distribution management company exclusively for Jusco stores. The company, known as Retail Support (Thailand) Co., Ltd., was formed jointly with a large Japanese wholesale company, Ryoshoku Co., Ltd., and the major Japanese general trading company Mitsubishi Shoji Co., Ltd. Jusco entrusted the company with the physical distribution of processed foods, daily necessities, and some fruits and vegetables, accounting for 60 percent of its total goods. It entrusted Logitem Thailand Co., Ltd., an overseas affiliated company of the Japan-based Nihon Logitem Co., Ltd., with the delivery from the distribution center to each store. Author interview with Mr. Iwasaki Yasuharu, president, Retail Support (Thailand) Co., Ltd. (Bangkok, September 20, 2006).

31. Author interviews with major supermarkets in Bangkok.

32. For example, see *TNSK* (June 25, 2006; February 8, 2007) and *PRCT-TK* (July 3 and 6, 2006). It is in the categories of processed foods and daily necessities, which can be stocked, that wet markets face stiff competition from new retail formats. In this respect, the real threats to wet markets are not supermarkets but hypermarkets and cash-and-carry stores.

33. Author interviews with major supermarket companies.

34. Even in Bangkok, wet markets are preferred to new retail formats (including hypermarkets) for perishable foods shopping. Niphon et al. (2002, 90–92).

35. However, there is a big difference between old-fashioned wet markets and modernized wet markets in which managers conduct quality inspection to monitor hygiene and sanitation conditions as well as the freshness of perishable foods. Author interviews with various wet market companies.

36. Ms. Chiranun Poopat of Tops said, "We need to educate consumers because many of them do not understand yet that Tops' perishable foods are of higher quality than those of wet markets" (author interview, Bangkok, February 20, 2007).

37. This is another example of consumer goods manufacturers attaching importance to traditional as well as modern distribution channels.

38. Jusco's general merchandise business had been losing market share due to competition with local, popular department stores located in the suburbs (author interview with Mr. Takani). It is an irony that the suburban department stores, which at one time had been very successful, should later be forced to withdraw from the market due to their inability to compete with hypermarkets.

39. Another example is Fuji Supermarket, which mainly aims at Japanese residents in Bangkok.

40. One good example of this, at the provincial level, is the Tantraphan Group's supermarket business in Chiang Mai, which is experiencing continuing growth by targeting the local upper-income strata and foreigners, including Japanese residents, and putting emphasis on an assortment of imported and high-quality goods to differentiate itself from wet markets and other supermarkets. Author interview with Mr. Phairoj

Phatsorpinyosakul, president, Tantraphan Supermarket (1994) Co., Ltd. (Chiang Mai, August 26, 2002). Based on the company's financial statements, total sales of Tantraphan Supermarket have been steadily increasing from 213 million baht in 2002, to 287 million baht in 2004, and 527 million baht in 2006.

41. Author interview with Ms. Chiranun.

42. In Thailand, 7-Eleven is managed by the CP Group that acquired trade rights (area licenses) for Thailand from the US-based Seven Eleven Inc. (a subsidiary of the Japan-based Seven and iHoldings), and basically adopted the operating system of Seven Eleven Inc. In October 2007, C. P. Seven Eleven Plc changed its name to CP All Plc and simultaneously concentrated all its affiliated retailing businesses into the new company (*TNSK*, October 18, 2007).

43. According to one Thai newspaper, the total number of convenience stores in Thailand as of the end of 2005 was 5,166 stores, about 77 percent of which were 7-Eleven and FamilyMart (*TNSK*, June 1, 2006). The newspaper reported that the number of V Shop stores had reached 900 stores, which is more than FamilyMart, but the details of the V Shop's business were unknown. For information on V Shop and Fresh Mart, see Phirawut (2004, 88–172).

44. However, a critical disagreement over the management policy emerged between the FamilyMart head office in Japan and Mr. Kanok who was inexperienced in the convenience store business. In 2005, Siam FamilyMart Company finally changed its management system by appointing a Japanese CEO. Author interview with Mr. Tsunematsu Hidenori, chief officer, Corporate Planning Office, Siam FamilyMart Co., Ltd. (Bangkok, July 25, 2006).

45. The head office of a convenience store chain sometimes gives local businesspersons, who have the necessary business contacts and skills, an area-limited business license in remote areas where the head office finds it difficult to directly control and manage the cost-effectiveness of the store. This is known as the sub-area license system. 7-Eleven is the only chain store to have adopted this system in Thailand's convenience store industry. The percentage of sub-area license stores to the whole of the 7-Eleven chain reached its peak in 1995 with 15.9 percent, but sharply decreased after the financial and currency crisis, and was at only 5.7 percent as of the end of 2006 (see table 4.9). For further details on sub-area license holders, see Endo (1998c, 170–71).

46. Author interview with Mr. Tsunematsu.

47. Mr. Tsunematsu, chief officer, Siam FamilyMart, also agreed with this view.

48. Takaoka (1999b) provides a useful viewpoint about this.

49. Author interviews with Ms. Hansa Taweeprapruth, deputy general manager, C. P. Seven Eleven Plc (Bangkok, March 13, 2007); Mr. Tsunematsu Hidenori, chief officer, Corporate Planning Office, Siam FamilyMart Co., Ltd. (Bangkok, July 25, 2006).

50. Contrary to 7-Eleven, FamilyMart opened new stores, mainly in the form of franchise stores, from the very beginning of its activity in Thailand. In the case of its franchise stores, however, the company found it was more difficult to seek franchisees than in Japan, and thus had to reduce the pace of its store openings. Under such

circumstances, Siam FamilyMart Company invited Mr. Kanok to serve as CEO and set out to actively expand the chain operation, mainly in the form of corporate stores under his leadership (Phirawut 2004, 9, 16–17).

51. Although the details are unknown between 1997 and 1999, the number of franchise stores decreased from 355 stores in 1997 to 303 stores in 2000, while the number of corporate stores rapidly increased from 415 stores in 1997 to 1,137 stores in 2000 (1997 figures are sourced from *GM Business*, August 1997, and 2000 figures are sourced from Thot 2005, 135).

52. To be more precise, in addition to the original Type A and the new Type B franchise system, there is also a modified Type A, in which Type A's requirements are relaxed a little, and a Type C, which is similar to Type B but with a longer term contract (Thot 2005, 48–51, 135–37). As for franchise stores, the company has come to open mostly Type C stores since October 2007 (*TNSK*, October 7, 2007).

53. There are few cases in which grocery stores and liquor shops were converted into FamilyMart convenience stores (author interview with Mr. Tsunematsu). On this point, too, the case of Thailand is very different from Japan.

54. Author interview with Ms. Hansa.

55. As of the end of 2011, CP All Plc had a total of 6,276 7-Eleven stores in Thailand, consisting of 2,926 corporate stores, 2,884 franchise stores, and 466 sub-area license stores (CP All Plc annual report, 2012).

56. Data in this section is primarily based on Arun (2002a); Sompratthan et al. (2000); Suriya et al. (1997); Thot (2005, 2008); author interviews.

57. Author interview with Ms. Hansa.

58. Ibid.

59. The POS system, which is one of the main logistics subsystems for both 7-Eleven and FamilyMart in Thailand, is still lagging behind that of convenience stores in Japan (author interview with Mr. Tsunematsu).

60. For example, Saha Pat Company delivers the bread of its original brand (Farm House) directly to each 7-Eleven store by route sales.

61. For example, Kodak and Fuji bid for the selection as an "exclusive brand" for camera film.

62. In addition to these points, 7-Elevens in Thailand are different from 7-Elevens in Japan in that most of the franchise stores in Thailand are not preexisting small-scale grocery stores.

63. Author interview with Ms. Hansa.

64. Ibid. According to CP All Plc website (www.cpall.co.th), the ratio of foods was 46.8 percent, while the ratio of non-foods was 53.2 percent, as of 2006.

65. In Thailand, the front of a convenience store is a rather good location for food carts. Food cart owners open their business by signing an agreement with the 7-Eleven head office and paying a small fee (author interview with Mr. Tsunematsu).

66. Based on Suriya et al. (1997, 99); author interview with Ms. Hansa.

CHAPTER 5

1. Statistical figures for Japan's retail and wholesale industries are based on various commercial statistics tables compiled by Japan's Ministry of Economy, Trade and Industry (see http://www.meti.go.jp/english/statistics/index.html). According to these statistics, the percentage of small-scale retail stores in Japan (of the same size as the case of Thailand) was 80.1 percent in 1988 and 69.3 percent in 2002.

2. See Ibid.

3. In Thailand, the commercial census has only been implemented three times. After an interval of a little more than twenty years between the first census (survey year 1965) and the second census (survey year 1987), the census was to be implemented every ten years, but the third census was postponed due to the curtailed national budget necessary to cope with the financial and currency crisis of 1997. Author interview with the Industrial Statistics Department, National Statistical Office, Bangkok, August 8, 1997. In addition to the commercial census, the National Statistical Office publishes the *Report of the Survey of Business Trade and Services* based on sampling every few years, but it lacks credibility since there is an unnatural fluctuation in statistical figures between the surveys (Endo 1998a).

4. Since 2002, the census has excluded from retail businesses such businesses as the sale and repair of motor vehicles and motorcycles as well as the sale of gasoline. Therefore, this figure is, in fact, underestimated. The same is also true of the number of wholesale establishments.

5. According to officials at the National Statistical Office in charge of the 2002 commercial census, although the industrial classification was changed from Thai standards to international standards, the survey coverage was not any different between the 1987 and 2002 census. Author interview with NSO, Bangkok, August 22, 2007. Yet the officials were unable to give the author convincing reasons for the unnatural gap in the number of establishments between 1987 and 2002. However, the change in statistical figures from 1996 onwards seems relatively natural.

6. The Nielsen survey pointed out that small-scale grocery stores were newly opened every year, but the details were not reported in the newspaper.

7. Author interview with Ms. Varaporn Namatra, executive director, Thai Retailers Association (Bangkok, October 27, 2006), including certain documents provided by her.

8. Although the Thai Retailers Association has recently released the number of retail establishments by retail format, the data unfortunately lacks sufficient reliability.

9. For example, an assistant professor on the Faculty of Economics, Thammasat University, estimated that new retail formats' sales represented 67.5 percent of total retail sales for all of Thailand, as of 2006 (*The Nation*, October 17, 2006), while the Thai Retailers Association estimated it to be 50 to 60 percent, as of 2007 (*TNSK*, November 11, 2007). Meanwhile, the Institute for Development of International Distribution and Franchise Business, Sri Pathum University, estimated that the share of modern retail businesses in Thailand would rise to 80 percent by 2011 (*TNSK*, January 14, 2007).

10. Author interview with Mr. Somchai Phonrattanajaroen, president, Thai Wholesale and Retail Association and president, So. Sapphakit Kha-song Co., Ltd., which is a leading wholesaler in Bangkok (Bangkok, September 1, 2004).

11. Unfortunately, there are too many reports on the difficulties faced by the traditional distribution industry in specific localities to enumerate. See, e.g., Uthikon and Sombun (1997); Worawan (2001); Khunathip (2001).

12. According to national income statistics issued by the National Economic and Social Development Board (NESDB), as of 2005, manufacturing accounted for 34.7 percent of Thailand's GDP, the largest percentage of all the industries, while retail and wholesale businesses accounted for 14.6 percent, the second largest percentage, followed by agriculture at 10.3 percent. The *2000 Population Census* by the National Statistical Office showed that, as of 2000, agriculture accounted for the largest part of the employed population (53.9 percent), followed by retail and wholesale businesses (11.6 percent), and manufacturing (9.0 percent).

13. All the major Thai, Western, and Japanese consumer goods manufacturers that the author interviewed attached importance to their business connections with modern retailers, especially hypermarkets. However, they simultaneously regarded traditional retailers and wholesalers as important partners as well.

14. A few manufacturers have refused direct transactions with new retail formats, and instead use sales agents as a kind of buffer between retailers and themselves.

15. Author interviews with major consumer goods manufacturers.

16. Hypermarket companies engage in a kind of informal selling activity known as *khai lang ran* or "selling behind the store." Every consumer goods manufacturer that the author interviewed confirmed this. This is an easy method for a hypermarket to achieve its target figures, given that strict sales quotas are imposed. It involves the store accepting orders for selling in bulk at a lower than ordinary price. The goods for sale are circulated to traditional wholesalers and others by way of a broker (*mu pun*). For further details, see Mr. Re-tell (2002, 83–91). However, this selling technique is not welcomed by manufacturers because they cannot participate in price decision-making processes and because it may bring confusion to traditional wholesalers purchasing goods for resale through a regular route. As a result, consumer goods manufacturers have taken various measures to control this practice (based on author interviews with each manufacturer). Consequently, the ratio of *khai lang ran* to the total sales of each store, which, at one time, had reached around 10 percent at its peak, has largely decreased. Author interview with Mr. Sombun Rujikhajon, co-editor, Brand Age Co., Ltd., Bangkok, December 22, 2006.

17. According to Suriya et al. (1997, 140), 7-Eleven had obtained strong bargaining power when the number of its stores reached around two hundred. As a result, suppliers/manufacturers began to compete for trade with 7-Eleven.

18. Private label goods are also referred to as "house brands," "store brands," "private brands," and so on.

19. Compared with Thailand, the sales percentage of private label goods to total goods in Western markets is relatively high (Mr. Re-tell 2002, 159). While it is almost impossible to accurately compare the sales percentage of private label goods between countries due to limited data, AC Nielsen, in 1997, did conduct a survey and found that the sales percentage figures for food brands in Europe were 50.7 percent in Switzerland, 34.0 percent in UK, 20.9 percent in Holland, and 16.5 percent in France and for household

articles were 49.6 percent in Switzerland, 44.4 percent in UK, 29.4 percent in Holland, and 28.0 percent in France (Yahagi 2000, 163–65, 202–3).

20. This is one of the unfair trade activities that large-scale retailers engage in, as per the Retail Business Guidelines based on the Trade Competition Act, B.E. 2542 (1999).

21. Using the example of dishwashing liquid, there is a kind of private label that uses a yellow container in imitation of the Unilever brand. Unilever Thai Trading Co., Ltd. not only protested in writing but also made efforts to differentiate its product by changing the design of its container (*TNSK*, September 10, 2006).

22. Some well-informed persons in the industry as well as many local newspapers and business magazines report that this trade practice is particularly hard on manufacturers of weaker brands. See Sombun (2002, 36–37); Sombun (2005a, 58); *TNSK* (July 20 and 27, 2006); *PRCT-TK* (September 11, 2006); Mr. Re-tell (2002, 158).

23. Wholesalers can participate in this merchandising activity, but there are few cases in Thailand in which they play a key role.

24. In the case of Ajinomoto's brand of seasoning, which is widely used by Thai families and restaurants, more than 90 percent of the product's total sales in Thailand are still sold via traditional distribution channels. Author interview with Mr. Akashi Okamoto, director, Ajinomoto Sales (Thailand) Co., Ltd. (Bangkok, August 1, 2006).

25. In addition to the major manufacturers represented in table 5.2, many other manufacturers generally attach great importance to traditional distribution channels as well as modern ones. Author interviews with ARS Chemical (Thailand) Co., Ltd. (Bangkok, August 20, 2002); Panasonic Siew Sales Co., Ltd., Battery Sales Division (Bangkok, September 13, 2006); Thai Glico Co., Ltd. (Bangkok, January 26, 2007). In addition, CP Meiji Co., Ltd., a milk manufacturer, is developing traditional distribution channels by using the sales network that the CP Group has built, since the company thought that depending only on modern distribution channels was insufficient to increase sales (*TNSK*, July 9, 2006).

26. For example, Breeze detergent, Sunsilk shampoo, Lux soap, and Sunlight dishwashing liquid are top-brand products in each category, according to various Thai-language newspapers and business magazines.

27. Author interview with Mr. Phairat Towiwat, a former concessionaire, Thai Unilever (Chiang Mai, January 3, 2007); see also *PRCT-TK*, December 17, 2001.

28. Author interview with Mr. Somchai; Sombun (2006c, 65–72); Thai-language newspapers, e.g., *PRCT-TK*, August 21, 2006 and January 4, 2007.

29. For example, Leng Seng Partnership Ltd., a leading wholesaler in Sakon Nakhon Province in the northeast, is putting a great deal of effort into human resources development and is, therefore, receiving employee training from specialists at Osotspa Co., Ltd., a local major manufacturer, as well as other companies (*TNSK*, April 20 and 23, 2006).

30. Unless other sources are cited, data in this section is based on author interviews with Mr. Samrerng Manoonpol, director, Saha Pathana Inter-holding Plc (Bangkok,

December 14, 2006); Ms. Pennapha Dhanasarnsilp, director, Saha Pathanapibul Plc (Bangkok, December 28, 2006).

31. In addition to Saha Pat, the Saha Group owns I. C. C. International Co., Ltd., which sells apparel and fashion-related commodities, and O. C. C. Co., Ltd. which mainly sells cosmetics as well as other sales companies. The group's Saha Pathana Inter-holding Plc also has many manufacturing subsidiaries. Together with this company, the group's three main sales companies—Saha Pat, I. C. C. and O. C. C.—play the role of a holding company as well, so that the ownership relations within the group are very complicated.

32. The regional breakdown of the number of *So. Ro.* is four in Bangkok and its vicinity, twelve in central Thailand, seventeen in the northeast, eighteen in the north, and twelve in the south. A few of the company's regional distribution centers still operate in certain regional cities such as Chiang Mai.

33. K. R S. Logistics Co., Ltd. was established in 1996 as a joint venture between the group and Japan's Q. P. Co., Ltd.

34. At the present time, Thai Unilever refers to a concessionaire as *sun chatchamnai* (selling center).

35. Unless other sources are cited, information regarding Unilever's concessionaire system is based on the author's interview with Mr. Phairat.

36. In the category of daily necessities, the coverage rate of Thai Unilever products is about ten times as high as that of Thai Kao products. Author interview with Mr. Fujimoto Takuro, director, Business Development, Consumer Business Division, Kao Commercial (Thailand) Co., Ltd. (Bangkok, September 26, 2006).

37. In the case of small-scale grocery stores in remote areas that concessionaires cannot cover and certain other similar cases, Thai Unilever allows concessionaires to appoint sub-concessionaires to execute some of their duties.

38. Generally, the sources from which small-scale grocery stores purchase goods consist of several channels, in which Thai Unilever and many other distribution-related companies have only temporary business connections.

39. Many trustees or concessionaires are complaining that profits are too small compared with the operations burdens (*TNSK*, November 25, 2001). This is why Mr. Phairat, a former concessionaire with Thai Unilever, cancelled his concessionaire contract with the company. Others are also complaining that the area in which they are in charge has shrunk because Thai Unilever has subdivided each concessionaire's area into smaller segments to enable Unilever products to more thoroughly penetrate the consumer market (*TNSK*, March 4, 2001).

40. According to one Thai newspaper, each distributor is offered 70,000 baht as a reward if he/she allocates more than 45 percent of shelf space to Thai Unilever's shampoo, more than 48 percent to its skincare lotion, more than 47 percent to its standard detergent, more than 66 percent to its concentrated detergent, and so on (*TNSK*, July 28, 2005).

41. According to well-informed sources in the industry, many local distributors who are entrusted with the operations of sales district offices are dissatisfied with this system

because the brand power of P&G is weaker than that of Unilever in Thailand's market. As a result, the company's sales offices are in a shaky financial state.

42. Information on Osotspa's marketing channels is based on author interviews with Mr. Vichai Vongsilpavattana, deputy director in charge of sales, Osotspa Co., Ltd. (Bangkok, August 15, 2006); Mr. Thawatchai Thammathiwat, director in charge of logistics, Osotspa Co., Ltd. (Bangkok, September 12, 2006).

43. Information on Thai Ajinomoto Sales' marketing channels is based on the author's interview with Mr. Okamoto, director of the company.

44. Information on Thai Kao Sales' direct sales system is based on the author's interview with Mr. Hirai Hiroshi, ex-president of the company, who took the lead in introducing the system (Chiba, February 27, 2006); Hirai (2003). Information on the recent changes in the system is based on the author's interview with Mr. Fujimoto, director of the company

45. According to several well-informed sources in the industry, Thai Unilever is making efforts to strengthen its relationship with leading wholesalers earlier than its rivals, e.g., by entering into a partnership contract with leading wholesalers.

46. Thai Unilever's shelf space management can be regarded as an attempt to "indirectly" control independent wholesalers.

47. Unless other sources are cited, information on Thai Diethelm is based on the author's interview with Mr. Sucheep Sriphrudtha, general manager in charge of sales and assistant vice president of the company (Bangkok, August 30, 2007).

48. Mr. Sucheep, general manager in charge of sales and assistant vice president of the company, emphasized that Thai Diethelm was not a general wholesaler (*phu kha song*) but a distributor, which has no direct equivalent in the Thai language (author interview, Bangkok, August 30, 2007).

49. However, the company entrusts the delivery activities to outside companies specializing in the business.

50. A typical case is trade with Nestle, a worldwide processed foods manufacturer. In 1973, Thai Diethelm became the sole sales agency for Nestle in Thailand, but in 1989 lost the big contract as Nestle began to build its own marketing channels (Suphattara 1993, 262).

51. Due to data limitations, details of other independent sales companies are unknown. By contrast, there are many sales companies, with Saha Pat as an example, which are related to specific manufacturers. In some cases, even manufacturer-related sales companies have recently begun to sell other manufacturers' products outside the group, but the percentages to the companies' total sales remain small.

52. As mentioned earlier in this chapter, major manufacturers of daily necessities and processed foods have built nationwide marketing channels of their own. As a result, the room for Bangkok-based independent wholesalers to play an active role in this field is becoming smaller than ever. It is at the provincial level that traditional wholesalers play an important role in the distribution channels of daily necessities and processed foods.

53. Unless other sources are cited, information on Tang Ngee Soon is based on the author's interviews with Mr. Milin Verarantanaroj, the first son of the third generation and managing director of the company (Udon Thani, August 23, 2007, August 12, 2008, March 9, 2009).

54. The percentage of the company's total sales from Lao customers is, however, not more than 10 percent of the company's sales base. Author interview with Mr. Milin.

55. Ibid.

56. Unless other sources are cited, information on Leng Seng is based on the author's interview with Mr. Somwang Dechsiriudom, the first son of the founding family's third generation and managing director of the company (Sakon Nakhon, August 13, 2008).

57. Unless other sources are cited, information on the Yongsanguan Group is based on the author's interview with Mr. Prakit Chaisongkhram, the first son of the founder family's third generation and managing director of the company (Ubon Ratchathani, August 14, 2008).

58. Unless other sources are cited, information on Ekkaphap Super Supply is based on the author's interview with Mr. Tuang Kuptivitdhayakul, managing director of the company (Saraburi, August 10, 2008).

59. Since comprehensive information on the wholesale business in Thailand is not available, the author selected these ten leading wholesalers from his own original database. To construct the database, the author first listed the leading wholesalers based on various Thai-language newspapers and business magazines, and then collected data from shareholders lists and financial statements of each company at the Business Development Department, the Ministry of Commerce. In selecting leading wholesalers, the author also added companies to his database based on advice from several persons connected with the industry. Due to methodological limitations, the ten companies listed in table 5.3 may not be the top ten wholesalers of daily necessities and processed foods in terms of sales. However, since the purpose here is to extract the characteristics of traditional leading wholesalers in Thailand, the author believes that even with the shortcomings of this methodological approach the essence of his argument is preserved.

60. Author interview with Mr. Sucheep.

61. One of the examples is ARS Chemical (Thailand) Co., Ltd. Author interview with Mr. Ong-art Prayoke, manager, Chiang Mai branch of the company (Chiang Mai, August 21, 2002).

62. One of the examples is Tang Ngee Soon (author interview with Mr. Milin).

63. Based on the author's interviews with various manufacturers and sales companies. Generally speaking, manufacturers and sales companies voluntarily dispatch product consultants, not because leading wholesalers and large-scale retailers request them to do so. It is also typically the case that each company employs local people as product consultants.

64. Information on product consultants for Tang Ngee Soon is based on the author's interview with a local thirty-year-old man that had been working for nine years as a

product consultant for Foremost Co., Ltd., a leading processed milk manufacturer (Udon Thani, August 23, 2007).

65. Then, how can provincial leading wholesalers be reconciled to such a low ordinary profit ratio, and what product assistance are they provided besides what is mentioned here? Due to data limitations, these points remain unclear.

66. Another important characteristic is that all of the leading provincial wholesale companies are family businesses. So, why, for example, have they carried out business reforms by rapidly and flexibly keeping up with the changes in business environment surrounding the distribution industry? And why have they entrusted the practical affairs of the business to the younger generation, with the first son as the leader? Also, why have they actively adopted modern retailers' new IT management systems? These matters ought to be related with the family business format. The author plans to further discuss in detail these particular questions in another study.

67. Big A Trading, a leading wholesale-cum-retail company in Chanthaburi, closed down its business in May 2009 due to a lack of cash flow, given that the company was selling goods on credit.

68. Unless other sources are cited, information here is based on author interviews with various manufacturers and sales companies.

69. Based on his field research in the lower north of Thailand, Preecha (1980) found that manufacturers (sales companies) in Bangkok, wholesalers at the provincial city level, wholesalers and medium-sized wholesale-cum-retail stores at the district level, medium-sized wholesale-cum-retail stores and small-scale grocery stores at the village level are all connected by their credit functions.

70. Author interviews with various major manufacturers and sales companies.

71. Author interviews with Mr. Somchai; Mr. Preecha Vejsupaporn, chief operating officer, Win Store Co., Ltd., a logistics service provider (Bangkok, August 19, 2002).

72. Some of the manufacturers with whom the author interviewed told him that they could not entrust retail and wholesale distributors to sell their products.

CHAPTER 6

1. Unless otherwise referenced, information regarding the distribution industry is based on author interviews with the following individuals: Mr. Manu Lilanuwat, director, Saha Pathana Inter-holding Plc belonging to the Saha Group (Bangkok, August 19, 2002); Mr. Pricha Wetchasuphaphon, chief operating officer, Win Store Co., Ltd., which conducts eCommerce of processed foods and daily necessities (Bangkok, August 19, 2002); Mr. Chalermchart Nakarungkul, vice president, Chiang Mai Province Chamber of Commerce and president, Denchai Trading Co., Ltd. (Chiang Mai, August 28, 2002, August 27, 2003, September 3, 2004); Mr. Niphon Nakhasuriyawong, operations director, Allied Retail Trade Co., Ltd. (Bangkok, August 22, 2003); Ms. Suchada Itthijarukun, president, Siam Makro Plc (Bangkok, December 24, 2003); Mr. Phitthaya Jiarawisitthakun, president, Thai Retailers

Association and vice president, C. P. Seven Eleven Plc (Bangkok, December 25, 2003); Ms. Thitima Bantraphiwat, vice president, Ek-Chai Distribution System Co., Ltd., running Tesco Lotus (Bangkok, December 26, 2003); Mr. Somchai Phonrattanajaroen, president, Thai Wholesale and Retail Association (Bangkok, September 1, 2004); Mr. Udomsak Loetthanaphok, director, Sutthiphan (1991) Co., Ltd., Chiang Mai's largest wholesaler of processed foods and daily necessities (Chiang Mai, September 3, 2004).

2. In March 2002, Deputy Commerce Minister Suwan resigned with the reshuffle of the cabinet.

3. The Saha Group organized small-scale retailers to develop the 108 Shop chain, where the group's products are sold at below market prices.

4. The enactment of the Retail and Wholesale Business Act was expected to take quite a long time because cabinet meetings and deliberations in parliament were needed. In the meantime, however, it was anticipated that foreign general mass merchandisers would be expanding their businesses, while the situation of local distributors would further deteriorate. The government thus decided to clarify the criteria for unfair trade practices on the basis of the Trade Competition Act already in force, and then attempted to control any unfair trade practices.

5. See, e.g., *TNSK* (October 10, 2002); *KTTK-RW* (October 11, 2002); *PJK-RS* (October 14, 2002). According to one Thai-language newspaper, new Deputy Commerce Minister Wattana, a lawyer, was elected to parliament as a member of the National Development Party from Prachin Buri Province in 1996. At the time of the second Chuan cabinet, he became secretary to Minister Phitak in the Office of the Prime Minister. Phitak was a coordinator between the National Development Party and the CP Group, and the general public thought that Phitak participated in the government as a representative of the CP Group. At the time of the 2001 election, Wattana moved over to the Thai Rak Thai Party and was appointed to the post of deputy secretary general to the Prime Minister for Political Affairs. He soon came to be trusted by Prime Minister Thaksin (*PJK-RS*, October 14, 2002).

6. Wattana was a son-in-law of Sumet Jiarawanon, one of the founding family members of the CP Group, while Thanin Jiarawanon, the leader of the CP Group, was an adviser on economic affairs to Prime Minister Thaksin.

7. Author interview with the Department of Internal Trade, Judicial Affairs Section, Ministry of Commerce (Bangkok, October 22, 2002).

8. In the draft, the government referred to the retail business-related laws of Japan, Indonesia, France, and Holland. Ibid.

9. Author interview with the Department of Internal Trade, Judicial Affairs Section, Ministry of Commerce.

10. Many newspapers called the seminar a public hearing (*prachaphichan*), but this was wrong. It was simply a seminar that was held to introduce the content of the new law. Ibid.

11. Author interview with the Business Support Office, Internal Trade Department, Ministry of Commerce (Bangkok, October 22, 2002).

12. Ibid.

13. At the time of the author's interviews in 2002 (August), 2003 (August and December), and 2004 (August and September), many persons concerned with the retail and distribution industries in Bangkok expressed doubts about the promise of the ART project.

14. The following discussion is based on the author's interview with Mr. Niphon Nakhasuriyawong, operation director, ART Co., Ltd. (Bangkok, August 22, 2003).

15. According to a local Thai newspaper, 82 percent of the goods at ART's member stores were, on average, priced 5.1 percent cheaper than the over-the-counter prices of general mass merchandisers' goods (*PJK-RW*, July 29, 2003).

16. Such local 3PL providers included Universal Co., Ltd. and WinStore Co., Ltd.

17. In addition, an applicant was required to register as a legal person to participate in the project. One Thai newspaper pointed out that such a requirement made small-scale grocery stores hesitate to apply because the tax payment was far more complicated for corporate stores than individual stores (*TNSK*, January 14, 2007).

18. Finally, WinStore decided to stop its dealings with ART.

19. Thailand's regional cooperatives, which consisted of six groups, had a plan to remodel the existing six thousand stores within three to five years, in accordance with their affiliation with ART (*KTTK-RW*, August 5, 2004).

20. Information on site plan regulations in this section is based on author interviews with the Urban Planning Department, Ministry of Interior (Bangkok, February 15 and 27, 2007) and various notices, ministerial ordinances, and Bangkok municipal ordinances (see References).

21. The notice lost validity on May 19, 2006. Since then, areas without urban planning in seventy-two provinces have not been under any site plan regulations.

22. Building area means the area measured from the inside of the building to the outside face (or structural sheathing) of the exterior walls. In the case of one-storey buildings, the building area should be larger than the store's floor space, excluding passages, lavatories, offices, and so on.

23. Wet markets (*talat*), established according to the law, are exempt from this regulation.

24. Carrefour also asked for deregulation, arguing that the company could not open its stores as originally planned due to the application process of the Urban Planning Act, and that hypermarkets did not directly compete with small-scale grocery stores (*PJK-RW*, May 18, 2004).

25. Author interview with Mr. Chalermchart Nakarungkul, vice president, Chiang Mai Chamber of Commerce (Chiang Mai, August 28, 2002).

26. Author interview with Mr. Somchai.

27. Only traditional grocery stores do not feel threatened by Tesco Lotus Express. Even 7-Eleven obviously keeps a watch on the developments of Tesco Lotus Express and strives to differentiate itself by strengthening its assortment of foods and selling original goods (*PRCT-TK*, July 20, 2006).

28. Specific cases were reported in *TNSK* (March 30, 2006); *TNSK* (June 11, 2006); *PRCT-TK* (July 3, 2006); *PRCT-TK* (September 4, 2006). Since the official notice went into force in 2003 and was valid until May 19, 2006, local self-governing bodies were sometimes confused as to whether they should obey the notice from May 20, 2006 onward.

29. Many other cases have been reported. Among them are cases in Lampang Province (*TNSK*, March 30, 2006), Mae Taeng District, Chiang Mai Province (*PRCT-TK*, July 6, 2006), Kaeng Khoi District, Saraburi Province (*PRCT-TK*, July 3, 2006), Chumphon Province (*TNSK*, July 16, 2006), Krabi Province (*PRCT-TK*, July 17, 2006), Ko Samui District, Surat Thani Province (*PRCT-TK*, August 31, 2006), and Mae Sot District, Tak Province (*TNSK*, September 7, 2006).

30. The 2002 guidelines for retail business were not put into practice in the end (*PRCT-TK*, October 5, 2006).

31. Points at issue were, in particular, that too much authority was given to the Retail and Wholesale Supervision Committee and that the committee members consisted heavily on representatives of small- and medium-sized distributors and consumer goods manufacturers. This led to doubts about the neutrality of the committee. Moreover, there was, for a time, a dispute between the Ministry of Commerce's version of the regulation and that of the National Legislative Assembly (NLA), which caused the government to spend a long time reconciling these two views. Some newspapers reported that the real dispute over the enactment of the bill lay in a fight for distribution channel leadership between the large-scale retailers and the major consumer goods manufacturers (see, e.g., *TNSK*, September 10, 2006; *PRCT-TK*, September 18, 2006; *PJK-RW*, October 17, 2008). While this view does capture one side of the actual situation, it remains a very simplistic and one-sided attempt to understand the relationship between distribution channel members (i.e., manufacturers and retailers, and wholesalers and retailers).

32. In September 2008, the then commerce minister, Chaiya Sasomsub, established the Research and Development Committee on Retail and Wholesale Business, whose aim was the enactment of the Retail and Wholesale Business Act (*PRCT-TK*, September 11, 2008). According to one newspaper, however, progress has fluctuated (*PJK-RW*, October 27, 2008).

33. The Network project for local stores that the Commerce Ministry's Business Development Department started in 2007 is an interesting attempt in this direction. This project encourages local wholesalers to: (i) cooperate with small-scale grocery stores in inventory reduction and management, (ii) consider reducing wholesale prices in accordance with the amount of goods purchased, and (iii) guide and mentor small-scale grocery stores on product display. The participants in this project are provided with a number of benefits, including sales-promotion staff that are regularly sent to participants' stores to provide advice on store management, delivery of goods to their stores, and assistance in seeking financial support from banks that is needed for capital improvement and business expansion (*TNSK*, October 7, 2007). Unfortunately, however, as of November 2012, this project has still not made remarkable progress.

CHAPTER 7

1. This is also true of the distribution of home electronics appliances. In this case, manufacturers and their sales companies maintain strict control over distribution channels by forcing retail customers, at the wholesale stage, to only buy goods from manufacturers' sales companies. Partly due to this channel strategy, the fundamental change in channel leadership shifting from manufacturers to retailers has not yet happened in Thailand, even though general mass merchandisers and mass home electronics retailers have substantially increased their sales volume (Endo 2006).

2. In the sense that the functions of new retail formats have partially spread into the traditional distribution sector, it may be said that the distribution revolution has indeed made some progress. As described in chapter 4, however, it is also true that new retail formats have never sufficiently expanded and developed.

3. The total retail industry sales for the entire country in 2010 were approximately 3,157,005 million baht (author's estimate).

4. Among the top five companies, CenCar (Carrefour), which had been behind its competitors in both sales volume and profitability, finally withdrew from Thailand in 2010 and sold its stores to Thailand's Big C Supercenter.

5. The number of 7-Eleven stores in Thailand as of the end of 2011 was 6,276 (www.cpall.co.th/). Thailand's 7-Eleven has also adopted the new concept "convenience food store," raising the proportion of ready-to-eat foods to the total sales of each store. However, these ready-to-eat foods are mainly bakery and "ready meal" items, which have a few days' shelf life, unlike Japan's convenience store chains that place great value on *bento* (box lunches) and rice balls, characterized by a much shorter shelf life and frequent, multiple deliveries.

REFERENCES

JAPANESE- AND ENGLISH-LANGUAGE SOURCES

Advanced Research Group Co., Ltd., ed. (annually). *Thailand Company Information*. Bangkok: Advanced Research Group.

Arai Nobuya. 荒井伸也. (1990). スーパーマーケット・チェーン [*Supermarket Chain*] (日本経済新聞社) [Published by Nihon Keizai Shimbun Sha].

Arai Yoshio. 荒井良雄.(1989). コンビニエンス・チェーンの物流システム ["Distribution System of Convenience Store Chains"]. 信州大学経済学論集 [*Economic Review Shinshu University]* 27: 19–43.

Baek Insoo. 白寅秀. (1999). 大衆消費市場の成立と小売業態の変容—後発国の韓国の事例を中心に— ["The Emergence of Mass Markets and the Dynamics of Retail Forms in Korea"]. 経営史学 [*Japan Business History Review*] 34(3): 49–75.

Brims, Jennieer Joy. (1979). "The Study of an Urban Market System in Chiang Mai, Thailand." Master's thesis, Australian National University.

Coe, Neil M. (2004). "The Internationalization/Globalization of retailing: Towards an Economic-Geographical Research Agenda." *Environment and Planning* 36(9): 1571–94.

Coe, Neil M., and Lee Yong-Sook. (2006). "The Strategic Localization of Transnational Retailers: The Case of Samsung-Tesco in South Korea." *Economic Geography* 82(1): 61–88.

Coe, Neil M., and Neil Wrigley. (2007). "Host Economy Impacts of Transnational Retail: The Research Agenda." *Journal of Economic Geography* 7(4): 341–71.

Davies, Ross, and Yahagi Toshiyuki, eds. (2000). *Retail Investment in Asia/Pacific: Local Responses and Public Policy Issues*. Oxford: Oxford Institute of Retail Management, Templeton College, University of Oxford. For the Japanese version, see デービス、ロス・矢作敏行編(外川洋子監訳)(2001)『アジア発グローバル小売競争』日本経済新聞社.

Dawson, John A. (2007). "Scoping and Conceptualising Retailer Internationalisation." *Journal of Economic Geography* 7(4): 373–97.

Dawson, John and Lee Jung-Hee, eds. (2004). *International Retailing Plans and Strategies in Asia*. New York: International Business Press.

Dawson, John, Masao Mukoyama, Sang Chul Choi, and Roy Larke, eds. (2003). *The Internationalisation of Retailing in Asia*. London: Routledge Curzon.

Dicken, Peter, and Anders Malmberg. (2001). "Firms in Territories: A Relational Perspective." *Economic Geography* 77(4): 345–63.

Endo Gen. 遠藤元. (1996). タイにおける地方実業家の事業展開—チエンマイを事例として—["The Development of Provincial Businessmen in Thailand: A Case Study of Chiang Mai"]. アジア経済 [*AJIA KEIZAI*] 37(9): 54–82.

———. (1998a). 商業・サービス業センサス ["Business Trade and Services Census"]. 末廣昭編 [In Suehiro Akira, ed.] タイの統計制度と主要経済・政治データ[*Statistics Systems and Principal Economic and Political Data*].〔調査研究報告書〕(アジア経済研究) [Published by Institute of Developing Economies].

———. (1998b). 消費市場・所得格差・地方経済—消費ブームからクレジット経済崩壊へ— ["Consumer Markets, Income Differentials, and the Provincial Economy: From Consumption Boom to Collapse of the Credit Economy"]. 末廣昭編 [In Suehiro Akira, ed.], 133–46. タイ—経済ブーム・経済危機・構造調整— [*Thailand: Economic Boom, Economic Crisis, and Structural Adjustment*]. (財団法人日本タイ協会) [Published by the Japan–Thailand Association].

———. (1998c). 大手流通資本の地方進出と地方流通企業の組織化—バンコク=地方都市関係の新たな展開— ["The Advance of Major Distribution Capital into the Provinces and Organization of Provincial Distribution Companies: A New Relationship between Bangkok and Provincial Cities"]. 田坂敏雄編 [In Tasaka Toshio, ed.], 163–90. アジアの大都市 1・バンコク[*Mega-Cities in Asia 1: Bangkok*]. (日本評論社) [Published by Nippon Hyoron Sha].

———. (2001). タイにおける地方小売財閥の形成と展開—タントラーパン・グループの事例—["The Development of a 'Local Retail *Zaibatsu*' in Thailand: The Case of Tantraphan Group in Chiang Mai City"]. 経営史学 [*Japan Business History Review*] 36(1): 28–59.

———. (2002). 小売業の構造変化と流通資本の再編—外資の台頭とセントラル・グループの対応— ["Structural Change in the Retail Industry and Reorganization of the Distribution Business: The Rise of Foreign Capital and Restructuring of the Central Group"]. 末廣昭編 [In Suehiro Akira, ed.], 255–312. タイの制度改革と企業再編—危機から再建へ— [*Institutional Reform and Corporate Restructuring in Thailand: From Crisis to Recovery*]. (アジア経済研究所) [Published by Institute of Developing Economies].

———. (2005). 経済危機後のタイにおける流通政策 [Distribution Policy in Thailand after the Economic Crisis in the Late 1990s]. 大東文化大学紀要 [*Bulletin of Daito Bunka University*] 43: 151–75.

———. (2006a). タイの家電市場と中国製品流入の影響 ["The Impact of 'Made in China' Goods on the Home Appliance Market in Thailand"]. 大西康雄編 [In Onishi Yasuo, ed.], 215–52. 中国・ASEAN経済関係の新展開—相互投資とFTAの時代へ— [*New Developments in Economic Relations between China and ASEAN: Entering an Era of Mutual Investment and FTAs*]. (アジア経済研究所) [Published by Institute of Developing Economies].

———. (2006b). タイ政府の大規模小売業規制とその背景["Large-Scale Retail Business Regulation by Thailand's Government"]. 所報 [*Shoho*] 535: 25–35.

———. (2008). タイにおける日用品・加工食品販売チャネルの再編 ["Reorganization of the Marketing Channel of Daily Necessities and Processed Foods in Thailand"]. 大東文化大学紀要 [*Bulletin of Daito Bunka University*] 46: 45–68.

Futagami Yasuro. 二神康郎. (2000a). 欧州小売業の世界戦略 [*World Strategy of European Retailers*]. (商業界) [Published by Shogyokai Publishing].

———. (2000b). 欧州小売業の国際化 ["Internationalization of European Retailers"]. 矢作敏行編 [In Yahagi Toshiyuki, ed.], 97–124. 欧州の小売りイノベーション [*Retailing Innovation in European Countries*]. (白桃書房). [Published by Hakuto-Shobo Publishing].

Hayashi Shuji. 林周二. (1962). 流通革命 [*Distribution Revolution*]. (中央公論社) [Published by Chuokoron-sha].

Hess, Martin. (2004). " 'Spatial' Relationships? Towards a Reconceptualization of Embeddedness." *Progress in Human Geography* 28(2): 165–86.

Higashi Shigeki. 東茂樹. (2001). タイ通貨危機後の経済社会政策—政策決定過程の政治経済分析— ["Socio-economic Policy in Post-Currency Crisis Thailand: A Political-Economy Analysis of the Policy Decision-Making Process"]. 佐藤幸人編 [In Sato Yukihito, ed.], 161–200. 新興民主主義国の経済・社会政策 [*Economic and Social Policy of Emerging Democratic Countries*]. (アジア経済研究所) [Published by Institute of Developing Economies].

———. (2002). 経済制度改革と企業グループの再構築—危機後の経済政策と産業再編— ["Institutional Reform and Change in the Corporate Sector: Economic Policy and Industrial Restructuring after the Crisis"]. 末廣昭編 [In Suehiro Akira, ed.], 3–62. タイの制度改革と企業再編—危機から再建へ— [*Institutional Reform and Corporate Restructuring in Thailand: From Crisis to Recovery*]. (アジア経済研究所) [Published by Institute of Developing Economies].

Hirai Hiroshi. 平井宏. (2003). 花王—タイにおける販売革新— ["Kao: Sales Innovation in Thailand"]. 吉原英樹他編 [In Yoshihara Hideki, ed.], 99–114. ケースブック国際経営 [*Case Book International Management*]. 有斐閣 [Published by Yuhikaku Publishing].

Hiranaka Teruo. 平中輝夫. (1995). 流通大戦争—タイ国小売業の現状と今後— ["The Great War of Distribution"]. 所報 [*Shoho*] 402: 15–20.

Ihara Motoi. 井原基. (2009). 日本合成洗剤工業のアジア進出—マーケティングと経営移転—[*The Advance of Japan's Synthetic Detergent Manufacturers into Asia: Marketing and Technology Transfer*]. (ミネルヴァ書房) [Published by Minerva Shobo].

Ikemoto Yukio. 池本幸生. (1997). タイの所得格差—1981 年から1994 年まで ["Income Disparities in Thailand: 1981–94"]. 所報 [*Shoho*] 428: 26–33.

Ingram, James C. (1971). *Economic Change in Thailand 1850–1970*. Stanford: Stanford University Press.

Ishihara Takemasa, and Yahagi Toshiyuki, eds. 石原武政・矢作敏行編. (2004). 日本の流通100年 [*Distribution of Japan: 100 Years*]. (有斐閣) [Published by Yuhikaku Publishing].

Ishii Junzo. 石井淳蔵. (1996). 商人家族と市場社会—もうひとつの消費社会論— [*Merchant Family and Market Society: Another View of Consumption Society*]. (有斐閣) [Published by Yuhikaku Publishing].

Ishii Kanji. 石井寛治. (2003). 日本流通史 [*Distribution History of Japan*]. (有斐閣) [Published by Yuhikaku Publishing].

Ishii Kanji, ed. 石井寛治編. (2005). 近代日本流通史 [*Distribution History of Modern Japan*]. (東京堂出版). [Published by Tokyodo Syuppan].

Japanese Chamber of Commerce, Bangkok. バンコク日本人商工会議所. (1993). 経済概況 (1992–93 年版)[*General Conditions of the Thai Economy: 1992–93*].

Kakizaki Ichiro. (2005). *Laying the Tracks: The Thai Economy and Its Railways 1885–1935*. Kyoto Area Studies on Asia, Volume 10. Kyoto: Kyoto University Press.

———. 柿崎一郎. (2009). 鉄道と道路の政治経済学—タイの交通政策と商品流通 1935–1975 年 [*Political Economy of Railway and Road: Transportation Policy and Commodity Distribution in Thailand*]. (京都大学学術出版会) [Published by Kyoto University Press].

———. (2012). *Rails of the Kingdom: The History of Thai Railways*. Bangkok: White Lotus.

Kanithar Pisitkasem. (1991). "The Competitive Behaviour of Department Stores in the Bangkok Metropolitan Area." Master's thesis, Thammasat University.

Kawabata Motoo. 川端基夫. (1999). アジア市場幻想論—市場のフィルター構造とは何か— [*A Critical View of the Asian Consumer Market: What is the Market Filter Structure?*]. (新評論) [Published by Shinhyoron].

———. (2000). 小売業の海外進出と戦略—国際立地の理論と実態— [*The Internationalization of Japanese Retailers: Location and Strategies*]. (新評論) [Published by Shinhyoron].

———. (2005). アジア市場のコンテキスト—グローバリゼーションの現場から— [*The Context of the Asian Market: From the Scene of Globalization*]. (新評論) [Published by Shinhyoron].

———. (2011). アジア市場を拓く—小売国際化の100年と市場グローバル化— [*Opening Up of Asian Markets: 100 Years of Retail Internationalization and Market Globalization*]. (新評論) [Published by Shinhyoron].

Kawabe Nobuo. 川辺信雄. (2003). 新版セブン−イレブンの経営史 [*A Business History of Seven Eleven, New Edition*]. (有斐閣) [Published by Yuhikaku Publishing].

Kikkawa Takeo. 橘川武郎. (1998).『消費革命と』『流通革命』—消費と流通のアメリカナイゼーションと日本的変容— ["'Consumption Revolution' and 'Distribution Revolution': The Americanization of Consumption and Distribution and its Japanese-style Transformation"]. 東京大学社会科学研究所編 [In Institute of Social Science, University of Tokyo, ed.], 99–137. 20世紀システム３・経済成長Ⅱ—受容と対抗— [*The Twentieth Century System 3—Economic Growth II: Acceptance and Opposition*]. (東京大学出版会) [Published by University of Tokyo Press].

Koyama Shuzo, and Togawa Yoko. 小山周三・外川洋子. (1992). (産業の昭和社会史７) デパート・スーパー [*Department Stores and Supermarkets*. Showa Social History of Industries 7]. (日本経済評論社) [Published by Nihon Keizai Hyoronsha].

Mieno Fumiharu. 三重野文晴. (2000). タイにおける企業金融構造と金融危機 ["The Corporate Finance Structure and the Financial Crisis in Thailand"]. 国宗浩三編 [In Kunimune Kozo, ed.], 111–45. 金融と企業の再構築—アジアの経験— [*Restructuring of Finance and Corporation: Experiences of Asia*]. (アジア経済研究所) [Published by Institute for Developing Economies].

———. (2002). コーポレート・ファイナンス—金融システムの機能後退と企業の対応— ["Corporate Finance: Accommodating Retrogression of the Financial System"]. 末廣昭編 [In Suehiro Akira, ed.], 215–53. タイの制度改革と企業再編—危機から再建へ— [*Institutional Reform and Corporate Restructuring in Thailand: From Crisis to Recovery*]. (アジア経済研究所) [Published by Institute for Developing Economies].

Miwa Yoshiro, and Nishimura Kiyohiko, eds. 三輪芳朗・西村清彦編. (1991).日本の流通 [*The Distribution of Japan*]. (東京大学出版会) [Published by University of Tokyo Press].

Nikkei Ryutsu Simbun, ed. 日経流通新聞編. (1993). 流通現代史—日本型経済風土と企業家精神— [*A Modern History of Distribution: The Japanese Economic Climate and Entrepreneurship*]. (日本経済新聞社). [Published by Nihon Keizai Shimbun Sha].

Ogawa Susumu. 小川進. (2003). 稼ぐ仕組み [*The Mechanism to Earn*]. (日本経済新聞社) [Published by Nihon Keizai Shimbun Sha].

Pasuk Phongpaichit and Chris Baker, eds. *Thai Capital after the 1997 Crisis*. Chiang Mai: Silkworm Books.

Preecha Kuwinpant. (1980). *Marketing in North-Central Thailand: A Study of Socio-Economic Organization in a Thai Market Town*. Bangkok: Chulalongkorn University Social Research Institute.

Reardon, Thomas, Spencer Henson, and Julio Berdegué. (2007). "Proactive Fast-Tracking Diffusion of Supermarkets in Developing Countries: Implications for Market Institutions and trade." *Journal of Economic Geography* 7(4): 399–431.

Robinson Planner Ltd., ed. (2000). "Robinson Department Store Public Company Limited Reorganisation Plan."

Sasaki Satoshi. 佐々木聡. (2007). 日本的流通の経営史 [*Business History of Japanese Distribution*]. (有斐閣). [Published by Yuhikaku Publishing].

Sato Hajime. 佐藤肇. (1971). 流通産業革命 [*The Distribution Industry Revolution*]. (有斐閣). [Published by Yuhikaku Publishing].

———. (1974). 日本の流通機構—流通問題分析の基礎— [*Distribution Systems in Japan: The Basis for Analysis of Distribution Issues*]. (有斐閣). [Published by Yuhikaku Publishing].

Sigetomi Shin'ichi. 重冨真一. (1998). 社会経済調査・家計調査 ["Household Socioeconomic Survey"] 末廣昭編 [In Suehiro Akira, ed.] タイの統計制度と主要経済・政治データ [*Statistics System and Principal Economic and Political Data*]. (〔調査研究報告書〕アジア経済研究所). [Published by Institute of Developing Economies].

Skinner, G. William. (1957). *Chinese Society in Thailand: An Analytical History*. Ithaca: Cornell University Press.

Society for the Study of Marketing History, ed. マーケティング史研究会編. (2001). 日本流通産業史—日本的マーケティングの展開— [*Japan's Distribution Industry History: The Development of Japanese Marketing*]. (同文舘) [Published by Dobunkan Shuppan].

Son, Il Sun. 孫一善. (1993).高度成長期における流通システムの変化—石鹸・洗剤業界を中心に— ["The Kao Corporation: A Case Study of Changes in Japan's Distribution of Channel Structure during a High Growth Period"]. 経営史学 [*Japan Business History Review*]. 27(4): 32–63.

———. (1994). 高度成長期における流通系列化の形成—松下販社制度の形成を中心に— ["Formation of the *Keiretsu* in the Distribution of Home Appliances at the Time of High Economic Growth: A Case of Matsushita Hansha"]. 経営史学 [*Japan Business History Review*] 29(3): 1–34.

Suehiro Akira. (1984). タイ系企業集団の資本蓄積構造—製造業グループを中心として— ["Capital Accumulation of Thai Business Groups: A Case Study of the Industrial Group"]. アジア経済 [*AJIA KEIZAI*] 25(10): 2–32.

———. (1989a). *Capital Accumulation in Thailand: 1855–1985*. Tokyo: The Center for East Asian Cultural Studies.

———. (1989b). バンコク：人口増加・経済集中・交通渋滞 ["Bangkok: Population Growth, Economic Concentration, and Traffic Congestion"]. 大阪市立大学経済研究所編 [In Institute for Economic Research, Osaka City University, ed.], 33–68.世界の大都市⑥バンコク・クアラルンプル・シンガポール・ジャカルタ [*Mega-cities in the World (6): Bangkok, Kuala Lumpur, Singapore, and Jakarta*]. (東京大学出版会) [Published by University of Tokyo Press].

———. (1995a). タイの『葬式本』—社会経済史研究の宝庫— ["'Crematory Books' in Thailand: A Treasure House of Socio-Economic History Studies"]. *UP* 24(3): 19–24.

———. (1995b). タイにおける拡大首都圏と地方経済圏 ["The Expanding Metropolitan Area and Provincial Economic Areas in Thailand"]. 総合的地域研究 [*Comprehensive Area Studies*] vol. 9.

———. (1998). 労働市場・労働政策・労働運動—制度化と非制度化の二極分化— ["Labor Market, Labor Policy, and Labor Movement: Bipolarization between Systematization and De-systematization"]. 末廣昭編 [In Suehiro Akira, ed.], 213–36. タイ—経済ブーム・経済危機・構造調整— [*Thailand: Economic Boom, Economic Crisis, and Structural Adjustment*]. (〔タイ国情報別冊〕財団法人日本タイ協会) [Published by The Japan-Thailand Association].

Suehiro Akira, and Nanbara Makoto. 末廣昭・南原真. (1991). タイの財閥—ファミリービジネスと経営改革— [*Zaibatsu in Thailand: Family Business and Management Reform*]. (同文館) [Published by Dobunkan Shuppan].

Tajima Yoshihiro. 田島義博. (2004). 歴史に学ぶ流通の進化 [*Evolution of Distribution from a Viewpoint of History*]. (日経事業出版センター) [Published by Nikkei Custom Publishing Center].

Takaoka Mika. 高岡美佳. (1997). 戦後復興期の日本の百貨店と委託仕入—日本的取引慣行の形成過程— ["Department Store Business in Japan between 1945 and 1956: Formation of Japanese-Style Trade Practices]. 経営史学 [*Japan Business History Review*] 32(1): 1–35.

———. (1999a). 高度成長期スーパーマーケットの資源補完メカニズム—日本の『流通革命』の実像— ["The Business Practices of Japanese Supermarkets During the Period of High Economic Growth from the Mid-1950s to the Early 1970s: A True Picture of Japan's 'Distribution Revolution'"]. 社会経済史学 [*Socio-Economic History*] 65(1): 3–24.

———. (1999b).日本のコンビニエンス・ストアの成長過程における資源補完メカニズム ["Resource Supplement Mechanism of the Convenience Store Business in Japan: Selection of the Franchise System"].経営史学 [*Japan Business History Review*]. 34(2): 44–73.

Tamura Masanori. 田村正紀. (1986). 日本型流通システム [*Distribution System of the Japanese Model*]. (千倉書房) [Published by Chikura Publishing].

Udagawa Masaru, Kikkawa Takeo, and Shintaku Junjiro, eds. 宇田川勝・橘川武郎・新宅純二郎編 (2000). 日本の企業間競争 [*Competition among Companies in Japan*]. (有斐閣) [Published by Yuhikaku Publishing].

Wrigley, Neil, Neil M. Coe, and Andrew Currah. (2005). "Globalizing Retail: Conceptualizing the Distribution-Based Transnational Corporation (TNC)." *Progress in Human Geography* 29(4): 437–57.

Yahagi Toshiyuki. 矢作敏行. (1994). コンビニエンス・ストア・システムの革新性 [*Innovation of the Convenience Store System*]. (日本経済新聞社) [Published by Nihon Keizai Shimbun Sha].

———. (2000). プライベート・ブランドの発展過程—イギリス・スーパーマーケットの場合— ["The Development Process of Private Brands: The Case of the UK's Supermarkets"]. 矢作敏行編 [In Yahagi Toshiyuki, ed.], 163–205. 欧州の小売りイノベーション [*Innovation in European Retailing*]. (白桃書房) [Published by Hakuto-Shobo Publishing].

———. (2001). アジアにおけるグローバル小売競争の展開 ["Developments of Global Retailing Competition in Asia"] ロス=デービス・矢作敏行編〔外川洋子監訳〕[In Davies, Ross and Yahagi Toshiyuki, eds.], 11–37. アジア発グローバル小売競争 [*Retail Investment in Asia/Pacific: Local Responses and Public Policy Issues*]. (日本経済新聞社) [Published by Nihon Keizai Shimbun Sha].

———. (2007). 小売国際化プロセス—理論とケースで考える— [*Retail Internationalization Process: Theory and Case Studies*]. (有斐閣) [Published by Yuhikaku Publishing].

Yahagi Toshiyuki, ed. 矢作敏行編. (2003). 中国・アジアの小売業革新 [*Retailing Innovation in China and Asia*]. (日本経済新聞社) [Published by Nihon Keizai Shimbun Sha].

Yui Tsunehiko, ed. 由井常彦編. (1991).セゾンの歴史―変革のダイナミズム― [*A History of Saison: Dynamism for Change*]. (上・下巻)リブロポート) [Published by Libro Port].

Yui Tsunehiko, and Hashimoto Juro, eds. 由井常彦・橋本寿朗編. (1998). 革新の経営史―戦前・戦後における日本企業の革新行動― [*Business History of Innovation: Innovative Actions of Japanese Companies before and after the War*]. (東京大学出版会) [Published by University of Tokyo Press].

THAI-LANGUAGE SOURCES

Abico Holdings Plc, ed. [บริษัท เอบิโก้ โฮลดิ้งส์ จำกัด (มหาชน)] (2000). [2543]. รายงานประจำปี 2542 แบบ 56–1 [Abico Holdings Plc prospectus 1999].

Anek Nawikkamun. (เอนก นาวิกมูล). (1999). [2542]. ตำนานห้างร้านสยาม [*The Origin of Thai Stores*]. กรุงเทพฯ: ต้นอ้อ ๑๙๙๙ [Published by Ton Oo 1999, Bangkok].

Arun Borirak, ed. อรุณ บริรักษ์ บก. (2002a). [2545]. *Logistics: A Case Study in Thailand*. กรุงเทพฯ: ไอทีแอล เทรดมีเดีย [Published by ITL Trade Media, Bangkok].

———. (2002b). [2545]. *Logistics: A Case Study in Thailand 2*. กรุงเทพฯ: ไอทีแอล เทรดมีเดีย [Published by ITL Trade Media, Bangkok].

———. (2004). [2547]. *Logistics: A Case Study in Thailand 3: Warehouse*. กรุงเทพฯ: ไอทีแอล เทรดมีเดีย [Published by ITL Trade Media, Bangkok].

Aruni Phonnoi. (อรุณี ผลน้อย). (2003). [2546]. เล่ห์เหลี่ยมค้าปลีก-ค้าส่ง [*Tricks of Retail and Wholesale*]. กรุงเทพฯ: ปันสัน [Published by Pan San, Bangkok].

Athiwat Sapphaithun. (อธิวัฒน์ ทรัพย์ไพฑูรย์). (2001). [2544]. คัมภีร์ "เจ้าสัว" ธนินท์ เจียรวนนท์ [*The Scripture of "Multimillionaire" Thanin Jiarawanon*]. กรุงเทพฯ: [Published by Super Touch Media Group].

———. (2002). [2545]. 6 อภิมหาอาณาจักรค้าปลีกค้าส่ง [*The Six Big Retailers and Wholesalers*]. กรุงเทพฯ: พึ่งตน [Published by Phoeng Ton, Bangkok].

Big C Supercenter Plc. [บริษัท บิ๊กซี ซูเปอร์เซ็นเตอร์ จำกัด (มหาชน)] (2000). [2543]. รายงานประจำปี 2542 แบบ 56–1 [Big C Supercenter Plc prospectus 1999].

———. (annually). รายงานประจำปี [Big C Supercenter Plc Annual Report].

Central Pattana Plc. [บริษัท เซ็นทรัลพัฒนา จำกัด (มหาชน)] (2000). [2543]. รายงานประจำปี 2542 แบบ 56–1 [Central Pattana Plc prospectus 1999].

Central Plaza Hotel Plc. [บริษัท โรงแรมเซ็นทรัลพลาซา จำกัด (มหาชน)] (2000). [2543]. รายงานประจำปี 2542 แบบ 56–1 [Central Plaza Hotel Plc prospectus 1999].

CP All Plc. [บริษัท ซีพี ออลล์ จำกัด (มหาชน)] (2009). [2552]. รายงานประจำปี 2552 แบบ 56–1 [CP All Plc prospectus 2009].

———. (annually). รายงานประจำปี [CP All Plc Annual Report].

C. P. Seven Eleven Plc. [บริษัท ซี.พี. เซเว่น–อีเลฟเว่น จำกัด (มหาชน)] (2006). [2549]. C.P. Seven Eleven Plc รายงานประจำปี 2549 แบบ 56–1 [C.P. Seven Eleven Plc prospectus 2006].

———. (annually). รายงานประจำปี [C.P. Seven Eleven Plc Annual Report].

Danut Tanthoetthit. ดนุช ตันเทอดทิตย์ . (2004). [2547]. "วอลเตอร์ ไมเยอร์ ยุคสุดท้ายที่เบอร์ลี่ ฯ [The Last Days of Walter Meyer at Berli Jucker]." (อรวรรณ บัณฑิตกุล และทีมงาน นิตยสาร ผู้จัดการ บก. [In Orawan Banditkun and Working Team Phujatkan, eds.], 96–110. บริษัท ๑๐๐ ปี. More than Old & Glory [*100 Year-Companies in Thailand: More than Old & Glory*]. กรุงเทพฯ: แมเนเจอร์ มีเดีย กรุ๊ป [Published by Manager Media Group, Bangkok].

Janjutha Sukkhi. จันทร์จุฑา สุขขี. (2006). [2549]. "สำเพ็ง: แหล่งรวมเศรษฐกิจ แหล่งรวมความบันเทิง [Sampheng: the Center of Economy and Entertainment]." (สุภางค์ จันทวานิช บก. [In Suphang Janthawanit, ed.], 93–121. สำเพ็ง: ประวัติศาสตร์ชุมชนชาวจีนในกรุงเทพฯ [*Sampheng: A History of Chinese Community in Bangkok*]. กรุงเทพฯ: ศูนย์จีนศึกษา สถาบันเอเชียศึกษา จุฬาลงกรณ์มหาวิทยาลัย [Published by Chinese Studies Center of the Institute of Asian Studies, Chulalongkorn University, Bangkok].

Jirapha Tosombun. (จีระภา โตสมบุญ). (2003). [2546]. วิวัฒนาการของช่องทางการจัดจำหน่ายสินค้าอุปโภคบริโภคในประเทศไทย [The Evolution of Distribution Channels for Consumer Goods in Thailand]. รายงานวิจัยเสริมหลักสูตร มหาวิทยาลัยธรรมศาสตร์ [A Monograph submitted to Thammasat University, Bangkok].

Kanjana Nopphaphan and Sanlaya Aksonmat. (กาญจนา นพพันธ์ และ ศัลยา อักษรมัต). (2001). [2544]. "เจาะลึก ธุรกิจค้าปลีกไทย: มุมมองประธานสมาคมผู้ค้าปลีก [Going into Thai Retail Business: A Viewpoint of President of the Thai Retailers Association]." วารสารส่งเสริมการลงทุน [*Thailand's Investment Promotion Journal*], ปีที่ 12 ฉบับที่ 3.

Kao Industrial (Thailand). [บริษัท คาโอ อินดัสเตรียล (ประเทศไทย) จำกัด]. (1986). [2529]. ประวัติไทยคาโอ ๒๐ ปี [20 Year History of Thai Kao].

Khomsan Rattanasimakun. (คมสัน รัตนะสิมากูล). (2006). [2549]. "ท่าน้ำราชวงศ์." (สุภางค์ จันทวานิช บก. [In Suphang Janthawanit, ed.], 359–71. สำเพ็ง: ประวัติศาสตร์ชุมชนชาวจีนในกรุงเทพฯ [*Sampheng: A History of Chinese Community in Bangkok*]. กรุงเทพฯ: ศูนย์จีนศึกษา สถาบันเอเชียศึกษา จุฬาลงกรณ์มหาวิทยาลัย [Published by Chinese Studies Center of the Institute of Asian Studies, Chulalongkorn Univeristy, Bangkok].

Khu Khaeng, ed. คู่แข่ง บก. (1995). [2538]. ผ่าทางตันธุรกิจค้าปลีก [*Breaking an Impasse of Retail Business*]. กรุงเทพฯ: คู่แข่ง [Published by Khu Khaeng, Bangkok].

———. (1998). [2541]. "เปิด 5 ค่ายยักษ์ใหญ่เจ้าตลาดสินค้าอุปโภค-บริโภค [Clarifying the Top 5 Consumer Goods Manufacturing Groups]." คู่แข่ง [*Khu Khaeng*], ปีที่ 18 ฉบับ 245.

Khunathip Saengchai. (คุณาธิป แสงฉาย). (2001). [2544]. "การขยายตัวของร้านค้าปลีกสมัยใหม่ และผลกระทบต่อร้านขายของชำดั้งเดิม [The Expansion of Modern Retail Stores and their Impacts on Traditional Grocery Stores]." วิทยานิพนธ์ปริญญาเศรษฐศาสตรมหาบัณฑิต, จุฬาลงกรณ์มหาวิทยาลัย [MA thesis (Economics), Chulalongkorn University, Bangkok].

Khunthong Loseriwanit. ขุนทอง ลอเสรีวานิช. (2004). [2547]. "121 ปี เบอร์ลี่ ยุคเกอร์ เกมนี้ยังไม่จบ [121 Years of Berli Jucker: This Game Is not Over Yet]." (อรวรรณ บัณฑิตกุล และทีมงานนิตยสารผู้จัดการ บก. [In Orawan Banditkun and Working Team Phujatkan, eds.], 65–84. บริษัท ๑๐๐ ปี More than Old & Glory [*100 Year-Companies in Thailand: More than Old & Glory*]. กรุงเทพฯ: แมเนเจอร์ มีเดีย กรุ๊ป [Published by Manager Media Group, Bangkok].

Krittaphon Lapphimon. กฤตพร ลาภพิมล. (2003). [2546]. "ปัจจัยที่มีผลต่อบทบาททางด้านพาณิชยกรรมของย่านสำเพ็ง กรุงเทพมหานคร [Factors to Influence Commercial Roles of Sampheng District, Bangkok Metropolis]." วิทยานิพนธ์ปริญญาการวางแผนภาค และเมืองมหาบัณฑิต, จุฬาลงกรณ์มหาวิทยาลัย [MA thesis (Regional and Urban Planning), Chulalongkorn University, Bangkok].

Niphon Phuaphongsakon et al. (นิพนธ์ พัวพงศกร และคณะ). (2002). [2545]. การค้าปลีกของไทย: ผลกระทบของการแข่งขันจากผู้ประกอบการค้าปลีกขนาดใหญ่จากต่างประเทศ [Retail in Thailand: The Impact of Competitiveness Brought about by Foreign Large-Scale Retailers]. กรุงเทพฯ: สถาบันวิจัยเพื่อการพัฒนาประเทศไทย [Thailand Development Research Institute, Bangkok].

Orawan Banditkun. อรวรรณ บัณฑิตกุล). (2004). [2547]. "วอลเตอร์ ไมเยอร์ ผู้คิดสูตรสบู่หอมนกแก้ว [Walter Meyer Who Invented Parrot Soap Products]." (อรวรรณ บัณฑิตกุล และทีมงานนิตยสารผู้จัดการ บก. [In Orawan Banditkun and Working Team Phujatkan, eds.], 115–22. บริษัท ๑๐๐ ปี More than Old & Glory [*100 Year-Companies in Thailand: More than Old & Glory*]. กรุงเทพฯ: แมเนเจอร์ มีเดีย กรุ๊ป [Published by Manager Media Group, Bangkok]).

Orawan Banditkun and Working Team Phujatkan, eds. (อรวรรณ บัณฑิตกุล และทีมงานนิตยสารผู้จัดการ บก. (2004). [2547]. บริษัท ๑๐๐ ปี: More than Old & Glory [*100 Year-Companies in Thailand: More than Old & Glory*]. กรุงเทพฯ: แมเนเจอร์ มีเดีย กรุ๊ป [Published by Manager Media Group, Bangkok].

Pandop Tangsiwong. ปัณฑพ ตั้งศรีวงศ์. (2000). [2543]. "Central Group: ถึงเวลาต้องผลัดรุ่น [Central Group: The Time of Generational Change Has Come]." ผู้จัดการ [*Phujatkan*] ปีที่ 18 ฉบับที่ 205.

———. (2002). [2545]. "ซิงเกอร์ขอเป็นฝ่ายรุกกลับหลังตั้งรับมาตลอด [Singer Makes a Counterattack after Facing All the Attacks]." ผู้จัดการ [*Phujatkan*] ปีที่ 20 ฉบับที่ 226.

PDS (Provincial Department Stores). [ชมรมห้างสรรพสินค้าภูธร] (1994). [2537]. ทำเนียบห้างสรรพสินค้าภูธร [*Membership List of Provincial Department Stores*] 1994. กรุงเทพฯ: คู่แข่ง [Published by Khu Khaeng, Bangkok].

Phanni Bualek. พรรณี บัวเล็ก. (2002). [2545]. ลักษณะของนายทุนไทยในช่วงระหว่าง พ.ศ. 2457–2482: บทเรียนจากความรุ่งโรจน์สู่โศกนาฏกรรม [*Characteristics of Thai Capitalists during 1914 to 1939: A Lesson from Downfall following Prosperity*]. กรุงเทพฯ: สำนักพิมพ์ พันธกิจ [Published by Phanthakit Publishing, Bangkok].

Phirawut Chattrakun Na Ayutthaya, ed. พีระวุธ ฉัตรกุล ณ อยุธยา บก. (2004). [2547]. ธุรกิจร้านสะดวกซื้อ [*Convenience Store Business*]. กรุงเทพฯ: สำนักพิมพ์ EDITOR 1999 [Published by EDITOR Publishing, Bangkok].

Phujatkan, ed. ผู้จัดการ บก. (2000). [2543]. "(Cover Story) CP ศตวรรษที่ 21: ภาระสุดท้าย ธนินท์ เจียรวนนท์ [(Cover Story) CP in 21 Century]." ผู้จัดการ [*Phujatkan*] ปีที่ 17 ฉบับที่ 197.

Phunphon Phuthajak. (พูนพร พูลทาจักร). (1987). [2530]. "การเปลี่ยนแปลงทางเศรษฐกิจในมณฑลพายัพหลังการตัดเส้นทางรถไฟสายเหนือ พ.ศ. 2464–2484 [Economic Change in Phayap Circle after the Opening of Northern Railroad: 1921–1941]." วิทยานิพนธ์ปริญญามหาบัณฑิต มหาวิทยาลัยศิลปากร [MA thesis, Silpakorn University, Bangkok].

Piyanat Bunnak. (ปิยนาถ บุนนาค). (2006). [2549]. "สำเพ็ง: ประวัติศาสตร์ชุมชนชาวจีนใน กรุงเทพมหานคร [Sampheng: A History of Chinese Community in Bangkok]" (สุภางค์ จันทวานิช บก. [In Suphang Janthawanit, ed.], 1–22. สำเพ็ง: ประวัติศาสตร์ชุมชนชาวจีนในกรุงเทพฯ [*Sampheng: A History of Chinese Community in Bangkok*]. กรุงเทพฯ: ศูนย์จีนศึกษา สถาบันเอเชียศึกษา จุฬาลงกรณ์ มหาวิทยาลัย [Published by Chinese Studies Center of the Institute of Asian Studies, Chulalongkorn Univeristy, Bangkok].

Plaio Chananon. (ปลายอ้อ ชนะนนท์). (1987). [2530]. นายทุนพ่อค้ากับการก่อและขยายตัวของ ระบบทุนนิยมในภาคเหนือของไทย พ.ศ. 2464–2523 [*Merchant Capitalists and the Expansion of Capitalism in Northern Thailand: 1921-1980*]. กรุงเทพฯ: สถาบันวิจัยสังคม จุฬาลงกรณ์มหาวิทยาลัย และสำนักพิมพ์สร้างสรรค์ [Published by Chulalongkorn University Social Research Institute and Sang San Publishing, Bangkok].

Prachachat Thurakit, ed. (ประชาชาติธุรกิจ บก.) (1989). [2532]. เฮง "เทียม" ผู้เยี่ยม วรยุทธ์ [*Prosperity of Thiam, the Best Strategist*]. กรุงเทพฯ: สำนักพิมพ์มติชน [Published by Matichon Publishing, Bangkok].

Prani Sirithon Na Phatthalung. ปราณี ศิริธร ณ พัทลุง. (1980). [2523]. ผู้บุกเบิกแห่งเชียงใหม่ [*Pioneers of Chiang Mai*]. กรุงเทพฯ: สำนักพิมพ์เรืองศิลป์ [Published by Rueang Sin Publishing, Bangkok].

———. (1995a). [2538]. เพ็ชร์ลานนา (๑) [*Lan Na's Diamonds Vol. 1*]. เชียงใหม่: ผู้จัดการ ศูนย์ภาคเหนือ [Published by Phujatkan Northern Center, Chiang Mai].

———. (1995b). [2538]. เพ็ชร์ลานนา (๒) [*Lan Na's Diamonds Vol. 2*]. เชียงใหม่: ผู้จัดการ ศูนย์ภาคเหนือ [Published by Phujatkan Northern Center, Chiang Mai].

Mr. Re-tell. (มร. รี-tell). (2002). [2545]. Dis3bution Channel: กลยุทธ์จัดการช่องทางจัดจำหน่าย [*Distribution Channel: Marketing Channel Strategies*]. กรุงเทพฯ: Brand Age Books [Published by Brand Age Books, Bangkok].

Rewadi Rattananuban and Sunantha Jaruwatthanachai. (เรวดี รัตนานุบาล และสุนันทา จารุวัฒนชัย). (2000). [2543]. "ทิศทางธุรกิจค้าปลีกไทย [The Direction of Thai Retail Business]." รายงานเศรษฐกิจและการเงินรายเดือน, ธันวาคม [*Bank of Thailand Monthly Economic Report, December 2000*]: 43–58.

Robinson Department Store Plc. [บริษัท ห้างสรรพสินค้าโรบินสัน จำกัด (มหาชน)]. (2007). [2549]. รายงานประจำปี 2549 แบบ 56-1 [Robinson Department Store Plc prospectus 2006].

———. (annually). รายงานประจำปี [Robinson Department Store Plc Annual Report].

Saha Pathanapibul Plc. [บริษัทสหพัฒนพิบูลจำกัด (มหาชน)]. (2006). [2549]. รายงานประจำปี 2548 (แบบ 56–1) [Saha Pathanapibul Plc prospectus 2005].

———. (annually). รายงานประจำปี [Saha Pathanapibul Plc Annual Report].

———. [n.d.] บริษัทสหพัฒนพิบูล ครบรอบ ๔๐ ปี [The Fortieth Anniversary of Saha Pathanapibul].

———. [n.d.] 50 ปี สหพัฒนฯ: มุ่งมั่นพัฒนา เพื่อคุณค่าชีวิตไทย [The Fiftieth Anniversary of Saha Pat: Aiming at the Development of Thai People's Daily Life].

Samrit Jirathiwat. (สัมฤทธิ์ จิราธิวัฒน์). (1992). [2535]. หนังสืออนุสรณ์ในงานพระราชทานเพลิงศพ นายสัมฤทธิ์ จิราธิวัฒน์ ต.ม., จ.ช. ณ เมรุวัดเทพศิรินทราวาส (ด้านใต้) 3 พฤศจิกายน 2535 [A Crematorium Book of Remembrance for Mr. Samrit Jirathiwat, November 3, 1992].

Santi Sawettawimon. (สันติ เศวตวิมล). (2001). [2544]. ตำนานตลาดไทย [*The Origin of Thai Wet Markets*]. กรุงเทพฯ: ประพันธ์สาส์น [Published by Praphan San, Bangkok].

Siam Makro Plc. [บริษัท สยามแม็คโคร จำกัด (มหาชน)]. (2000). [2543]. รายงานประจำปี 2542 แบบ 56-1 [Siam Makro Plc prospectus 1999].

———. (annually). รายงานประจำปี [Siam Makro Plc Annual Report].

Sombun Rujikhajon. (สมบุญ รุจิขจร). (2002). [2545]. *Thai Grocer.* กรุงเทพฯ: Tipping Point Press.

———. (2005a). [2548]. "Store War: สงครามกินรวบค้าปลีกไทย [An All-Out War among Thai Retailers]." *FOUR P*, ปีที่ 2, ฉบับที่ 22, กรกฎาคม.

———. (2005b). [2548]. "เพาเวอร์ออฟเซลส์ฟอร์ซ: นี่แหละ... พลังอำนาจค้ำบัลลังก์แชมป์ของยูนิลีเวอร์ [Power of Sales Force: This is Supporting for Unilever to Maintain the Position of Champion]." *FOUR P*, ปีที่ 2, ฉบับที่ 24, กันยายน.

———. (2006a). [2549]. "7-อีเลฟเว่น - เทสโก้ โลตัส เอ็กซ์เพรส-แฟมิลี่มาร์ท [7-Eleven, Tesco Lotus Express, and FamilyMart]." *FOUR P*, ปีที่ 3, ฉบับที่ 33, มิถุนายน.

———. (2006b). [2549]. "อายิโนะ เอฟเฟกต์ [The Ajinomoto Effect]." *FOUR P*, ปีที่ 3, ฉบับที่ 35, สิงหาคม.

———. (2006c). [2549]. "สงคราม 'ยื้ออำนาจ': ซัพพลายเออร์ vs. ค้าปลีก [Struggle for the Leadership: Supplier vs. Retailer]." *FOUR P*, ปีที่ 3, ฉบับที่ 36, กันยายน.

Somjai Wiriyabanditkun. (สมใจ วิริยะบัณฑิตกุล). (1990). [2533]. สหพัฒนฯ โตแล้วแตก และ แตกแล้วโต [Saha Pat Grows and then Splits, and Splits and then Grows]. กรุงเทพฯ: ผู้จัดการ [Published by Phujatkan, Bangkok].

———. (2004). [2547]. "97 ปี ดีทแฮล์มลงทุนเพื่อซื้ออนาคต [Diethelm's Investment for Future: 97 Years]" (อรวรรณ บัณฑิตกุล และทีมงาน นิตยสารผู้จัดการ บก. [In Orawan Banditkun and Working Team Phujatkan, eds.], 229–54. บริษัท ๑๐๐ ปี More than Old & Glory [*100 Year-Companies in Thailand: More than Old & Glory*]. กรุงเทพฯ: แมเนเจอร์ มีเดีย กรุ๊ป [Published by Manager Media Group, Bangkok]).

Sompratthana Khlaiwichian et al. (สมปรารถนา คล้ายวิเชียร, ฒนพันธุ์ วงษ์พันธุ์ และ วทัญญู รณชิต-พานิชยกิจ). (2000). [2543]. มหัศจรรย์ธุรกิจ 7-Eleven ภาค ๒ [*The Wonders of 7-Eleven (Part 2)*]. กรุงเทพฯ: สำนักพิมพ์มติชน [Published by Matichon Publishing, Bangkok].

Suphang Janthawanit. (สุภางค์ จันทวานิช). (2006). [2549]. "การค้าและการขนส่งในย่านสำเพ็ง: จากท่าเรือสำเภาสู่ท่าเรือกลไฟ [Trade and Transportation in Sampheng: From the Port for Junks to the Port for Steamships]." (สุภางค์ จันทวานิช บก [In Suphang Janthawanit, ed.], 67-92. สำเพ็ง: ประวัติศาสตร์ชุมชนชาวจีนในกรุงเทพฯ [*Sampheng: A History of Chinese Community in Bangkok*]. กรุงเทพฯ: ศูนย์จีนศึกษา สถาบันเอเชียศึกษา จุฬาลงกรณ์ มหาวิทยาลัย [Published by Chinese Studies Center of the Institute of Asian Studies, Chulalongkorn Univeristy, Bangkok].

Suphaphan Khophon. (สุภาพรรณ ขอผล). (1991). [2534]. "การเปลี่ยนแปลงทางเศรษฐกิจของภาคเหนือตอนล่างในช่วงปี พ.ศ. 2448–2484 [Economic Change in the Lower North of Thailand: 1905-1941]." วิทยานิพนธ์ปริญญามหาบัณฑิต มหาวิทยาลัยธรรมศาสตร์ [MA thesis, Thammasat University, Bangkok].

Suphattara Saenprasoet. (สุพัตรา แสนประเสริฐ). (1993). [2536]. "บทเรียนที่ไม่มีวันจบของดีทแฮล์ม [An Everlasting Lesson of Diethelm]." ผู้จัดการ [*Phujatkan*] ฉบับที่ 122.

Supphachai Amphut. (ศุภชัย อัมพุช). (2006). [2549]. หนังสืออนุสรณ์ในงานพระราชทานเพลิงศพ นาย ศุภชัย อัมพุช ณ ฌาปนสถานกองทัพอากาศ วัดพระศรีมหาธาตุ 19 มีนาคม 2549 [A Crematorium Book of Remembrance for Mr. Supphachai Amphut, March 19, 2006].

Suriya Pradapsamut et al. (สุริยา ประดับสมุทร, สมปรารถนา คล้ายวิเชียร, และ จุฑารัตน์ เหลืองศรีพงศ์). (1997). [2540]. มหัศจรรย์ธุรกิจ 7-Eleven [*The Wonders of 7-Eleven*]. กรุงเทพฯ: สำนักพิมพ์มติชน [Published by Matichon Publishing, Bangkok].

Sutjanya Sunthonraphonjaroen and Saran-ya Daenginthawat. (สุจรรยา สุนทรพรเจริญ และ สรัญญา แดงอินทวัฒน์). (2006). [2549]. กลยุทธ์ Brand Building สยามพารากอน vs. เซ็นทรัลเวิลด์ [*Brand Building Strategy: Siam Paragon vs. Central World*]. กรุงเทพฯ: ฐานการพิมพ์ [Published by Than Kanphim, Bangkok].

TDRI (Thailand Development Research Institute). [สถาบันวิจัยเพื่อการพัฒนาประเทศไทย]. (1999). [2542]. การค้าส่งค้าปลีกไทย [*Wholesale and Retail in Thailand*]. กรุงเทพฯ: กระทรวงพาณิชย์ [Published by Ministry of Commerce, Bangkok].

Thai Retailers Association. (สมาคมผู้ค้าปลีกไทย) (n.d.) ทำเนียบสมาคมผู้ค้าปลีกไทย [Membership List of the Thai Retailers Association].

Thanawat Sapphaibun. (ธนวัฒน์ ทรัพย์ไพบูลย์). (2000). [2543]. 55 ตระกูลดัง ภาค 1 [55 *Well-Known Families Vol. 1*]. กรุงเทพฯ: สำนักพิมพ์เนชั่น [Published by The Nation Publishing, Bangkok].

———. (2001). [2544]. ตำนานชีวิตเจ้าสัว: 55 ตระกูลดัง ภาค 2 [*Life Histories of Multimillionaires: 55 Well-Known Families Vol. 2*]. กรุงเทพฯ: สำนักพิมพ์เนชั่น [Published by The Nation Publishing, Bangkok].

Thanit Duangkrommana. (ธนิต ดวงกรมนา). (2001). [2544]. ใต้เงากิเลน [*In the Shade of Kilen*]. กรุงเทพฯ: สะเพียรชัย [Published by Saphianrachai, Bangkok].

Thapana Bunla. (ฐาปนา บุญหล้า). (2006). [2549]. โลจิสติกส์ประเทศไทย [*Logistics in Thailand*]. กรุงเทพฯ: สำนักพิมพ์ สมาคมส่งเสริมเทคโนโลยี (ไทย-ญี่ปุ่น) [Published by Technology Promotion Association (Thailand-Japan) Publishing, Bangkok].

Thiam Chokwatthana. (เทียม โชควัฒนา). (1991). [2534]. อนุสรณ์ในงานพระราชทานดินฝังศพ นายเทียม โชควัฒนา ท.ม. วันพุธที่ 14 สิงหาคม พ.ศ. 2534 ณ สุสานมังกรทอง จังหวัดชลบุรี [A Crematorium Book of Remembrance for Mr. Thiam Chokwatthana, August 14, 1991].

Thot Khananaphon. (ทศ คณนาพร). (2005). [2548]. กลยุทธ์ เซเว่น อีเลฟเว่น: คัมภีร์ธุรกิจค้าปลีกยุคใหม่ [*Strategies of 7-Eleven: The Scripture of Modern Retail Business*]. เชียงใหม่: บลูพริ้น ดีซายน์ [Published by Blue Print Design, Chiang Mai].

———. (2008). [2551]. มหัศจรรย์ เซเว่น อีเลฟเว่น [*A Threat of 7-Eleven*]. กรุงเทพฯ: สำนักพิมพ์กู๊ดลัค [Published by Good Luck Publishing, Bangkok].

Van Roy, Edward (วราภรณ์ จิวชัยศักดิ์ แปล). (2006). [2549]. "จากผืนน้ำสู่แผ่นดิน จากตรอกเล็กสู่ถนนใหญ่ คลอง ถนน ซอย สะพาน และการคมมาคมในสำเพ็ง [From Water to Land, from Lane to Road: Waterway, Road, Lane, Bridge, and Transportation in Sampheng]." (สุภางค์ จันทวานิช บก. [In Suphang Janthawanit, ed.], 23–66. สำเพ็ง: ประวัติศาสตร์ชุมชนชาวจีนในกรุงเทพฯ [*Sampheng: A History of Chinese Community in Bangkok*]. กรุงเทพฯ: ศูนย์จีนศึกษา สถาบันเอเชียศึกษา จุฬาลงกรณ์มหาวิทยาลัย [Published by Chinese Studies Center of the Institute of Asian Studies, Chulalongkorn Univeristy, Bangkok].

Waraphon Panprasong. (วราภรณ์ ปานประสงค์). (2000). [2543]." ภาพรวมธุรกิจค้าปลีกในปี 2543 [An Outlook of Thai Retail Business as of 2000]." เศรษฐกิจปริทัศน์ [*Economic Review*], ปีที่ 6, ฉบับที่ 6, มิถุนายน.

Warunrat Chaisut. (วรุณรัตน์ ชัยสุทธ์). (2001). [2544]. "ธุรกิจค้าปลีกในประเทศไทย [Retail Business in Thailand]." เศรษฐกิจปริทัศน์ [*Economic Review*], ปีที่ 7, ฉบับที่ 8, สิงหาคม.

Wirat Saengthongkham, Pandop Tangsiwong, and Somsak Damrongsunthonrachai. (วิรัตน์ แสงทองคำ ปัณฑพ ตั้งศรีวงศ์ และ สมศักดิ์ ดำรงสุนทรชัย). (2003). [2546]. 70 ปี จิราธิวัฒน์ Central ยิ่งสู้ ยิ่งโต [*The Growing Jirathiwat Family and Central Group for 70 Years*]. กรุงเทพฯ: แมเนเจอร์ มีเดีย กรุ๊ป [Published by Manager Media Group, Bangkok].

Wirayut Kanchuchat. (วีระยุทธ กาญจน์ชูฉัตร). (2006). [2549]. "สองนคราค้าปลีกไทย [Two Dragons of Thai Retail]." (ผาสุก พงษ์ไพจิตร บก. [In Pasuk Phongpaichit, ed.], 217–79. การต่อสู้ของทุนไทย เล่ม 2 [*A Struggle of Thai Capital Vol. 2*]. กรุงเทพฯ: สำนักพิมพ์มติชน [Published by Matichon Publishing, Bangkok]).

Worawan Kirati-adun (วรวรรณ กีรติอดุลย์). (2001). [2544]. "ร้านโชวห่วยอยู่กัน อย่างไรเมื่อห้างใหญ่เปิดตัว [How can Grocery Stores Coexist with Large-Scale Stores?]." วารสารส่งเสริมการลงทุน [*Thailand's Investment Promotion Journal*], ปีที่ 12, ฉบับที่ 2, กุมภาพันธ์.

Yutthasak Khanasawat. (ยุทธศักดิ์ คณาสวัสดิ์). (1997a). [2540]. "ภาพรวมธุรกิจค้าปลีกไทย [An Outlook of Thai Retail Business]." วารสารส่งเสริมการลงทุน [*Thailand's Investment Promotion Journal*], ปีที่ 8 ฉบับที่ 6.

———. (1997b). [2540]. "ห้างสรรพสินค้ากับสถานการณ์ที่ล่อแหลม [Department Stores and their Critical Conditions]." วารสารส่งเสริมการลงทุน [*Thailand's Investment Promotion Journal*], ปีที่ 8 ฉบับที่ 7.

———. (2001a). [2544]. "ตำนานธุรกิจค้าปลีกในไทย [The Origin of Retail Business in Thailand]." วารสารส่งเสริมการลงทุน [*Thailand's Investment Promotion Journal*], ปีที่ 12 ฉบับที่ 2.

———. (2001b). [2544]. "ธุรกิจค้าปลีกไทยยุควิกฤติเศรษฐกิจ [Thai Retail Business during the Economic Crisis]." วารสารส่งเสริมการลงทุน [*Thailand's Investment Promotion Journal*], ปีที่ 12 ฉบับที่ 2.

———. (2001c). [2544]. "บีโอไอเป็นต้นเหตุแห่งการล่มสลายของโชวห่วยหรือไม่? [Did BOI Cause Grocery Stores to Fall?]." วารสารส่งเสริมการลงทุน [*Thailand's Investment Promotion Journal*], ปีที่ 12 ฉบับที่ 2.

NEWSPAPERS AND MAGAZINES

Brand Age

FOUR P

GM Business

KTTK-RW: กรุงเทพธุรกิจรายวัน [The Daily Bangkok Business]

Khu Khaeng: คู่แข่ง [The Competitor]

PRCT-TK: ประชาชาติธุรกิจ [The Business Newspaper for the People]

PJK-RS: ผู้จัดการรายสัปดาห์ [The Weekly Manager]

PJK-RW: ผู้จัดการรายวัน [The Daily Manager]

The Nation

TNSK: ฐานเศรษฐกิจ [The Base of Economy]

GOVERNMENTAL STATISTICS

Bank of Thailand. www.bot.go.th

BOI (Board of Investment). (1989). *Key Investment Indicators of Thailand 1989.*

———. (1998). Press release, 210/2541 (25 December, 1998).

NESDB (National Economic and Social Development Board). www.nesdb.go.th

NSO (National Statistical Office). *Population and Housing Census*, annually.

———. *Report of the Census of Business Trade and Services*, annually.

———. *Report of the Household Socio-Economic Survey*, annually.

———. *Report of the 1996 Listing of Industrial and Business Establishments (The 1997 Industrial Census) Whole Kingdom.*

———. *Retail Survey*, annually.

———. *The 2002 Business Trade and Services Census Basic Information: Municipal Areas Whole Kingdom.*

———. *The 2002 Business Trade and Services Census Basic Information: Sub-district Administration Organization Whole Kingdom.*

———. *The 2007 Industrial Census (Basic Information: Municipal Area) Whole Kingdom.*

———. *The 2007 Industrial Census (Basic Information: Non-municipal Area) Whole Kingdom.*

LAWS AND OFFICIAL DOCUMENTS

กรมโยธาธิการและผังเมือง [2546] "ประกาศกรมโยธาธิการและผังเมือง เรื่อง กำหนดหลักเกณฑ์การใช้ประโยชน์ในทรัพย์สินเพื่อประโยชน์ในการวางและจัดทำผังเมืองรวม ในท้องที่จังหวัดเชียงใหม่ พ.ศ. ๒๕๔๖."

กระทรวงมหาดไทย [2546] "ประกาศกระทรวงมหาดไทย เรื่อง กำหนดบริเวณห้ามก่อสร้าง ดัดแปลง หรือ เปลี่ยนการใช้อาคารบางชนิดหรือบางประเภท ในพื้นที่บางส่วนในท้องที่จังหวัดเชียงใหม่ พ.ศ. ๒๕๔๖."

กระทรวงมหาดไทย [2547a] "ประกาศกระทรวงมหาดไทย เรื่อง กำหนดบริเวณห้ามก่อสร้าง ดัดแปลง หรือ เปลี่ยนการใช้อาคารบางชนิดหรือบางประเภท ในพื้นที่บางส่วน ในท้องที่กรุงเทพมหานคร พ.ศ. ๒๕๔๗."

กระทรวงมหาดไทย [2547b] "กฎกระทรวงกำหนดบริเวณห้ามก่อสร้าง ดัดแปลง หรือเปลี่ยนการใช้อาคารบางชนิดหรือบางประเภท ในพื้นที่บางส่วนในท้องที่จังหวัดเชียงใหม่ พ.ศ. ๒๕๔๗."

กรุงเทพมหานคร [2548] "ข้อบัญญัติกรุงเทพมหานคร เรื่อง กำหนดบริเวณห้ามก่อสร้าง ดัดแปลง หรือ เปลี่ยนการใช้อาคารบางชนิดหรือบางประเภท ในพื้นที่บางส่วนในท้องที่กรุงเทพมหานคร พ.ศ. ๒๕๔๘."

กรุงเทพมหานคร, สำนักผังเมือง [2549] "ผังเมืองรวมกรุงเทพมหานคร."

คณะกรรมการการแข่งขันทางการค้า [2549] "ระเบียบสำนักงานคณะกรรมการการแข่งขันทางการค้าว่าด้วยแนวทางพิจารณาการปฏิบัติทางการค้าระหว่าง ผู้ประกอบธุรกิจค้าส่งค้าปลีกกับผู้ผลิตหรือผู้จำหน่าย พ.ศ. ๒๕๔๙."

คณะกรรมการการแข่งขันทางการค้า [2550] "ประกาศคณะกรรมการการแข่งขัน ทางการค้า เรื่อง หลักเกณฑ์การเป็นผู้ประกอบธุรกิจซึ่งมีอำนาจเหนือตลาด."

"ประกาศของคณะปฏิวัติฉบับที่ ๒๘๑."

"พระราชกฤษฎีกากำหนดเขตที่จะทำการสำรวจเพื่อการวางและจัดทำผังเมืองรวมในท้องที่ ๗๒ จังหวัด พ.ศ. ๒๕๔๖."

"พระราชบัญญัติการแข่งขันทางการค้า พ.ศ. ๒๕๔๒."

"พระราชบัญญัติการการค้าส่งและการค้าปลีก พ.ศ. ...."

"พระราชบัญญัติการประกอบธุรกิจของคนต่างด้าว พ.ศ. ๒๕๔๒."

INDEX